James Bloom

Half Cheetah

Skin in the game
Bronac Ferran

A decentring of human subjectivity into the multi-agented otherness of machinic systems is a game being played today by the most contemporary of artists. James Bloom's *Half Cheetah* illuminates this territory.

Despite carrying resonances of thousands of years of animal-human entanglings and transgenic creations, *Half Cheetah* has a quality of unfamiliarity that causes us to look and look again. Bloom here is crossing into new territory in ways that disarm and unsettle us, with intimations of new lifeforms that viscerally draw us into an emerging world, one that is beginning to be inhabited and yet seems somewhere out of our conscious reach. Both simple and complex, these are bewitchingly contemporary icons for our metamorphic times.

They retrieve a sense of the mystery or praxis of embodiment, or the felt texture of material substance, over and above the efficacy of elite performance-orientated systems. He has added the texture of skin back onto the void of abstracted data.

What we encounter is a symbiotic composite. To make this, Bloom appropriated an existing algorithm, the Half Cheetah Task, devised for commercial and military robotics training, and harnessed it to more poetic and humane ends. Conceived after two bereavements in his close family, Bloom developed a series of code-based creatures that mutate, radiate and emote.

These works have taken time to find their feet. Features have been added almost daily over months in a heuristic process of trial and error. A painstaking endeavour, made in liaison with a brilliant coder, *Half Cheetah* probes the potential of Deep and Reinforcement Learning to look beyond the fitness function. As such it throws some shade on a sense of time as a foward-facing progression, so prevalent in the sphere of unilinear technological innovation.

Conceptualised initially in the late 1950s, when machine learning was in its infancy, genetic algorithms are fundamental to the effective workings of neural networks. They were first named in 1975 by John Holland, author of *Adaptation in Artificial and Natural Systems*. Closely associated with Darwin's Theory of Natural Selection is the concept of 'the survival of the fittest', introduced in the 1860s by philosopher Herbert Spencer. He argued that this theory went beyond biology into the domains of society and economy, a view that left him significantly open to criticism.

But we can see the legacy of his thinking in the relentlessly feed-forward configuring of today's AI.

Yet Bloom's *Half Cheetah* distinguishes itself through what he describes as "taking an antagonistic approach to innovation." His Reinforcement Learning creatures duly lean towards the forward-facing, frictionless qualities of artificial lifeforms. But he has gone further also, as he has explained of the process: "By setting the initial challenge of making an artwork that innovates technologically, I've already created problems for myself. I then go a step further and innovate again, this time against the original innovation, so to progress it by breaking it. This is something that happens intuitively, maybe as a reaction against the first step. But it creates its own problems too, for myself and also a viewer."

In making these dimensions find new forms in their interaction, a laborious task of coding one onto the other, Bloom has made a conceptual breakthrough that seems to me to change the rules of the game. His view of what he has been doing is that he has created a 'functional provocation'. This seems to me to be why, as viewers and interlopers, we feel we are invited into this curious landscape.

We are offered privileged glances into the habitats of not yet fully evolved creatures, that are incommensurably on their way to somewhere, though quite how they will get there remains open to speculation. What is the world they might be inhabiting? Is the other half of the *Half Cheetah* a machine or a human being? What is it that makes us want to reach into their space of otherness and to commune with their alienation?

Within the patterns and behaviours that are being engendered is a zone of displacement, disequilibrium and deterritorialisation that, critically, has no centre. It is only the temporal-spatial parameters of the information architecture, manifest in various modes of transmission, including this book, that holds these decentring energies together. We are interacting with new lifeforms held in the compressed transference from code into material language. What was once (de)void now has a skin. We can touch the chimera.

The flipside of becoming

In his essay, 'Encore des Changements' [Still More Changes] (1935), Henri Michaux stated: "I was sorry not to be a boa or a bison anymore. A little later I had to shrink to fit on a saucer. Endless sudden changes, everything had to be done all over again, and it wasn't worth the trouble, it was only going to last a few moments, and yet you had to adapt, and there were always these sudden changes."[1] Having first experimented with drugs in 1928, Michaux took to using LSD and mescaline from the middle of the 1950s, exploring aspects of the dark side of the human mind, as a reservoir for mutant creativity.

Sudden change was also core to Bloom's formative years, moving between his parents, one of whom lived in Glastonbury and the other in London. He was thrown out of three different schools, before beginning and not finishing a foundation course in art. He then suddenly found his tribe with the emergence of networked media, as a hybrid spin-off from the countercultural forces of the postwar decades. By the age of nineteen he was writing articles for *The Guardian* about new technological forces of creative destruction, and at twenty, he was an editor at *GQ* magazine. He then went on to build some of the earliest interactive experiences for brands. Of this period of development he recalls: "I didn't stay in one place – was very much at home with the 'move fast and break things' mentality."

Bloom was also early to recognise the potential of blockchains as contexts in which he might probe the monetisation of art, as well as modes of flipping and domains of technological collapse and slippage. His *GOLD* series has become a paradigmatic art intervention in the value-shifts of the Ethereum blockchain, engaging critically in on-chain systems of exchange and transaction, reflexively mirroring these back in a real-time feedback loop. Bloom released it initially under the moniker of 'crashblossom': a term poetically redolent of both falling and flowering, signifying also, in machine-language learning modelling, a point of ambiguity demanding human input. Like Half Cheetah, it presents us with a dynamic scenario in which art is part of a volatile system that might veer towards collapse, or might recover, but which is constantly in a state of disequilibrium.

Bloom has amplified this narrative further within *Half Cheetah*, heightening recognition of how points of mutation may signify progress, or be evolutionary dead ends that might throw us back to drawing bison in our caves.

Fleeing backwards?

To achieve this destabilising effect, Bloom fully taps into the sphere of emotional ambivalence that many are now feeling about the limits or otherwise of so-called technological advancement. Is there hope here in our capacity for evolved mutation? Or try as we might to learn, will there only ever be a sense of racing, and falling short, and constantly failing to catch up?

> For Bruno Latour, as expressed in 2010, "the moderns never looked to the future; they always looked to the past they were afraid of. Now the moderns are actually turned towards the future, ever aware of what is behind them. They always have 'ruptures' at their backs and they are continuously moving forward. They flee backwards." Latour adds, "And you turn around, and suddenly you realise, that first, you have destroyed the whole planet – I mean this is cause for a little hesitation."[2]

This seems to me to be right on the nose with respect also to what Bloom is doing with his multiplying chimera, who are neither here nor there but somewhere in between beginning and ending. What he has conjured up are perfect creatures for our present-day contemplative musings on where we might be going as human beings. Our race to create indelible future memories has brought us to these decomposed recompositions, held in the infinitely hollow space of becoming. But what then might follow? Is there an exit-route beyond this complicity with our own erasure?

1 From a translation of Henri Michaux, ‘Encore des Changements’ (Paris: Editions Gallimard, 1935) by John Tittensor, reproduced as ‘Still More Changes’, in *Animism*, Vol. 1, Anselm Franke (ed.), The Sternberg Press, Berlin, 113–114, 113.

2 Bruno Latour, in ‘Angels Without Wings. A conversation between Bruno Latour and Anselm Franke’, in *Animism*, Vol. 1, 86–96, 96.

James Bloom and Mark Leckey in conversation

Mark Leckey Hello.

James Bloom It's been a while.

ML Yes.

JB I was thinking about Online Magic.

ML Yeah, yeah.

JB The web agency. I worked there a while after you worked there, and I got fired fairly quickly. But one of the things I did while I was there was an early interactive TV ad. And it was really shit. But it went on to win all these awards because it was one of the first interactive TV ads. The point being that working with technology is a good sales tool because of the novelty value.

ML I think novelty was something I was conditioned into when I was younger, the idea that pop music as it innovated culture was exciting and things were happening and inevitably, that would lead to like better and brighter things. So I was kind of duped by consumerism into associating novelty with innovation. But I can never fully be that cynical about it. Even if these things are orchestrated by capitalism in entirely cynical marketing moves,

I believe that there's something that you can extract out of that for yourself.

JB Yeah. There's a lot of focus on the new. We're surrounded by that, it's part of our milieu, right? There's just so much. We live inside it, in fact.

ML Right. But you in turn use these things to produce an effect beyond whatever is being marketed. There's something that can become useful in terms of fulfilling a sort of imaginative landscape that fulfils you and is potentially transformative.

JB The world of art works a little like marketing too. Quite often technology is used for its novelty value, I think. There's a kind of fetishisation of technology, a sort of future gazing. There's also another whole school who set up technology as a straw man to knock down. But having the technology at the very centre gets a bit boring. I don't want to work with all the shiny new AI image generation models, for example.

ML Right, when you're prompting it.

JB Yeah. It's not really something that I'm interested in personally.

ML It's quite unsatisfactory, isn't it? I've been playing around with it recently. That's how we started talking, isn't it? And at first I was like, "Oh, I can really do something with this." On a metaphysical level, when I first saw those images, there was so much verisimilitude between them and a dream. I've always been looking for the kind of transition that's dreamlike. I used Runway AI. But the more I learned to control it, the more I was able to create the images I wanted to, the less satisfying they became. I just got bored of them, you know?

JB Yeah.

ML In the learning curve, I thought there's going to be a point where I get the images I want, and when I did, they were just quite dull. Maybe I was trying to control it too much.

JB Maybe. Personally, my process is to use things the wrong way, mostly because I don't know the tools well enough, and even if I'm working with proper coders, I'll end up breaking things at a structural level. I am essentially innovating with the technology;

I get deep in the weeds, but in the process I'm breaking the innovations. And it's really through that I think I can reveal something else.

ML Yeah. But with that technology – AI image prompting – I don't know how you could break things any more than it already does. It's kind of breaking reality. It's abstracting or distorting the body, or figurative imagery and making it really plastic, isn't it? It's very much a realisation of surrealist ideas, drawing on a kind of dreamscape to realise things in the world. But for the surrealists the hope was those things, once in the world, would be destabilising and ultimately political. The surrealists were Marxists, but now it feels more like the right have adopted those same tactics with AI. Or AI has adopted those tactics itself.

JB The surrealists were making these disruptions to upset our rational assumptions. But prompted-AI imagery is mostly just a product of the technology itself. Actually all the weird image splicing and distortions are just due to errors in the nascent technology. One day soon AI won't produce 'surrealism by default' anymore;

it'll splice things together perfectly. For now, the artist has become a kind of servant or facilitator of the current state of AI.

ML Right, okay. When these sorts of techniques have been appropriated or are part of the apparatus itself, I think that makes it very hard as an artist to figure out what you're meant to do.

JB If you look at the Impressionists or Abstract Expressionists, you feel a sense of the person who was painting that painting. The Abstract Expressionists literally used their body as a tool. Or, say, Bruce Nauman. My process with Reinforcement Learning AI is quite antagonistic. I had to learn various models, 3D real-time environments, it's pretty technologically-involved. I ran into many obstacles and by the time I was done, even though the end-product is these technological figures running and failing, I think something else is in the pieces. I think it contains a trace of me as a person.

ML I'm very much for that. I guess your metaphor is a cyborg. It's not a cyborg, but some kind of form you try and operate within, within this kind of robot you figuratively try and speak through. You're trying to speak through the technology and the matter becomes bigger than you. You use the tech to try and amplify the way you feel.

JB Yeah.

ML Like Kanye West at the end of 'Runway'? 'Runaway'. He has auto-tune and then he puts the auto-tune through some kind of distortion pedal and then he just kind of starts wailing. You can't hear what he's saying but it goes through this process that amplifies whatever trauma he's trying to communicate. But somehow to align yourself with the tech... To make yourself in this moment a kind of cyborg and use that cyborg to express something vulnerable or something animalistic, I really love that.

JB I'm interested in the behavioural level of things. Body movements and their motivations. Because we're in motion as people, we're in motion as a society, we have these goals that we strive for. Objectives we're aiming towards. And technology systematises a lot of that. So when you start breaking the structure of that goal-seeking and passage of progress, you start seeing these failures.

These are the moments that are usually made invisible, so showing the failures reveals something.

ML For me, this idea of progress at the moment is quite anxiety inducing. I think of the internet as a kind of doomsday device. It's a longer conversation, but I think the internet produces apocalyptic thinking. It's born of a kind of eschatological moment, born of the end times.

JB Bloody hell, right. Well these networks are so big and the data is so complicated that they're impossible for us to understand. We just look at it all and go 'wow' or 'oh shit'. So then people built these other systems, AI models, which can understand and analyse all that big data for us. Now the problem is who owns those structures, who's structuring the data and how the direction of our lives is based on that.

ML Yeah, yeah. Totally. You were talking at the beginning about either fetishising technology or being overly critical of it, either over-determining or under-determining it. But I look at the art world as it is now... There was post-internet art, which I find hilarious, like it was just this brief blip. But post-internet art failed within the gallery, because the gallery structure is nineteenth-century. And then art sort of retreated back into painting. I don't look for progress in the art world anymore.

JB I'm optimistic. I think people keep moving, they're moving towards their goals but there's always a bias effect where what comes out in the end is conditioned by the goals you had at the start. So then you try again. It's good for artists, and not only artists, but people to work inside those structures and break them down. You know, according to your own motivations and feelings. Maybe that's real innovation. It's something anyway.

ML Innovation is coming from people working online, with these kind of tools we've been talking about. I've been listening to a lot of Plug Rap lately. These nineteen-year-olds aren't even singing or rapping. It's like if you clean up a vocal digitally, there are artifacts that are left over. They're making songs from those artifacts. They're making these tracks from the digital waste.

JB I love artifacts. You get really interesting results just from technology being used badly. The artifacts have something about them that can be more meaningful than the rest of it.

ML Definitely. I'm trying to write this piece about the twentieth century and counterculture. A lot of the counterculture energy came from waste, you know? Just things that were left over. It begins in the ruins of World War II and then all the waste from '50s and '60s consumerism gets adapted.

JB Yeah, yeah.

ML It gets expressed best with punk, right? Punk's an expression of kind of like waste. And then once you get to the twenty-first century and the internet, waste gets kind of smoothed away. Everything becomes efficient. But artifacts are kind of like the digital waste, right? So the excess or surplus in whatever you're trying to do. As long as that still exists, we're alright.

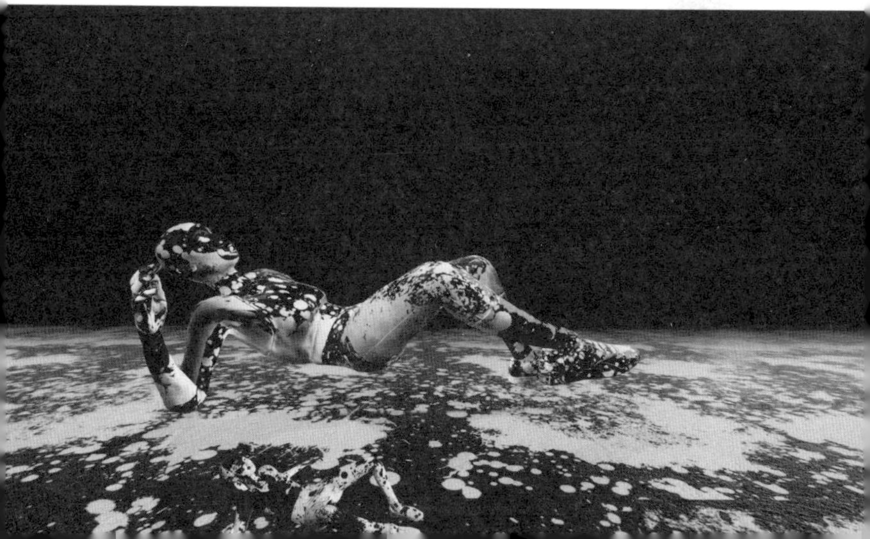

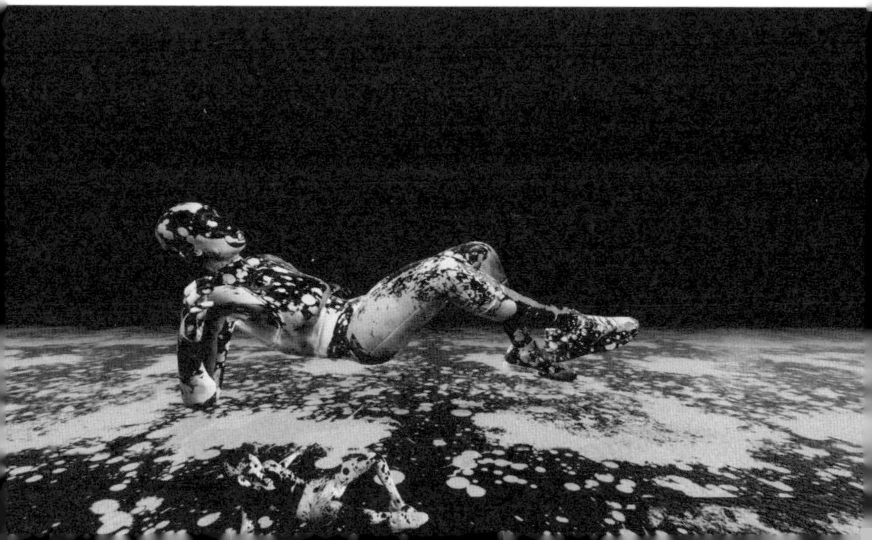

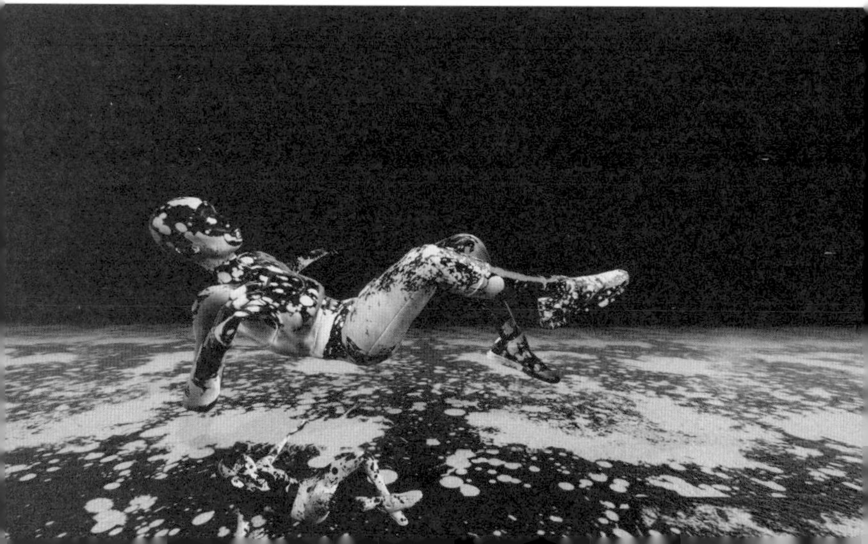

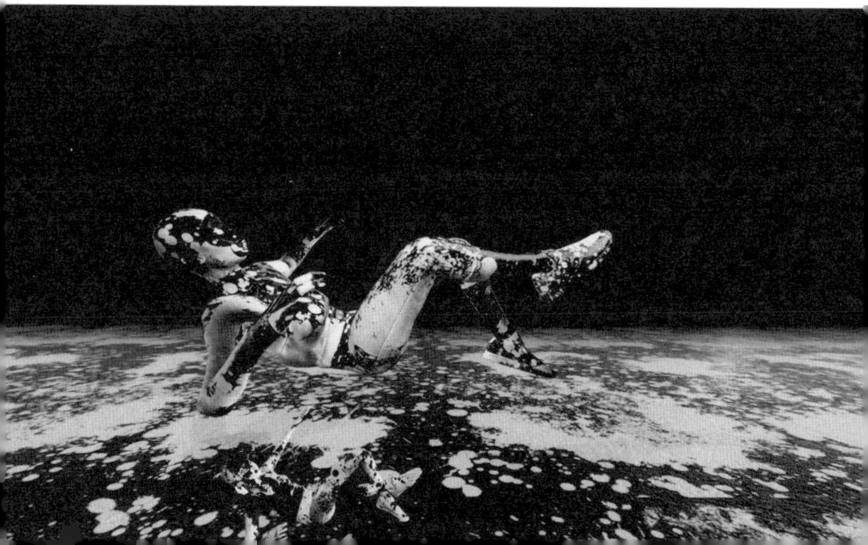

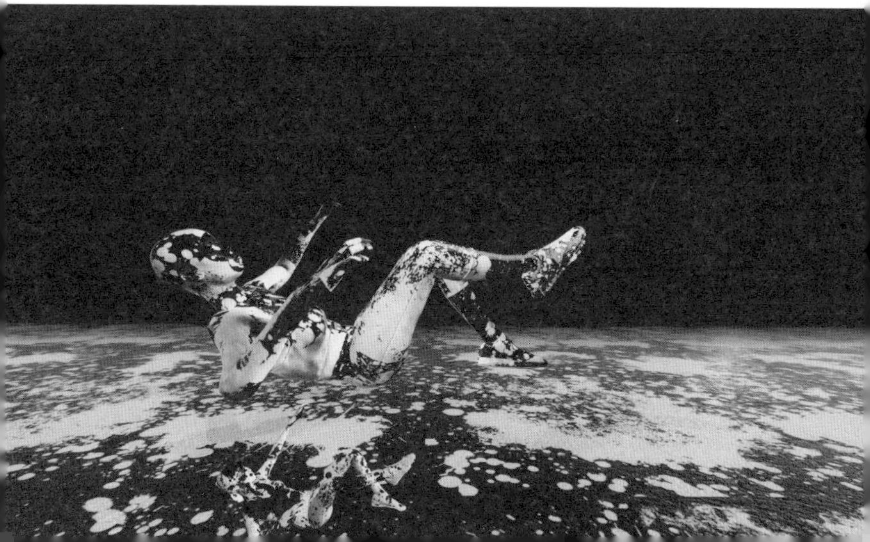

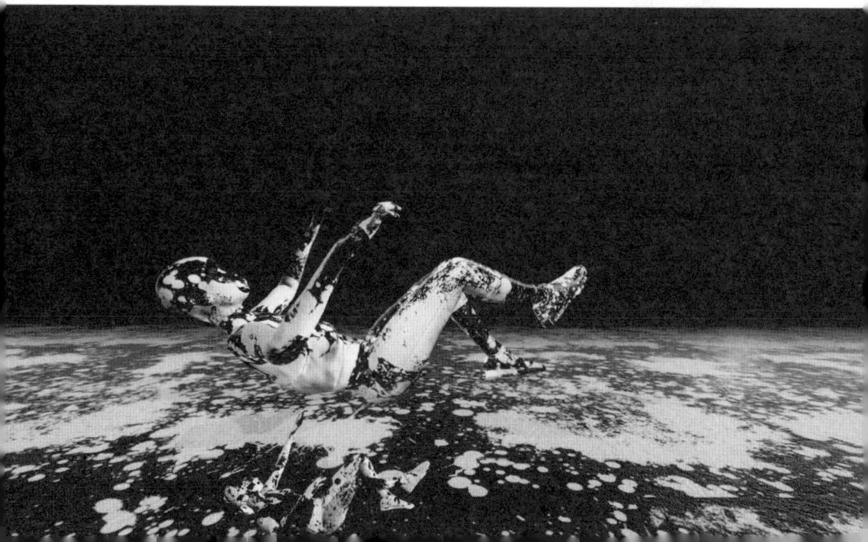

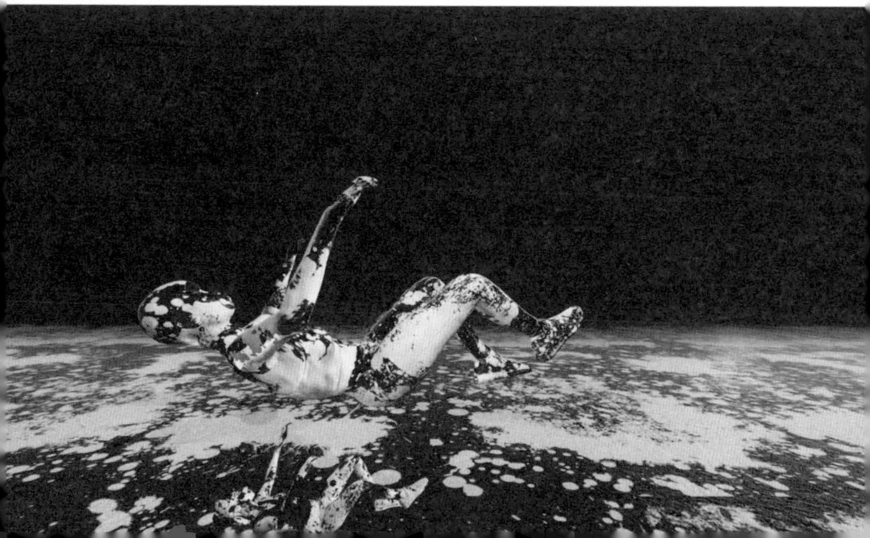

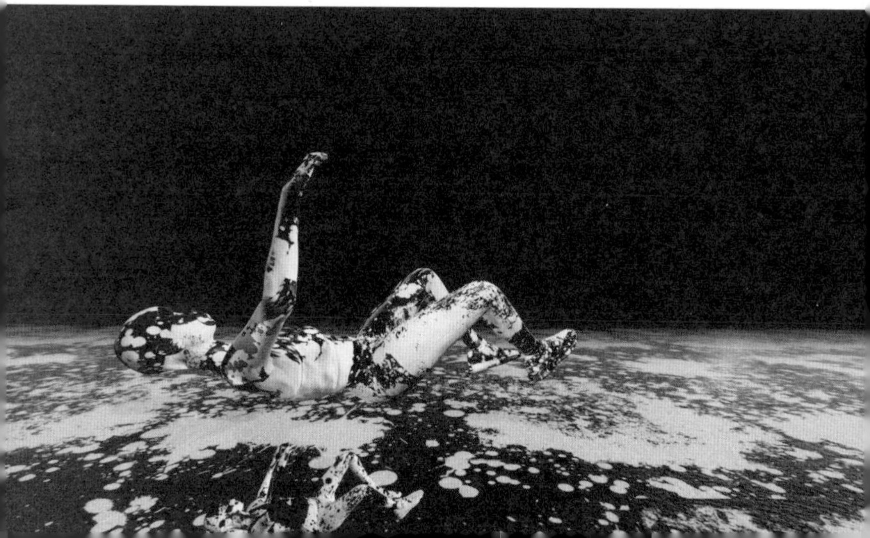

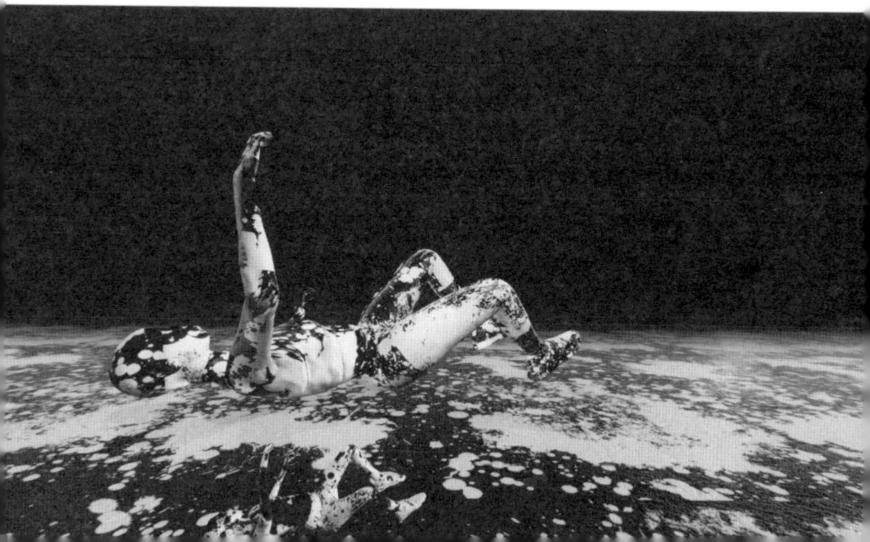

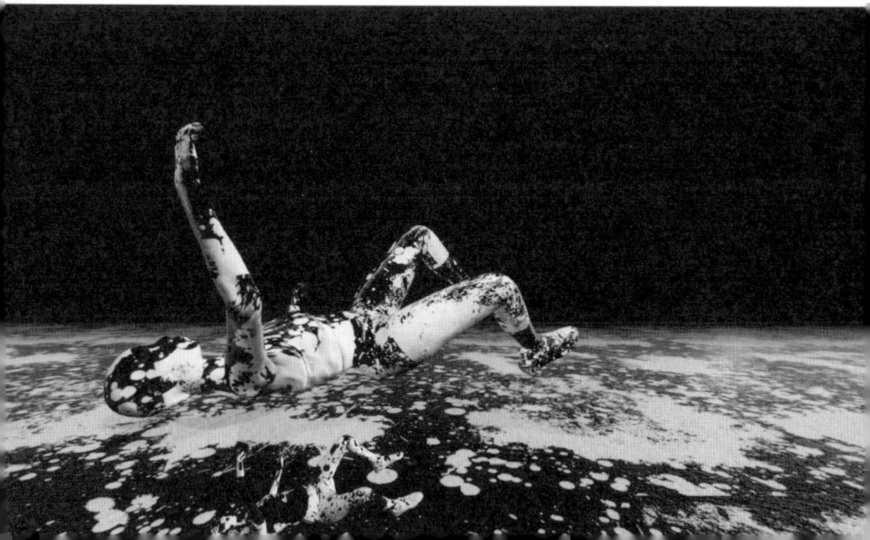

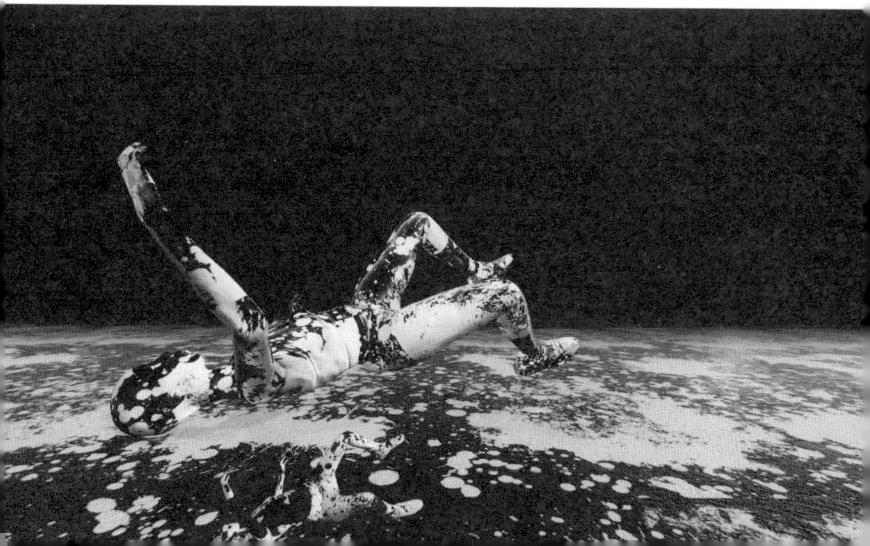

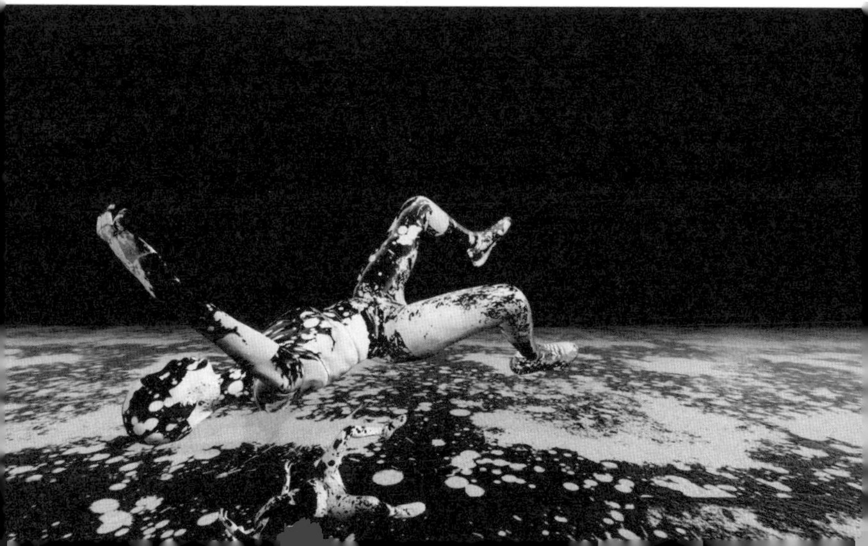

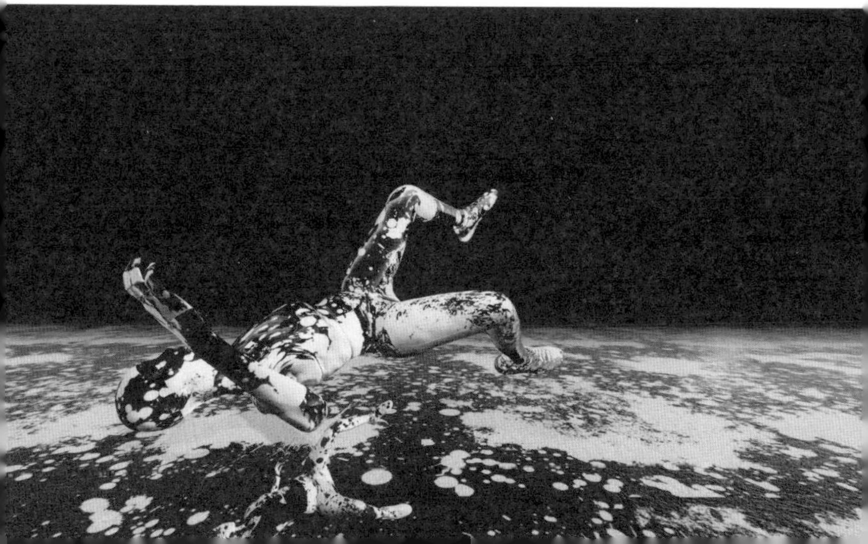

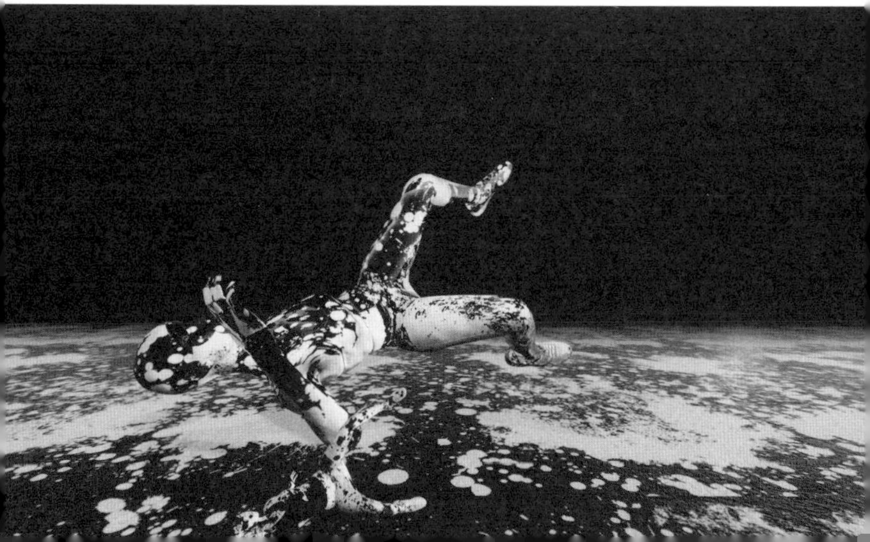

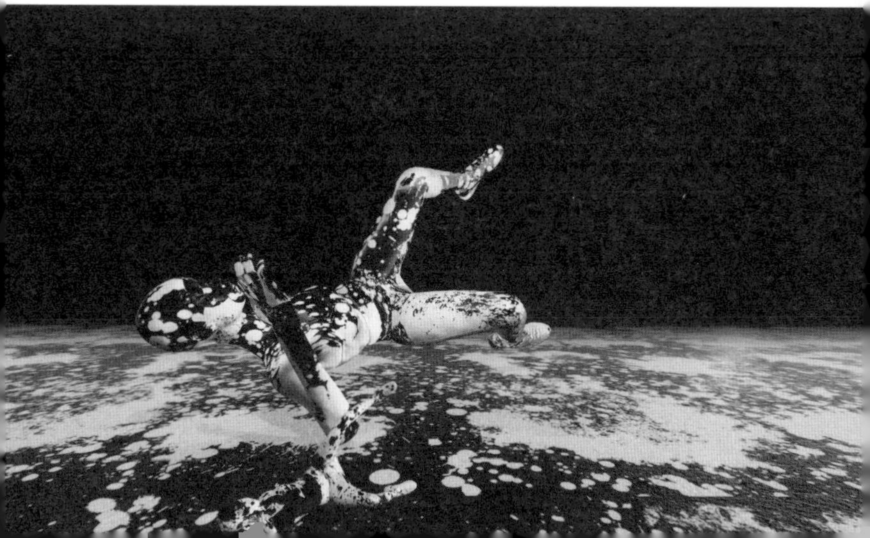

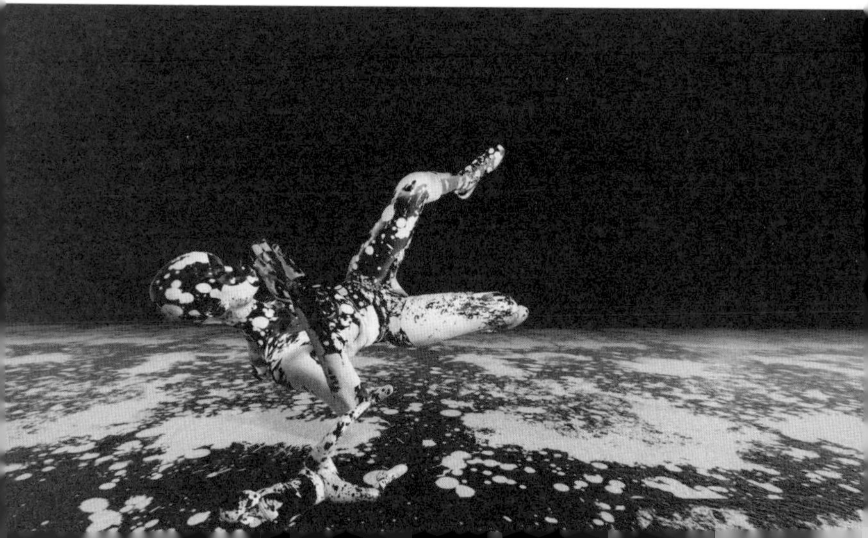

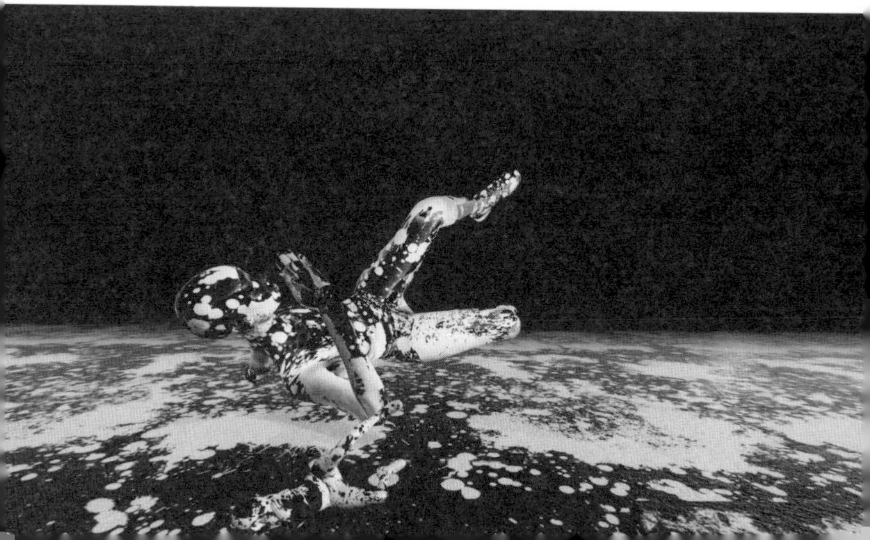

09

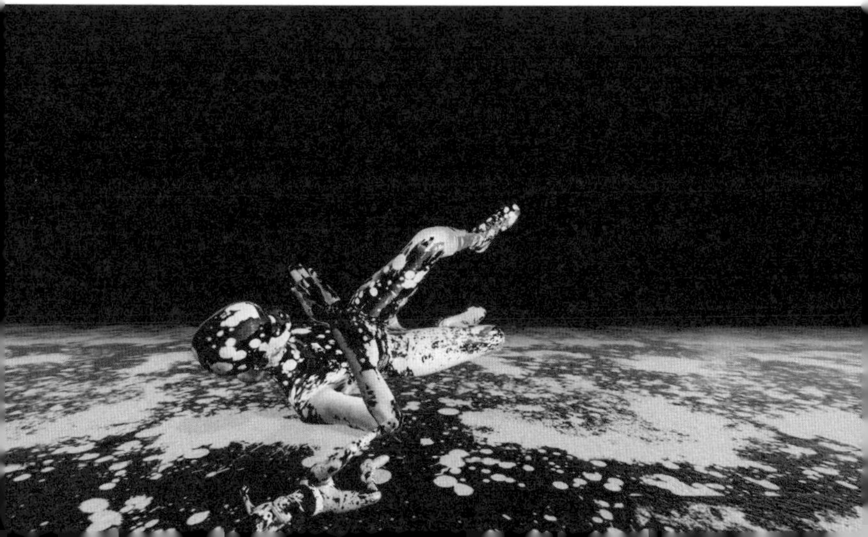

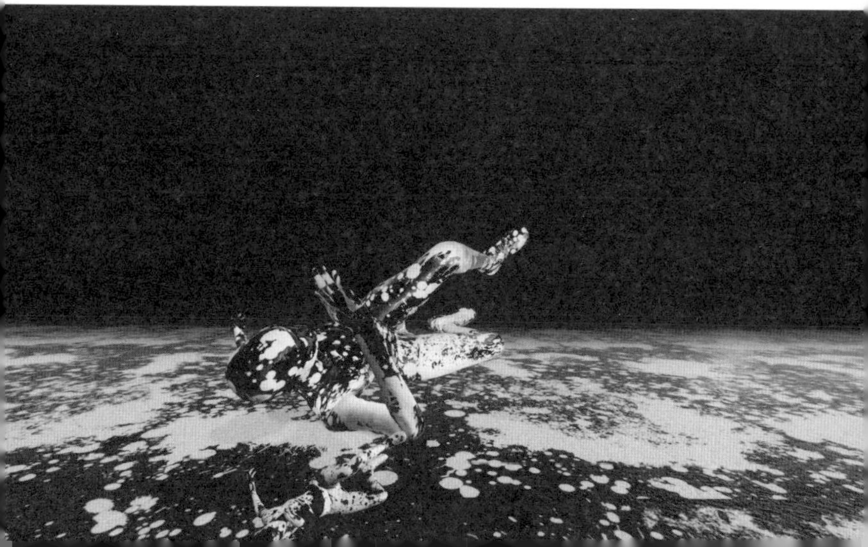

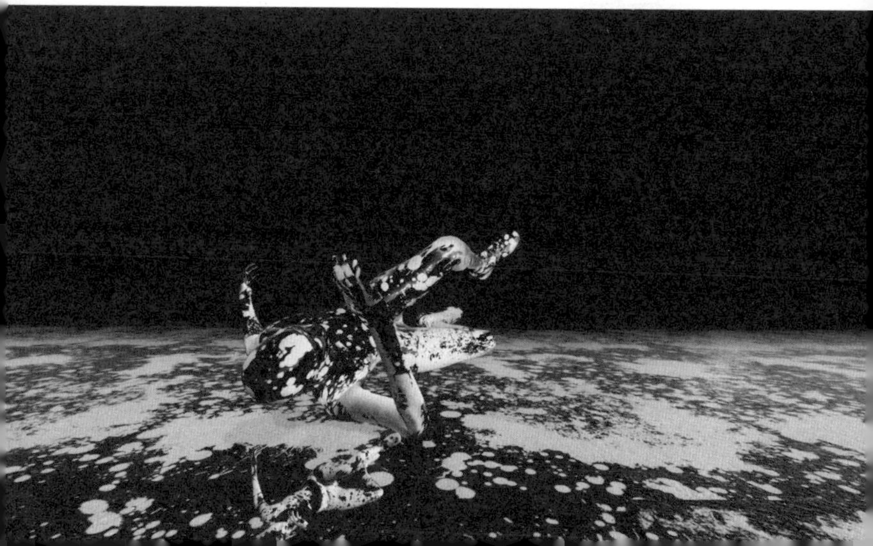

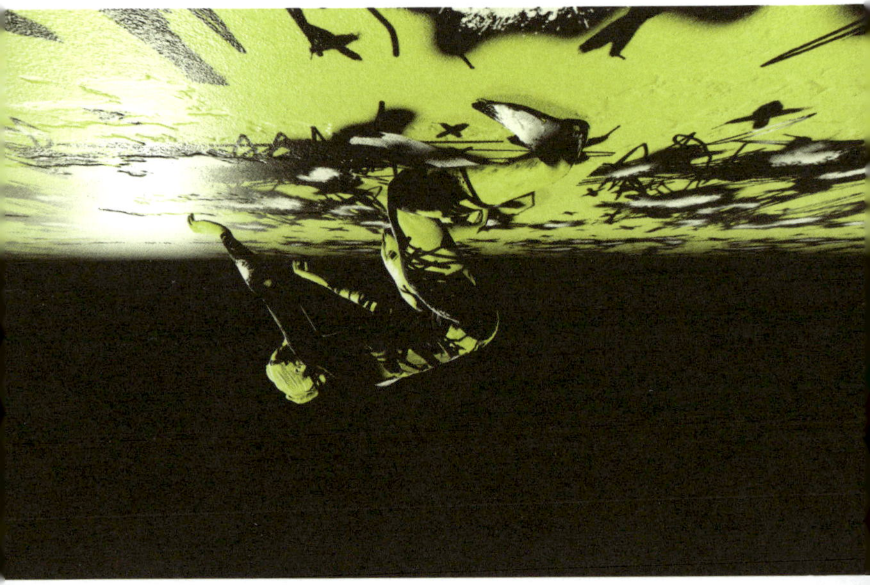

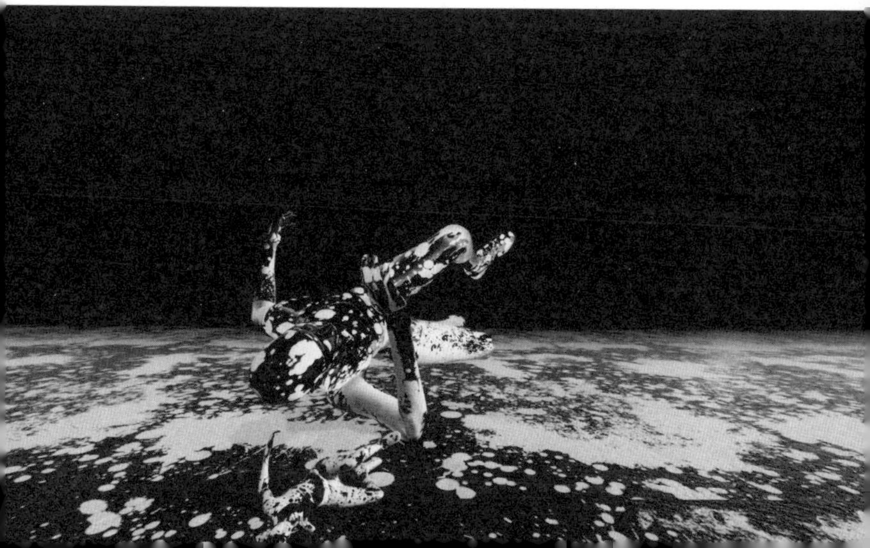

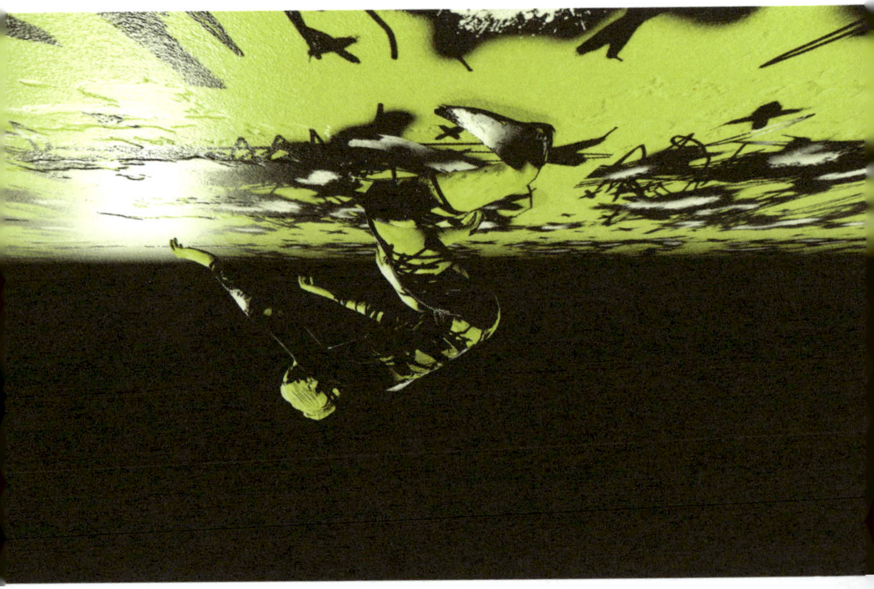

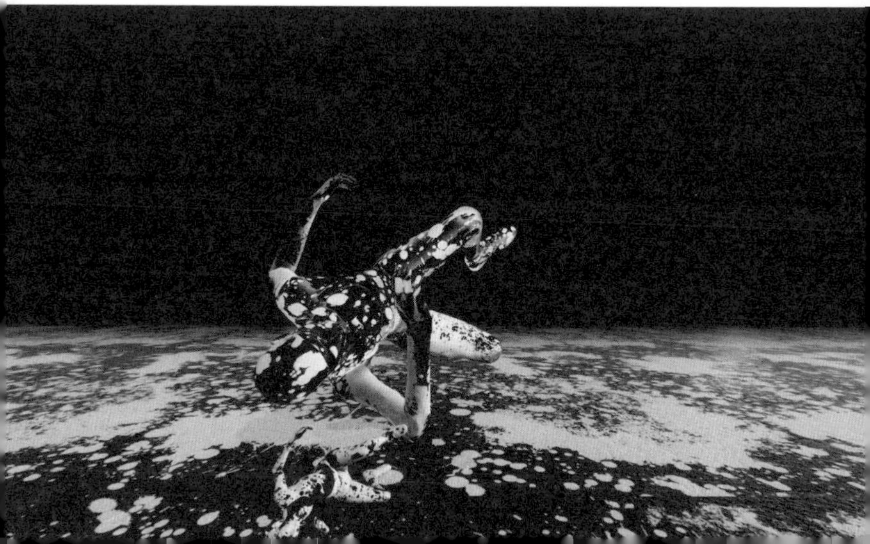

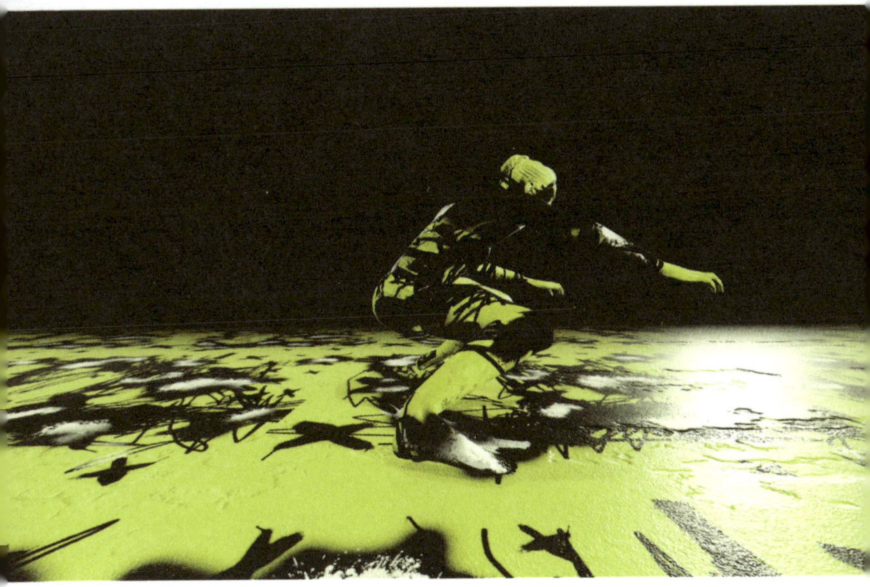

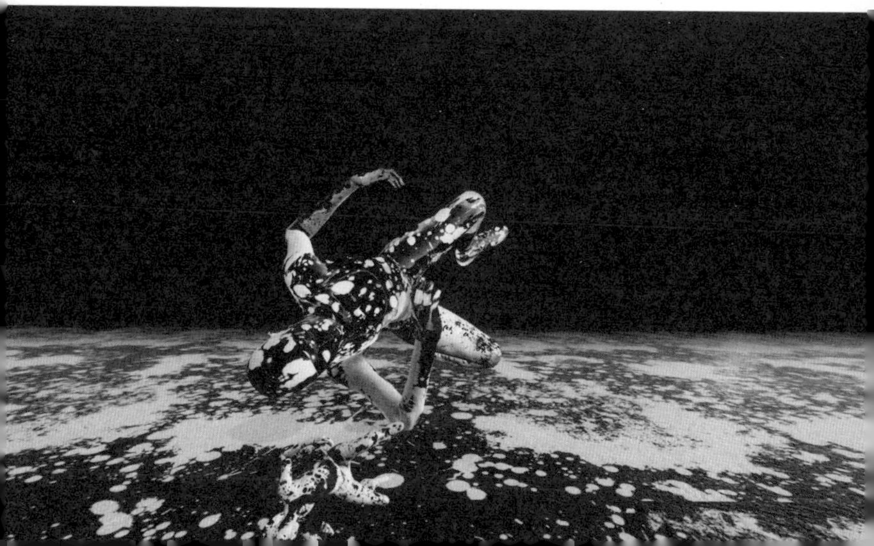

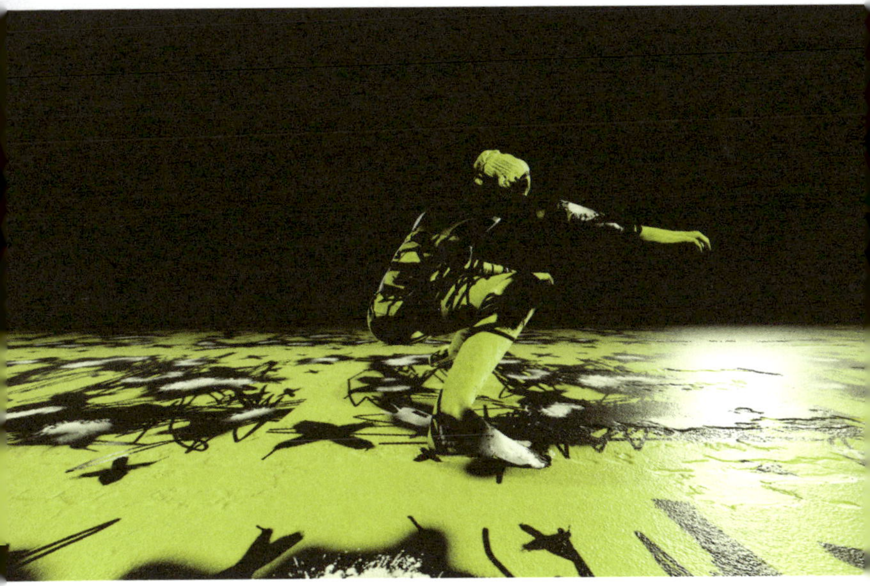

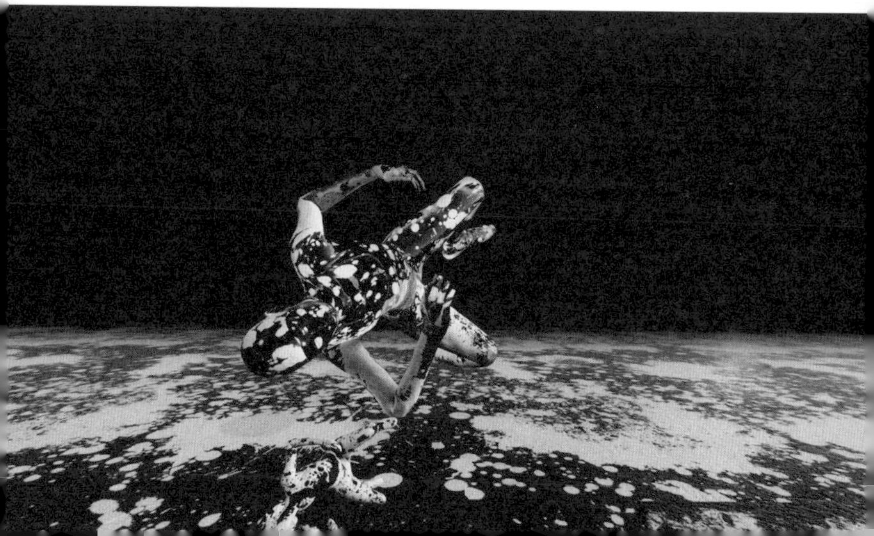

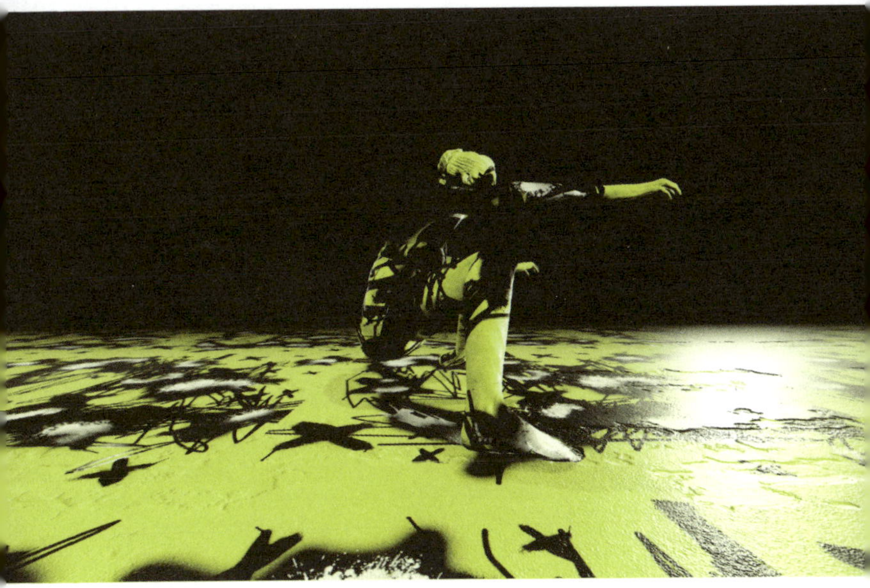

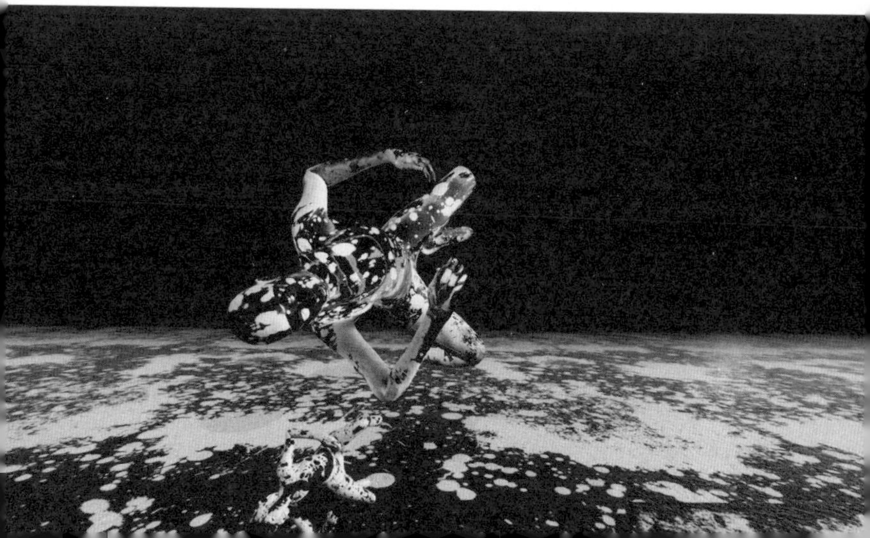

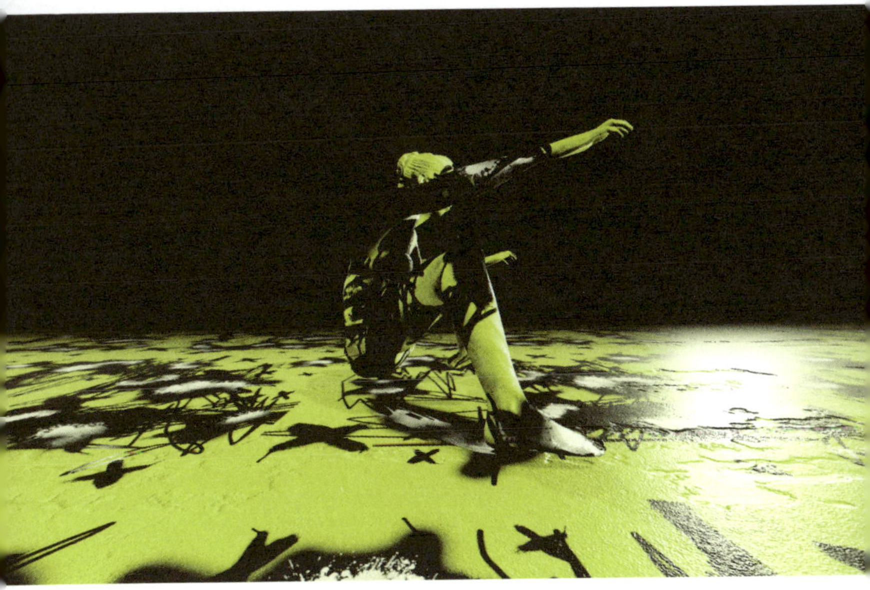

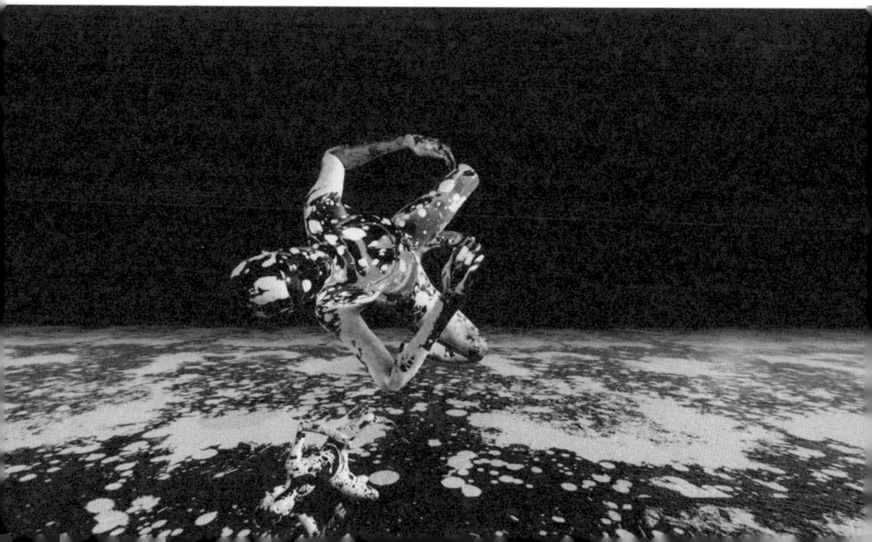

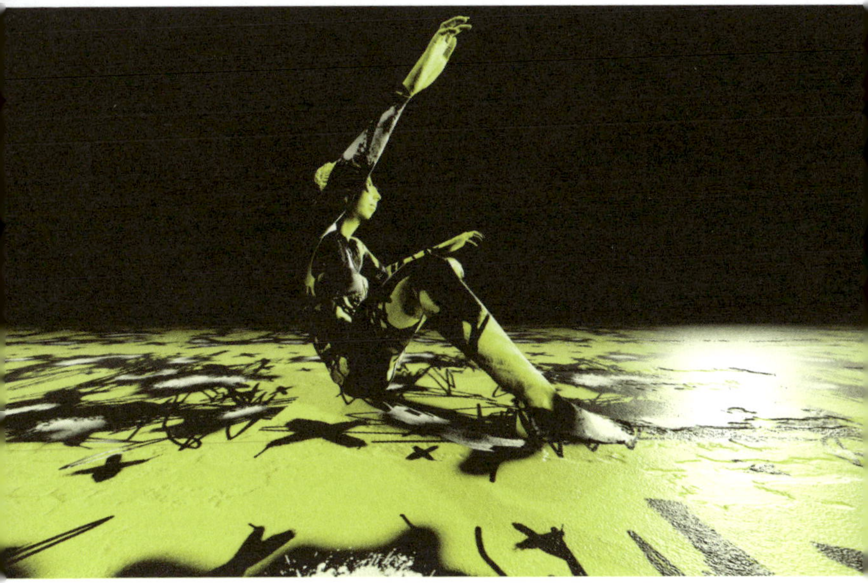

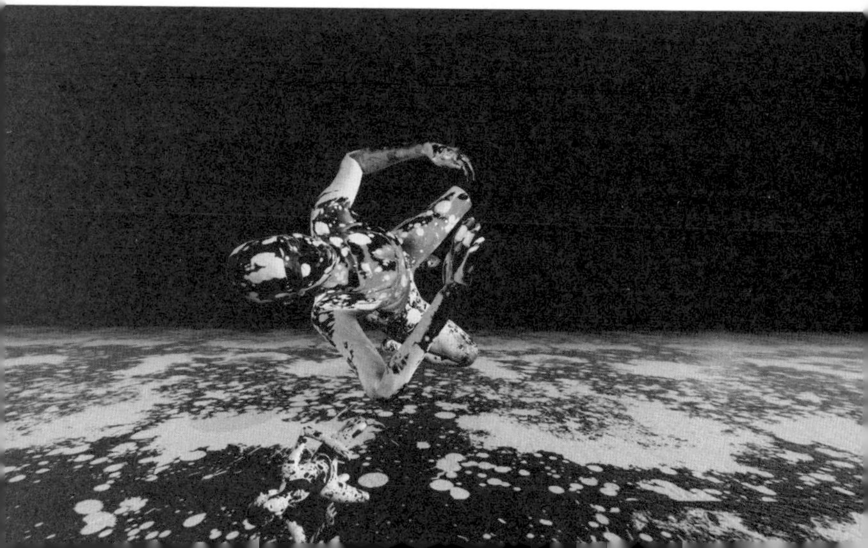

08

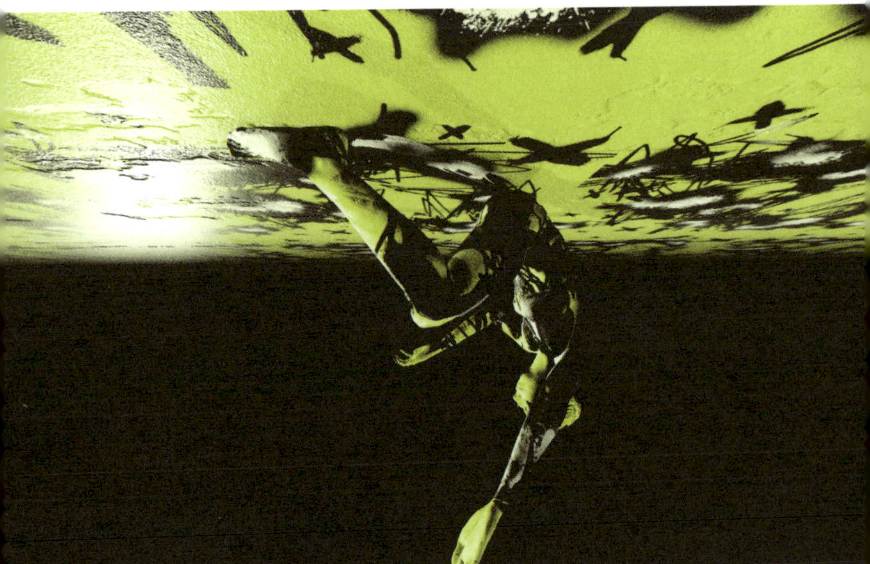

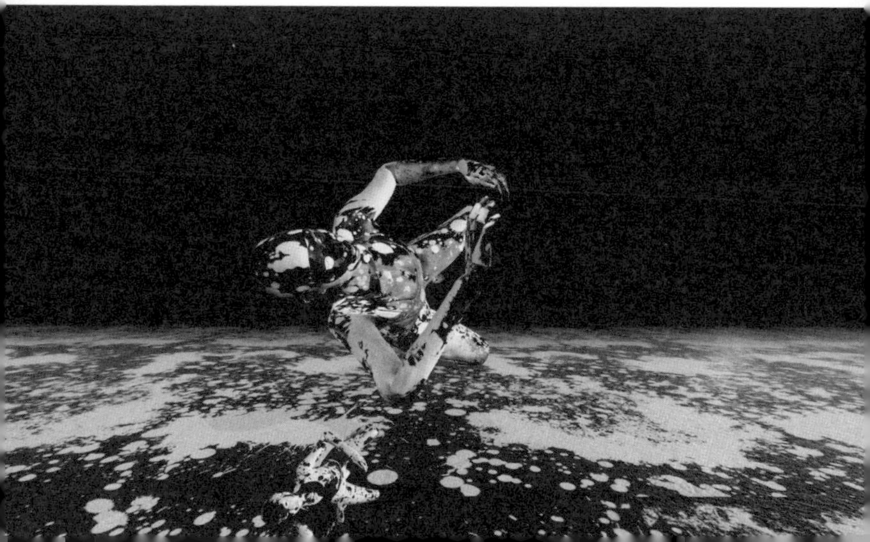

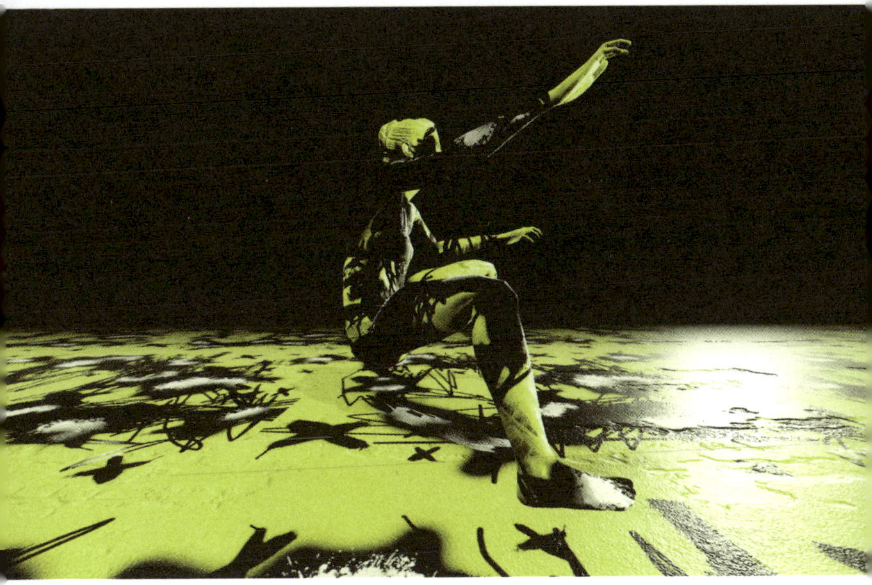

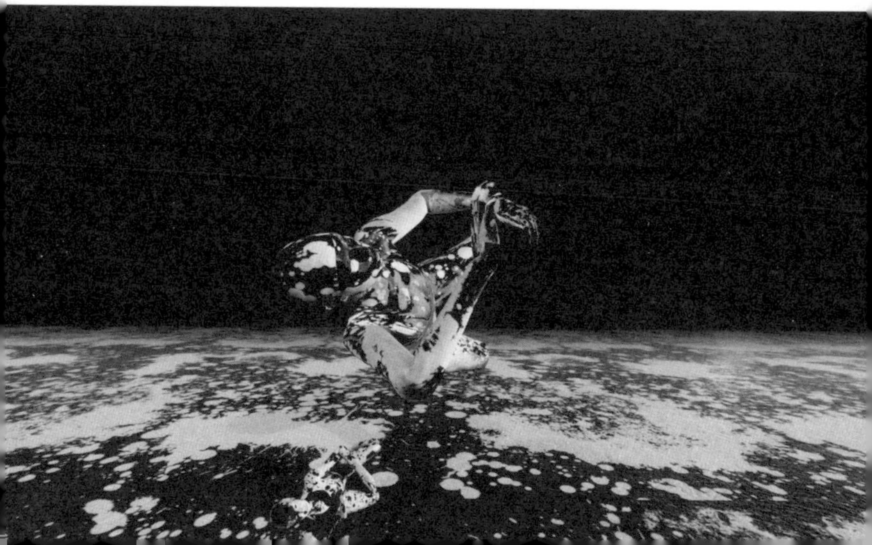

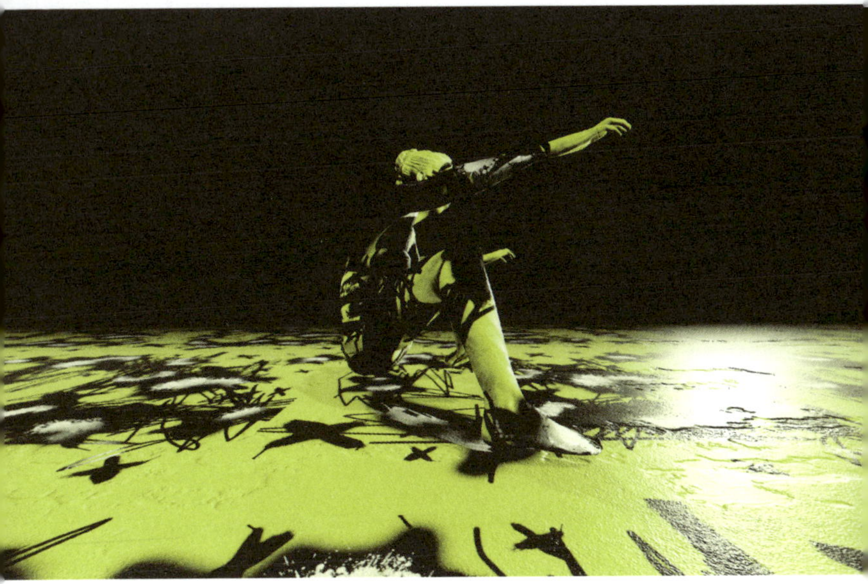

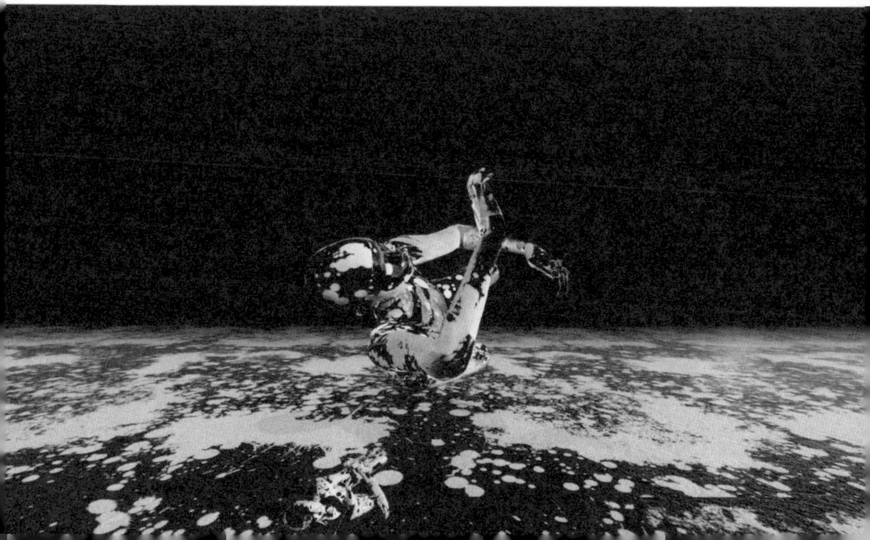

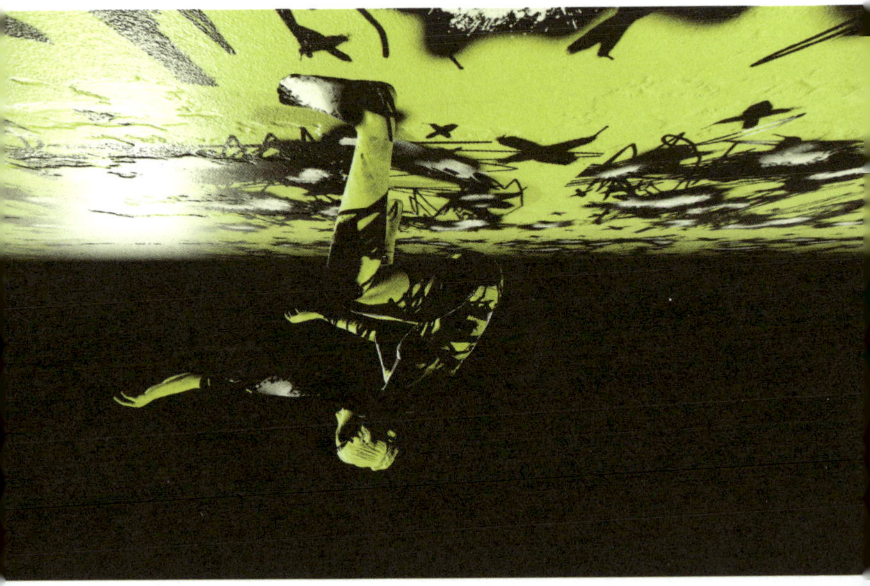

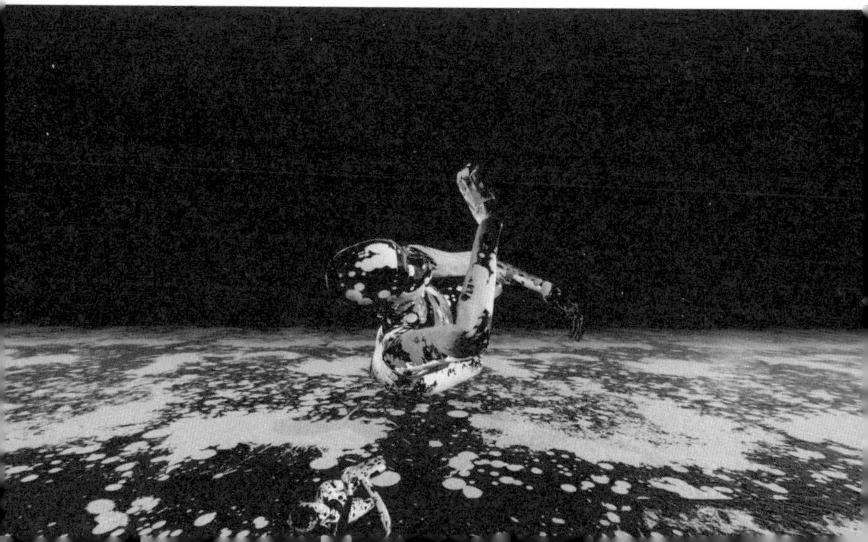

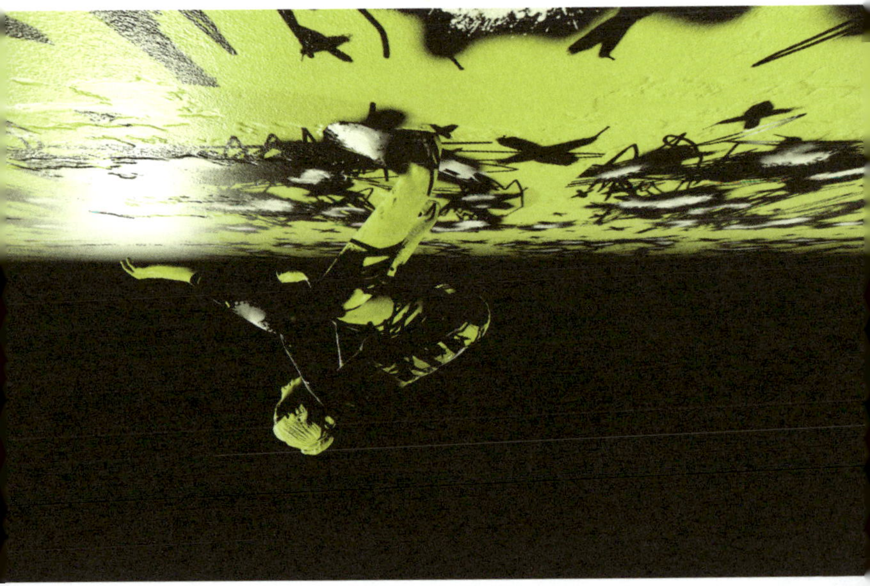

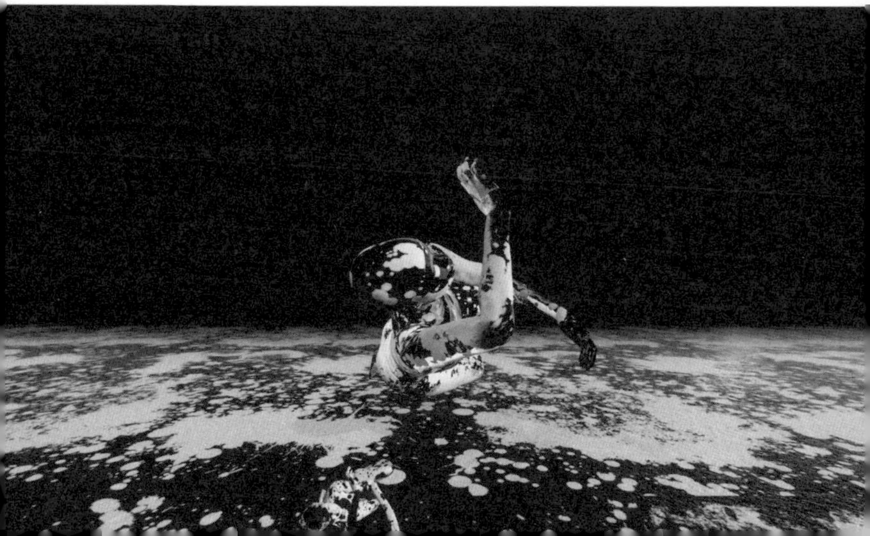

06

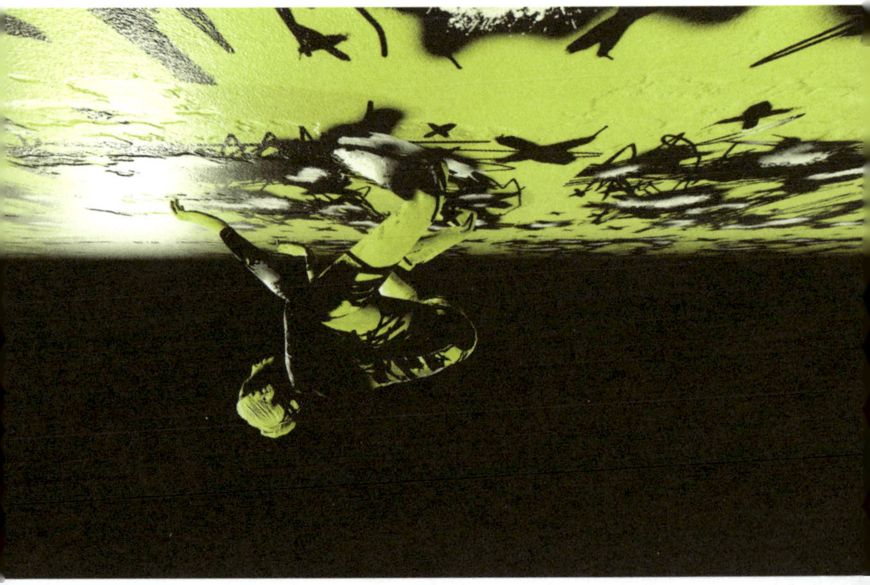

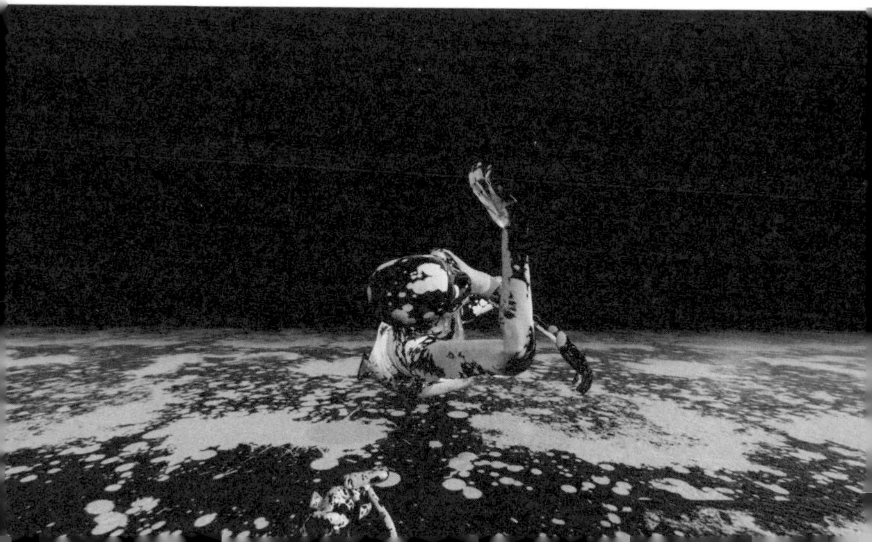

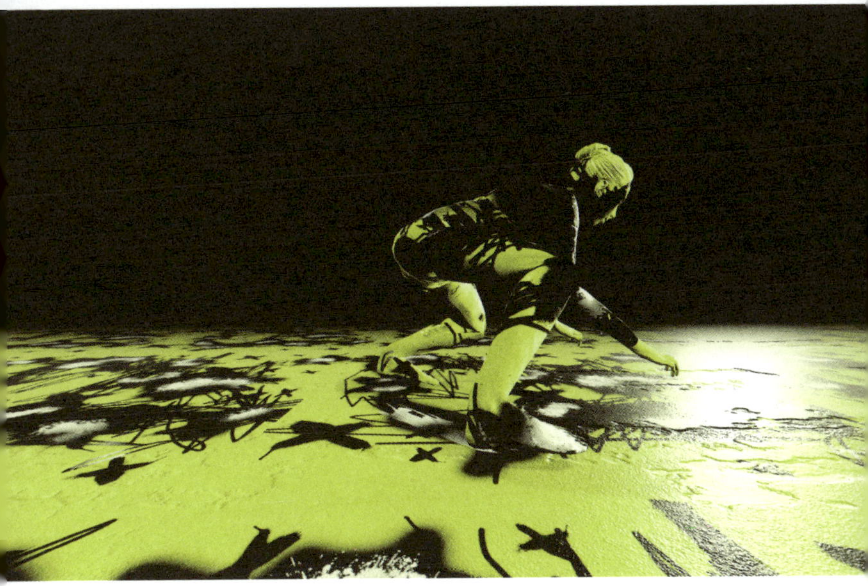

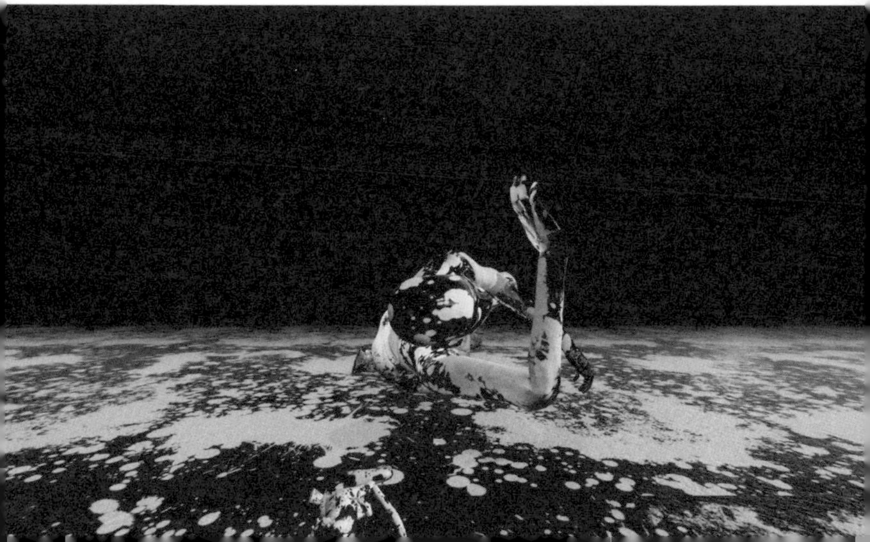

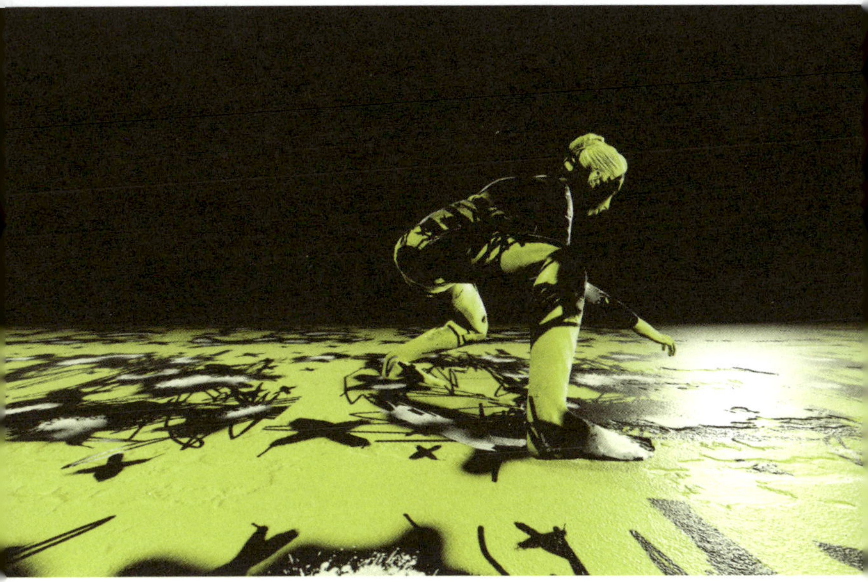

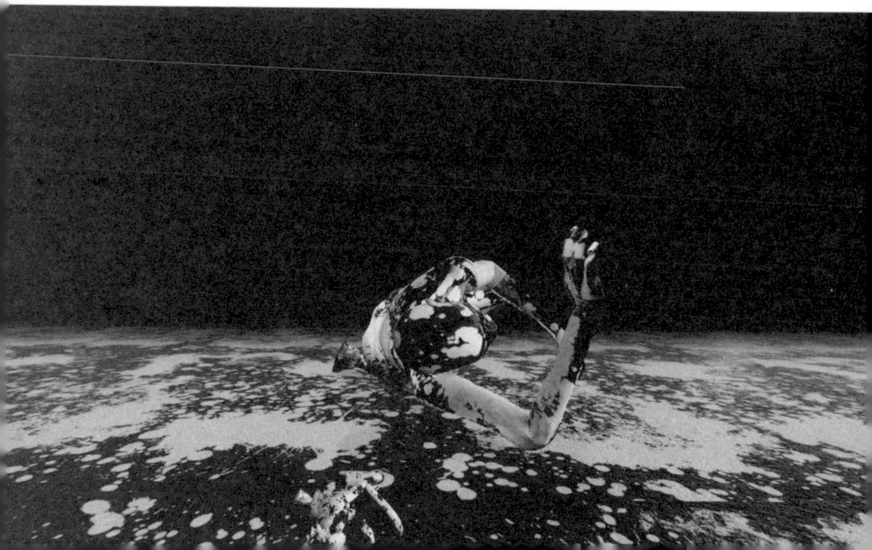

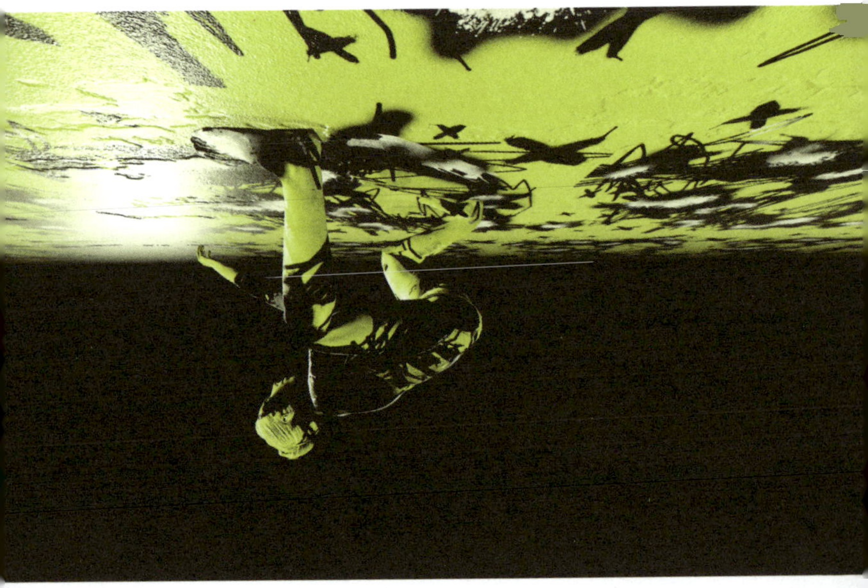

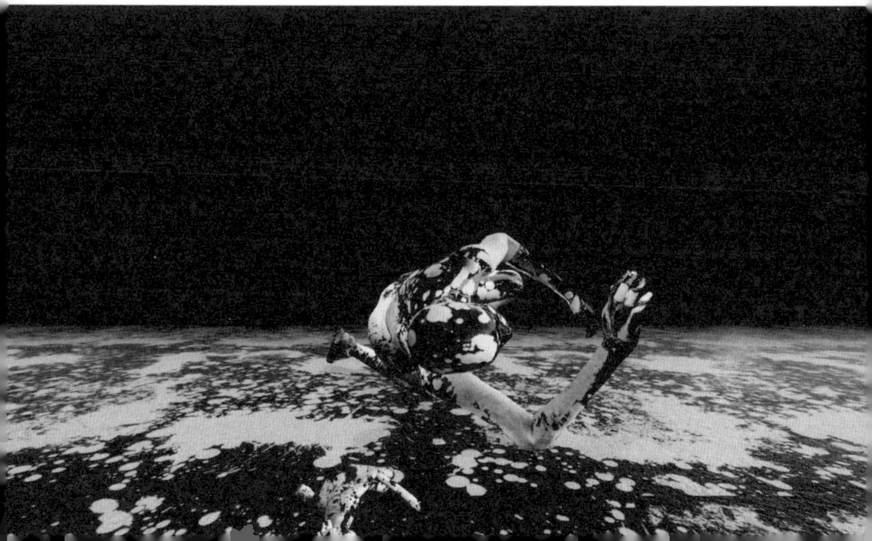

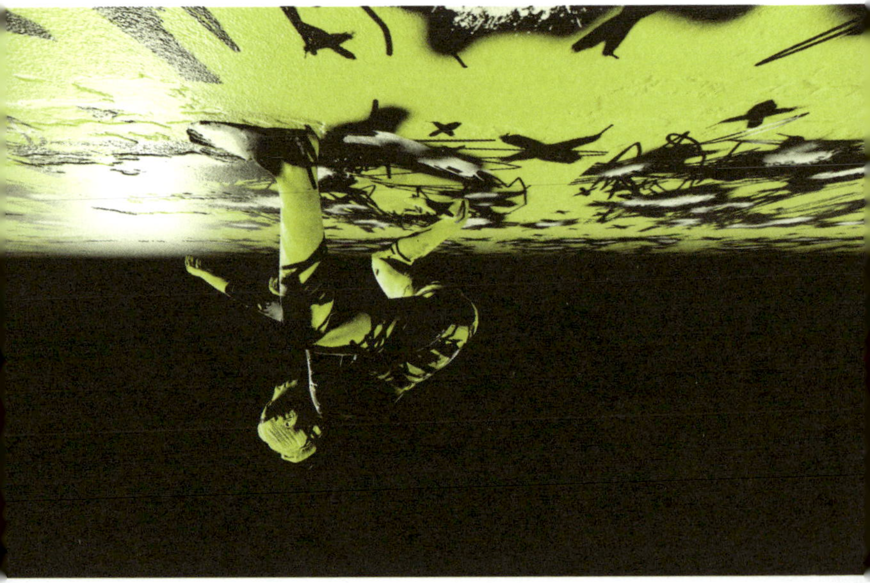

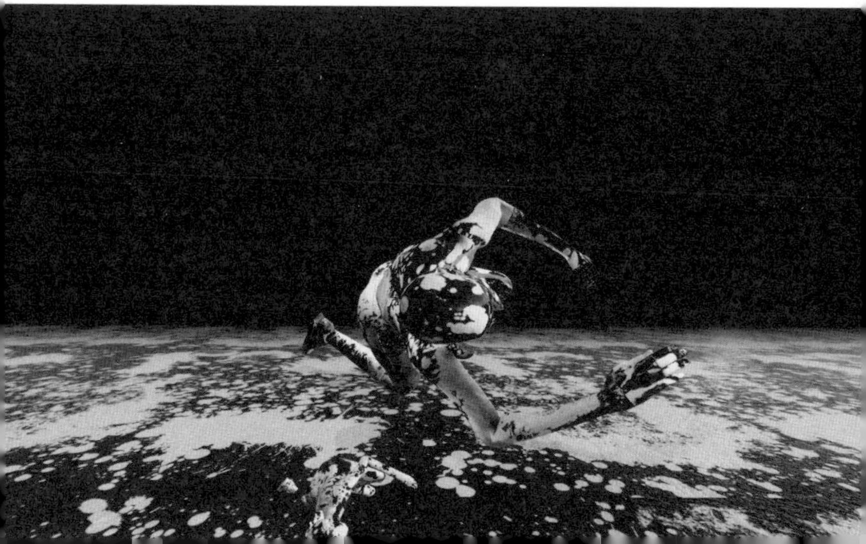

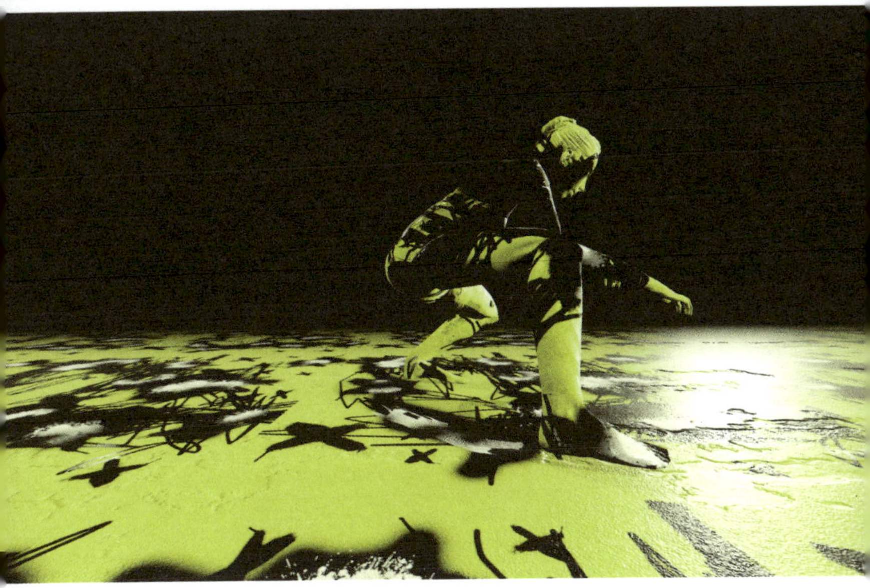

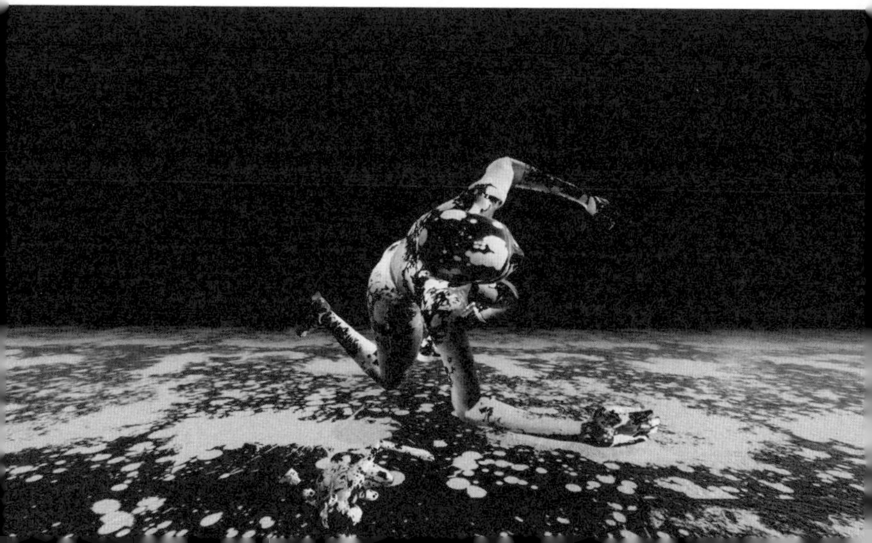

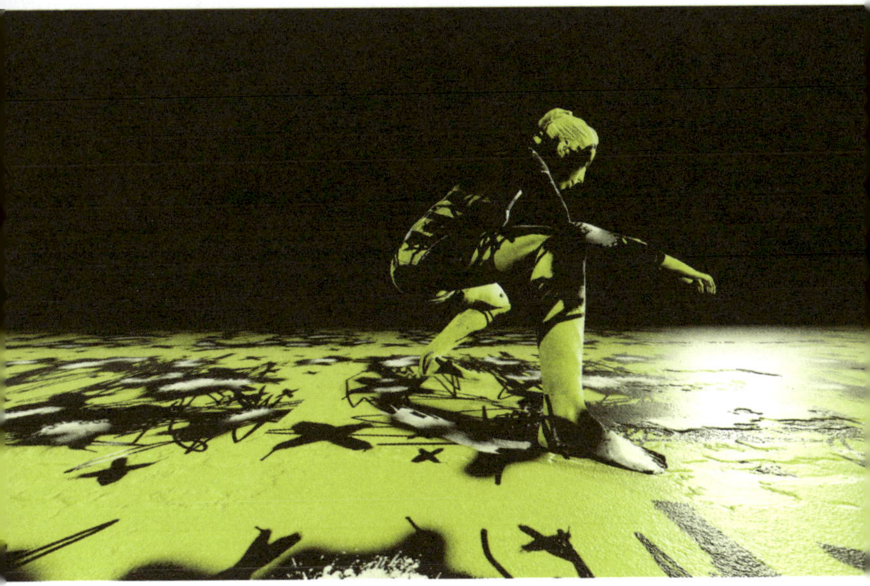

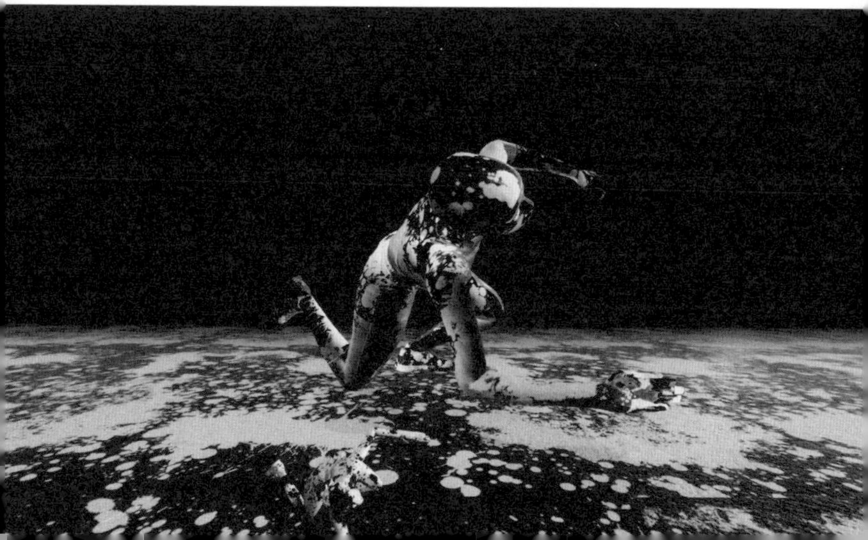

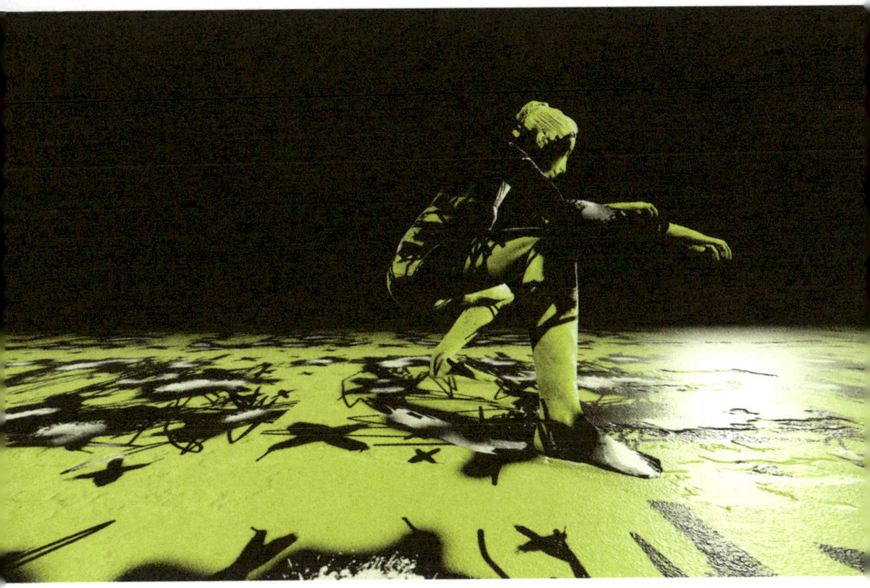

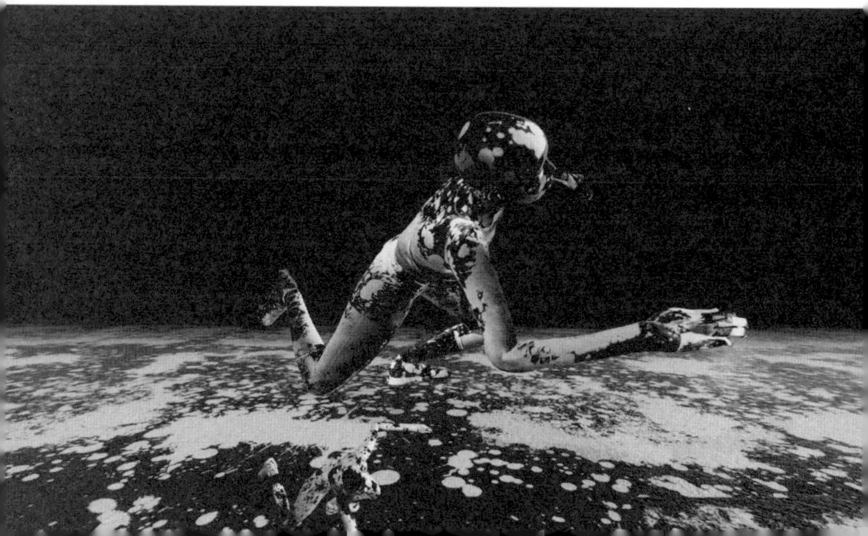

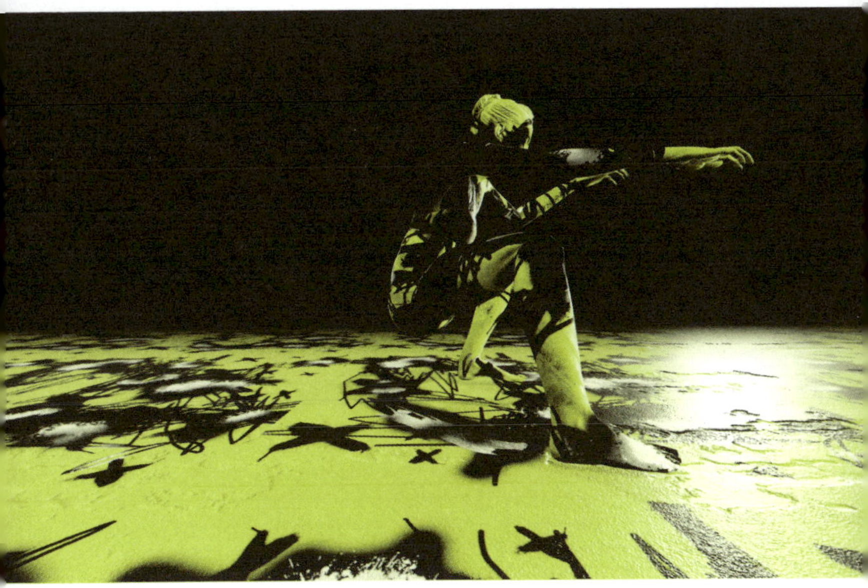

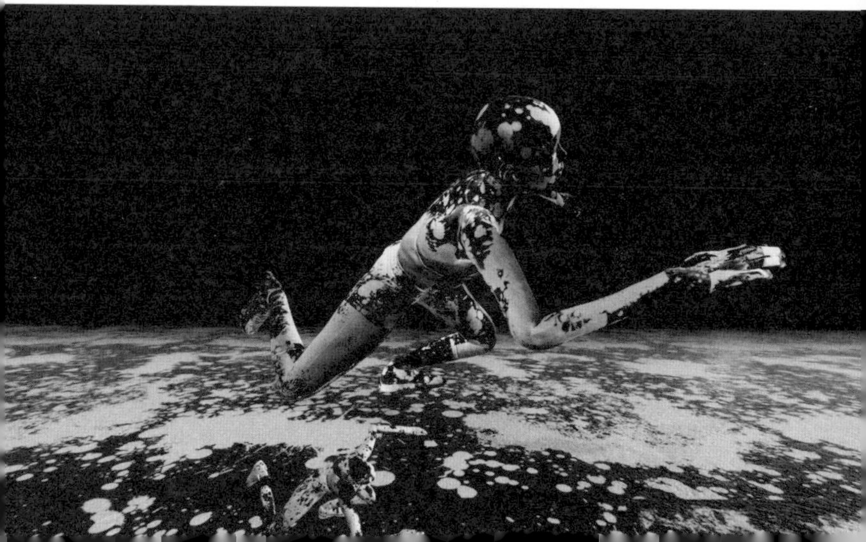

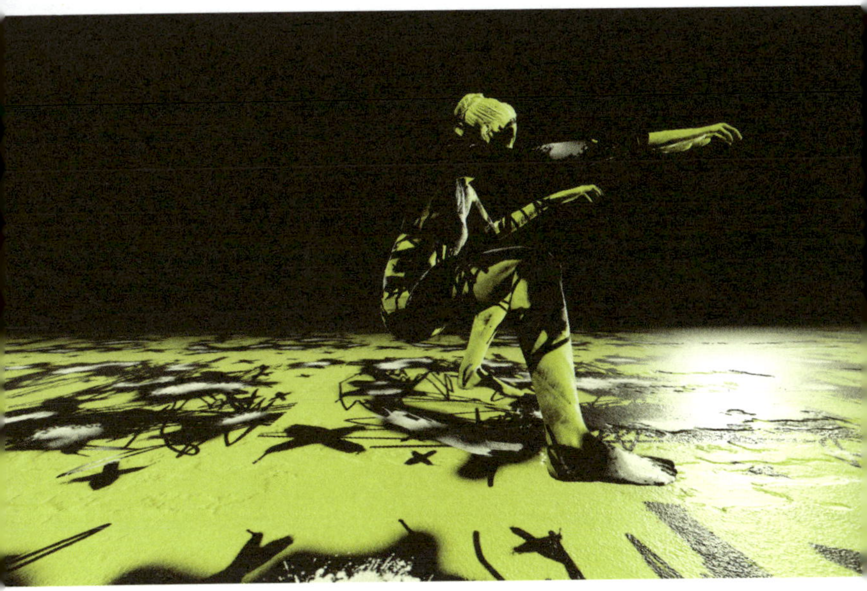

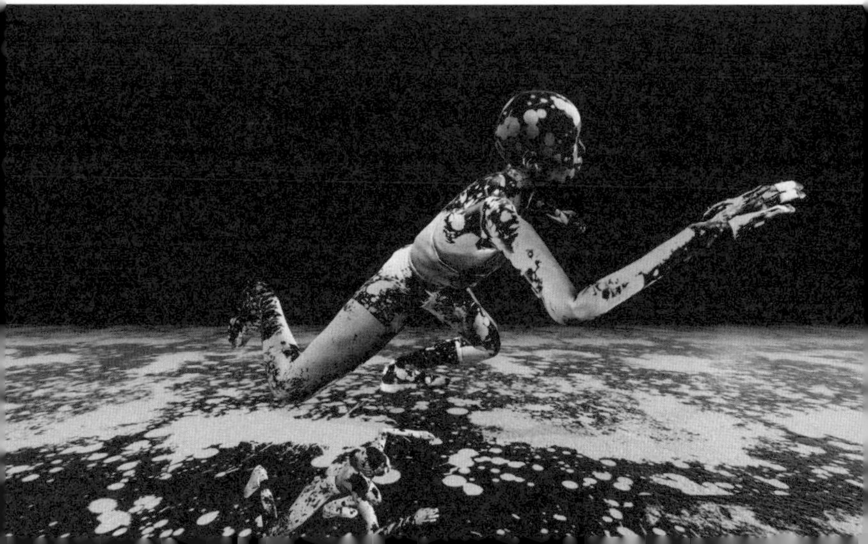

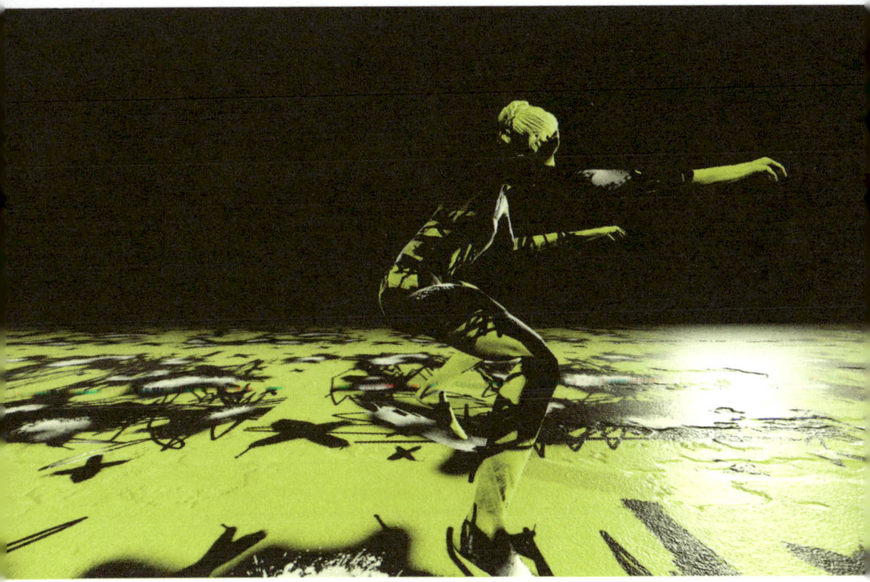

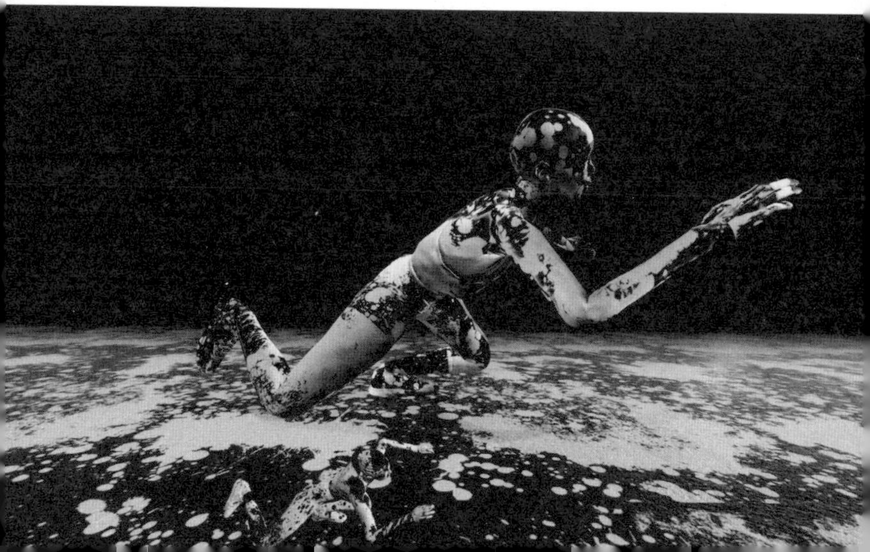

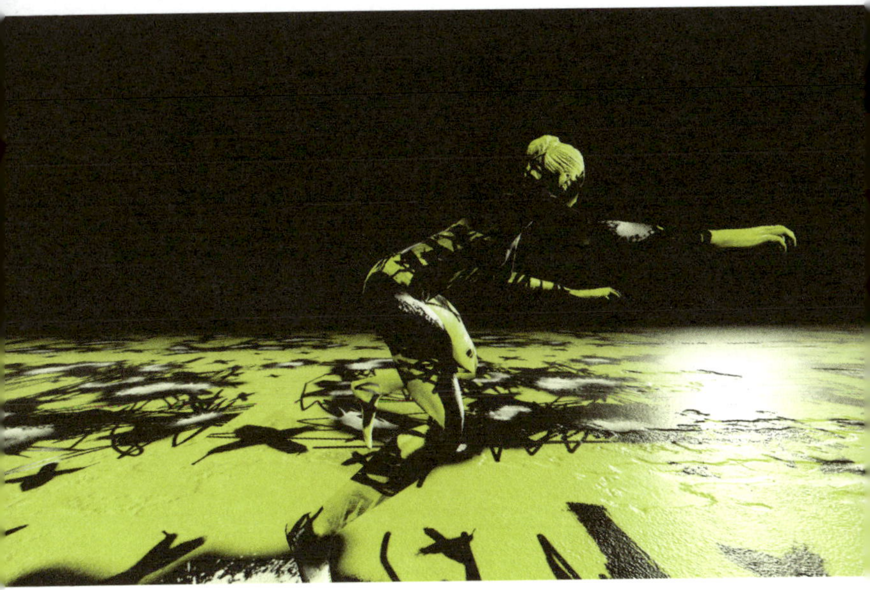

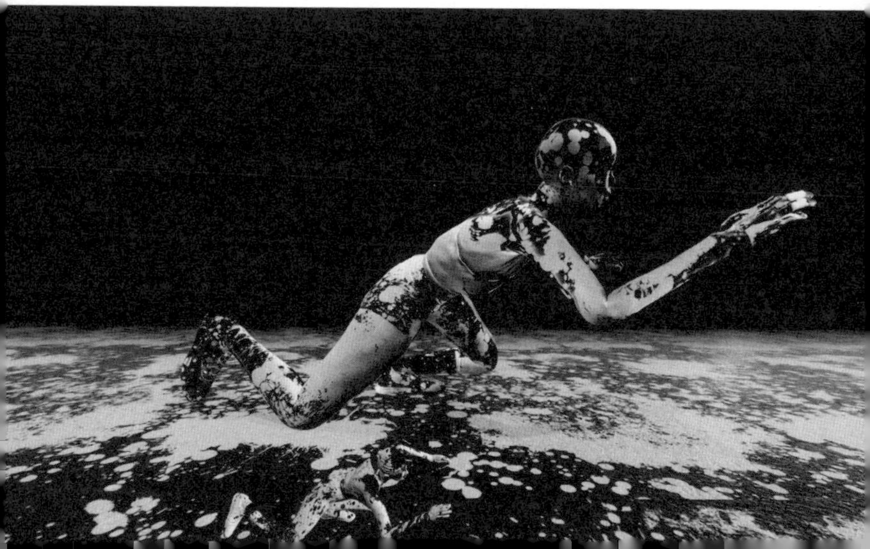

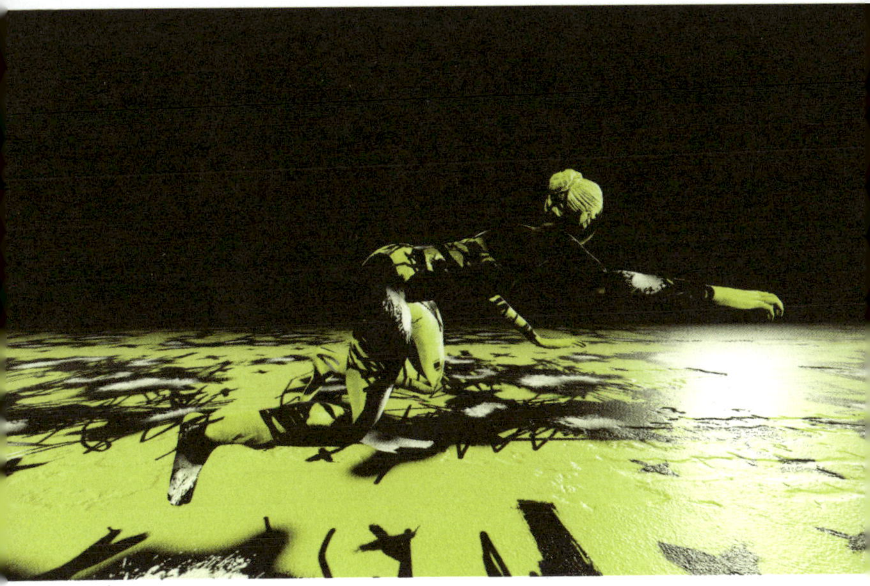

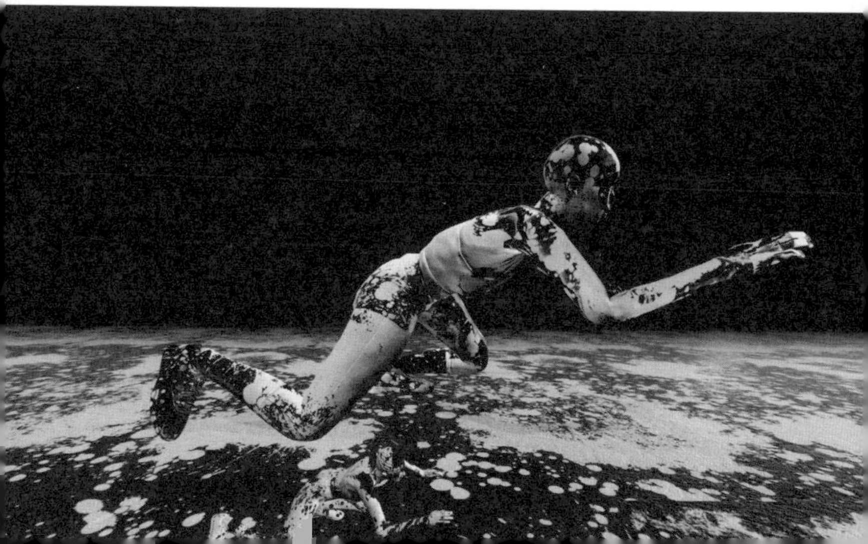

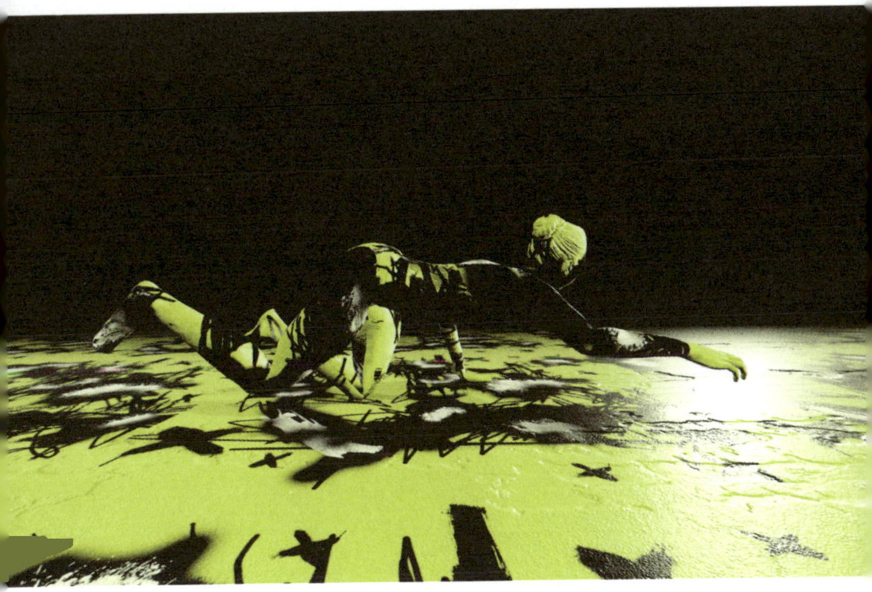

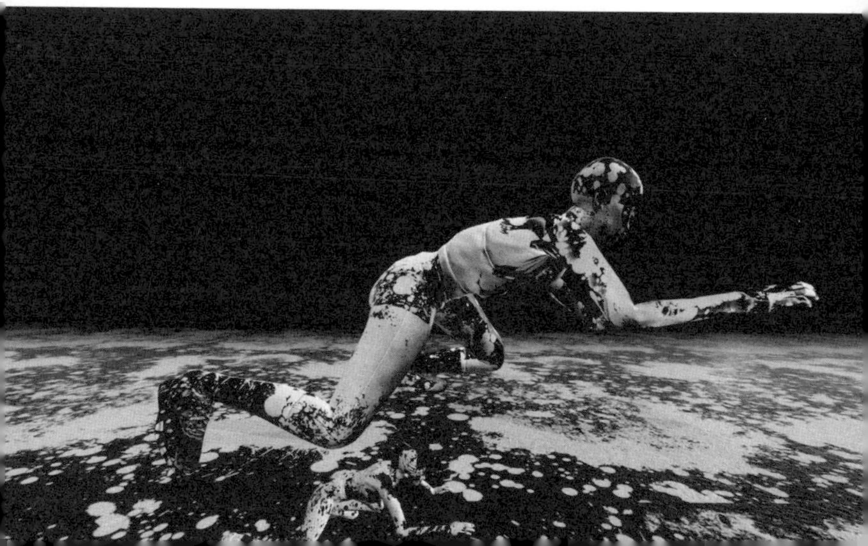

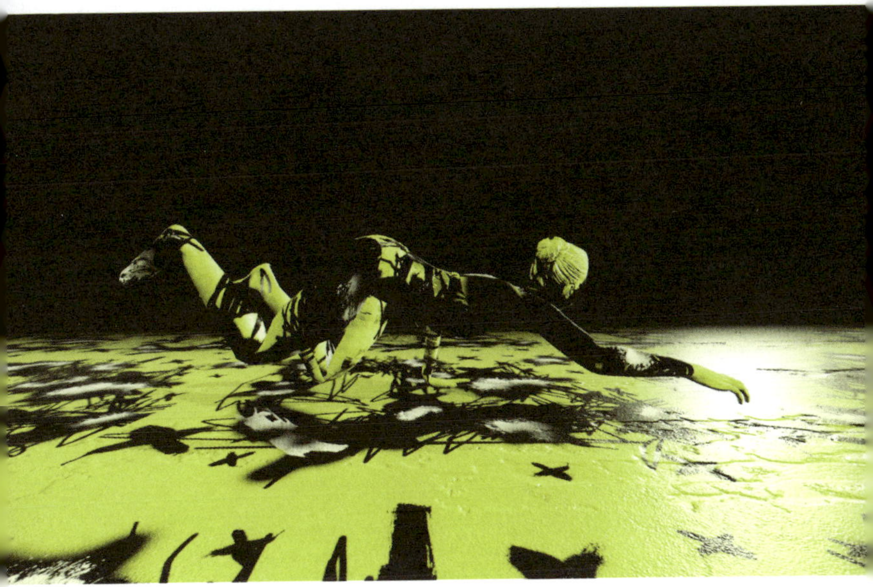

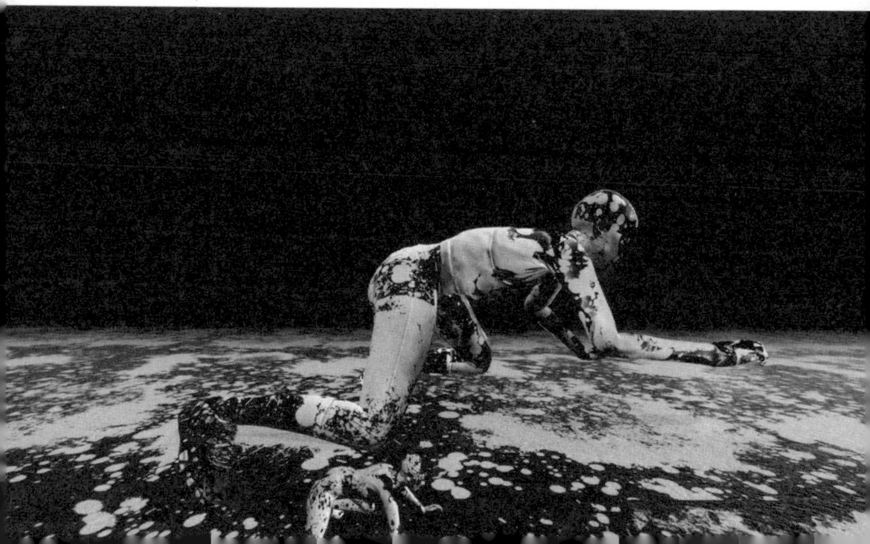

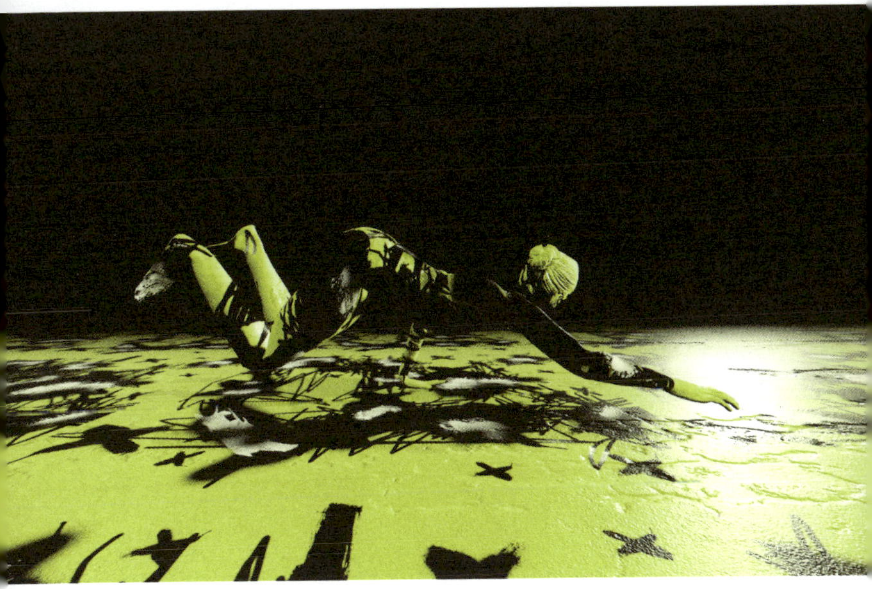

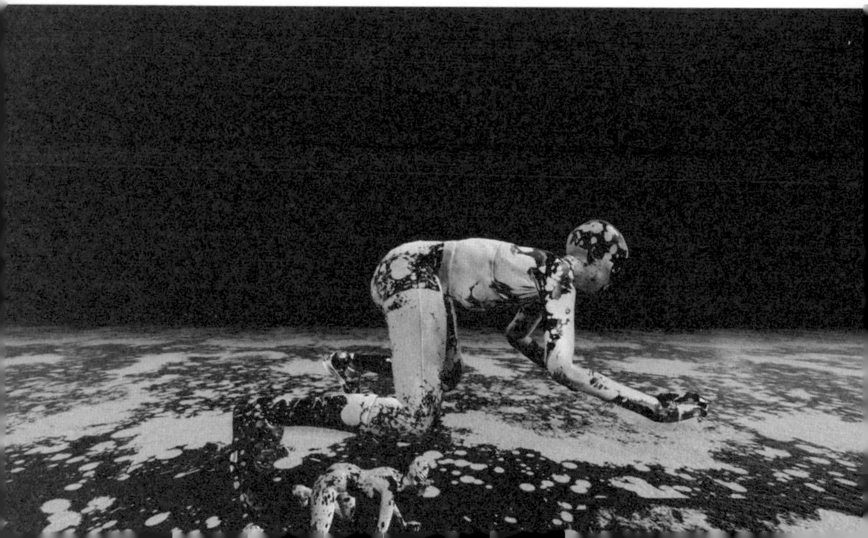

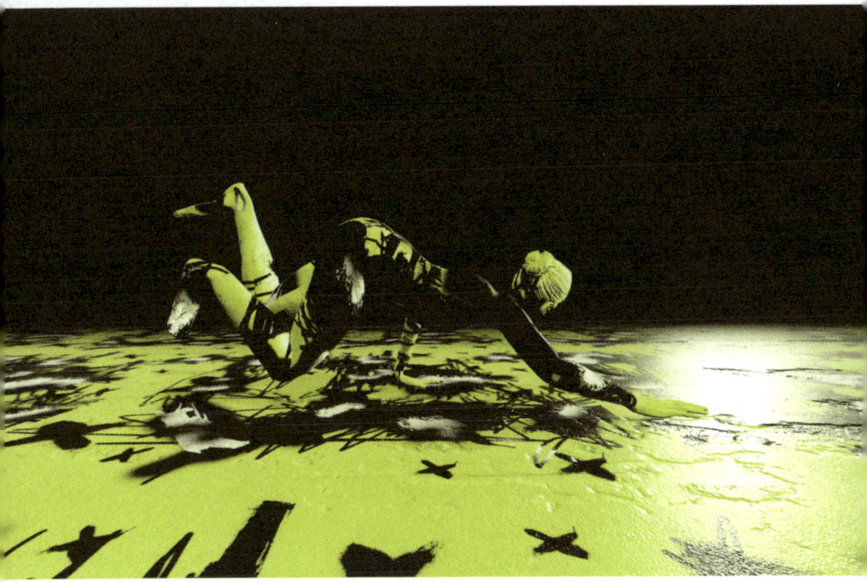

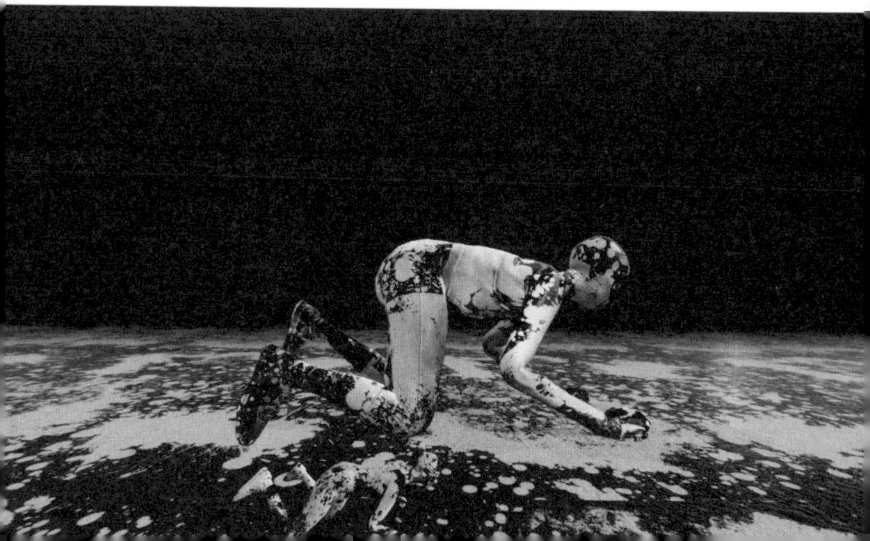

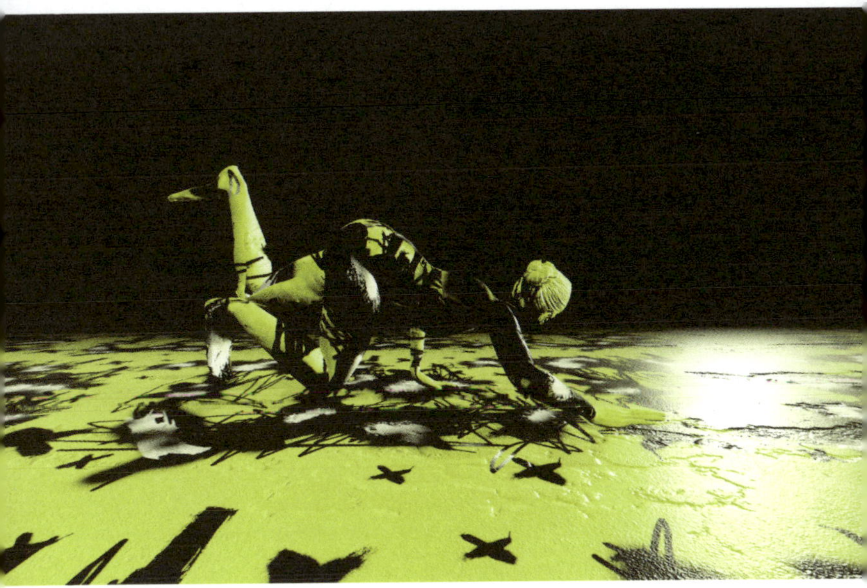

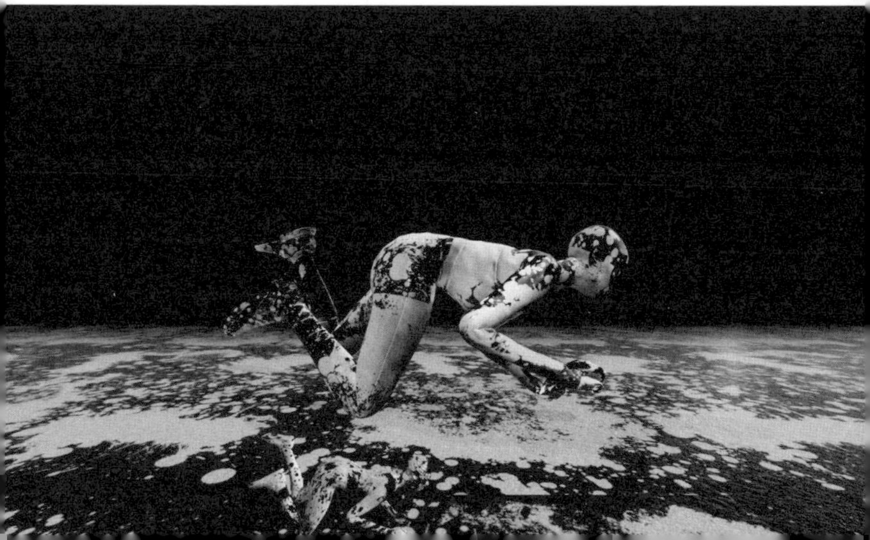

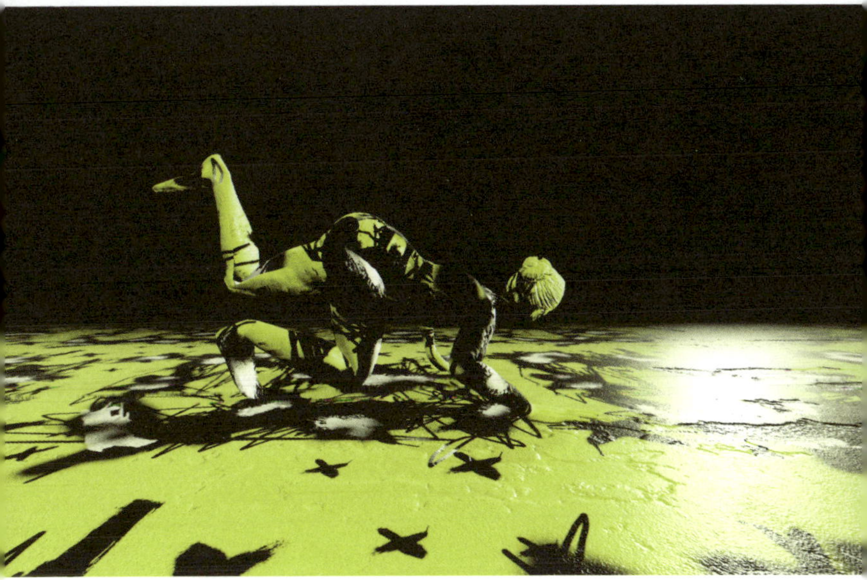

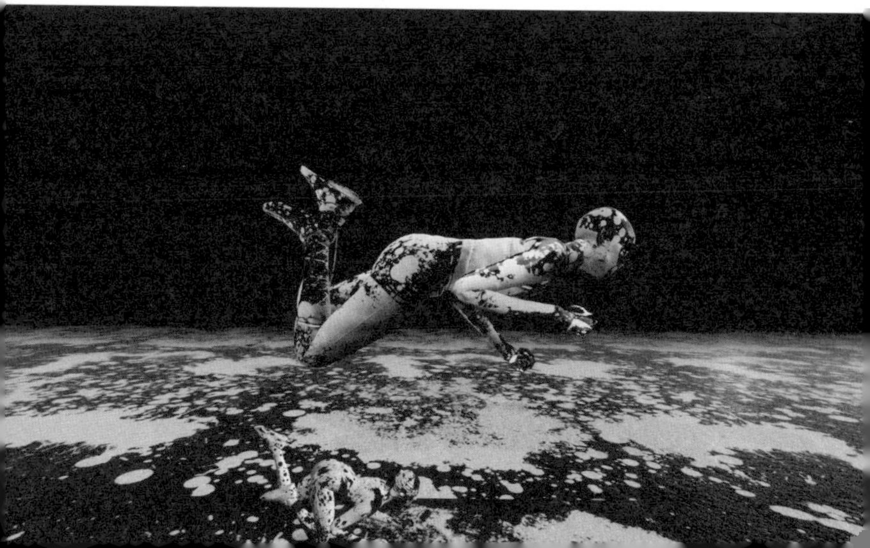

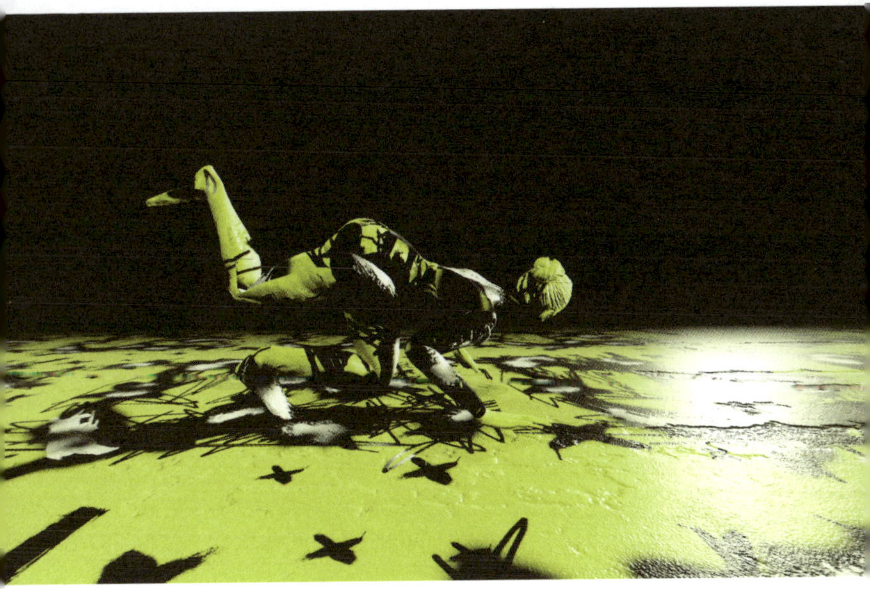

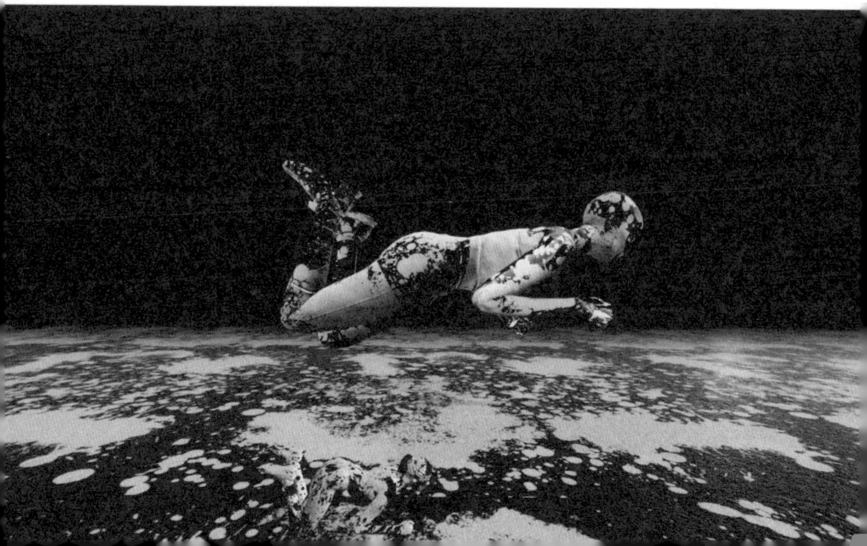

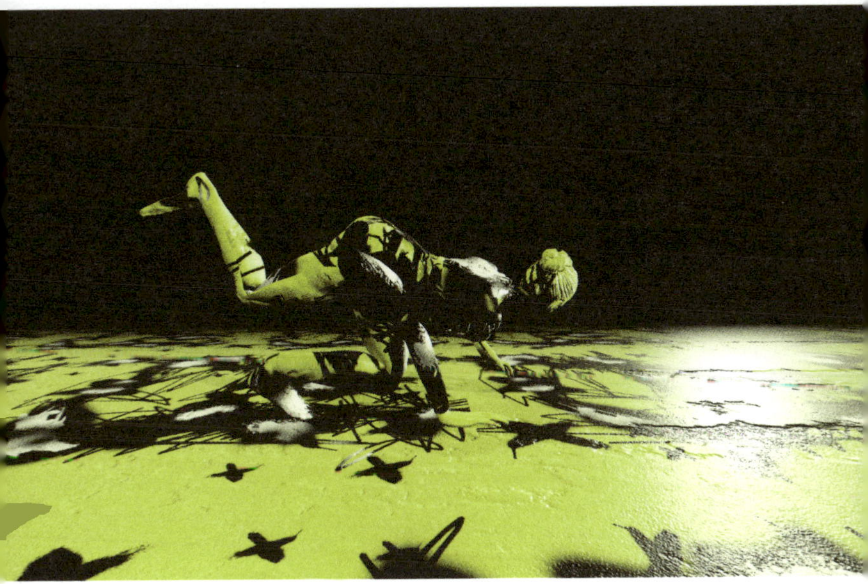

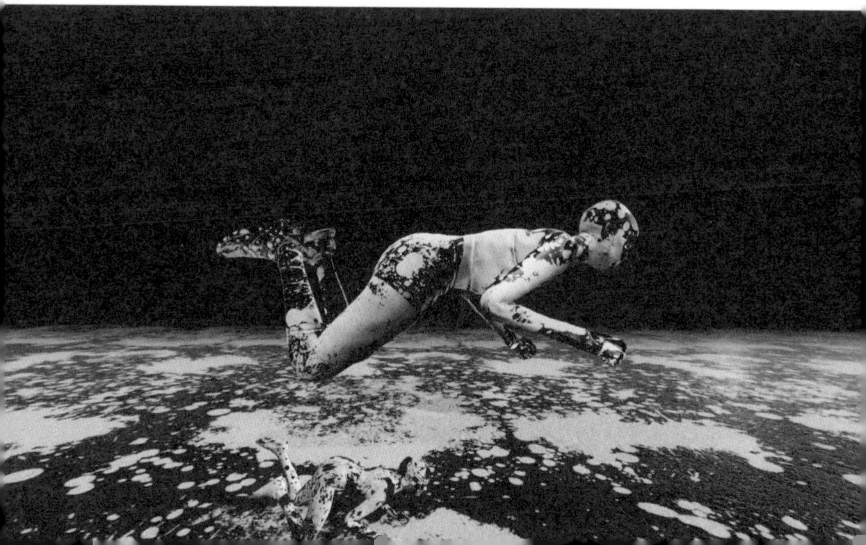

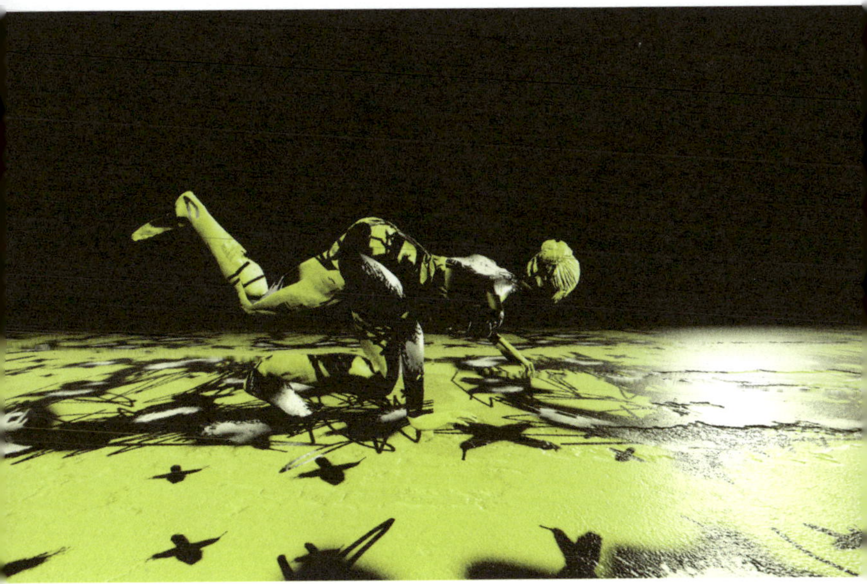

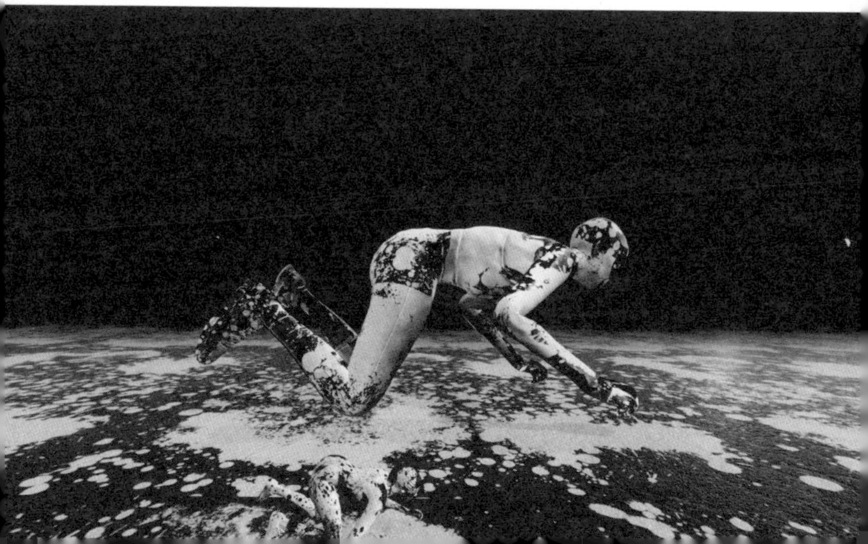

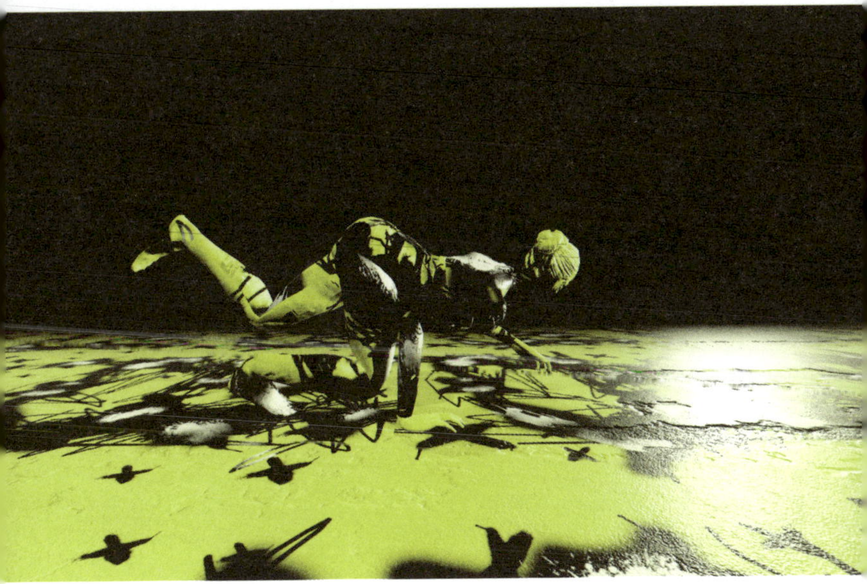

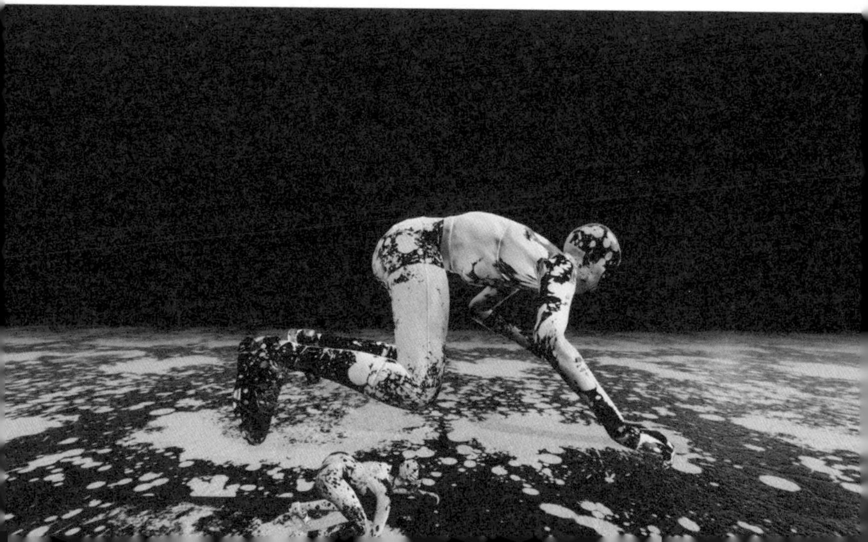

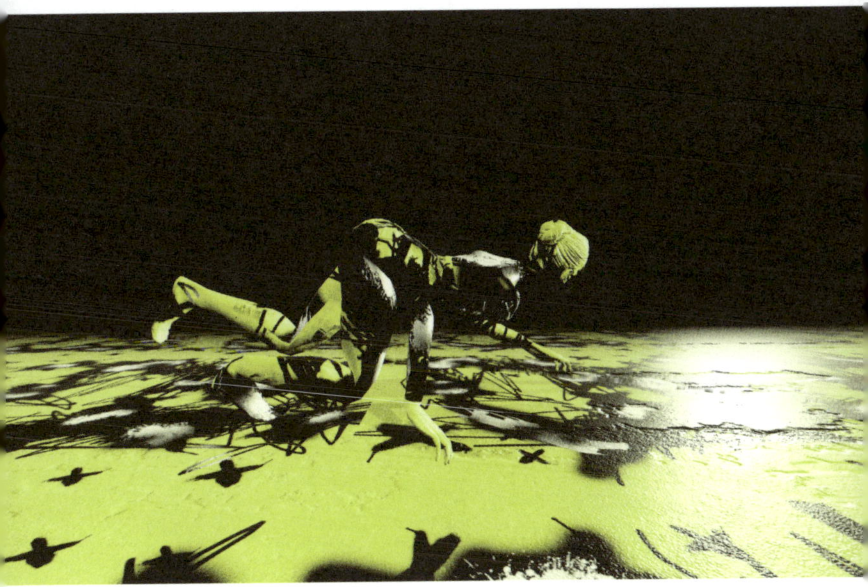

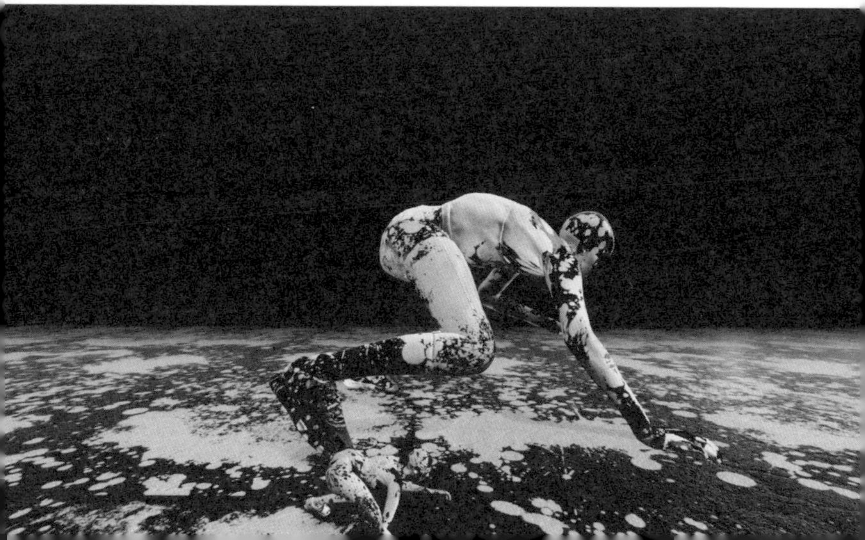

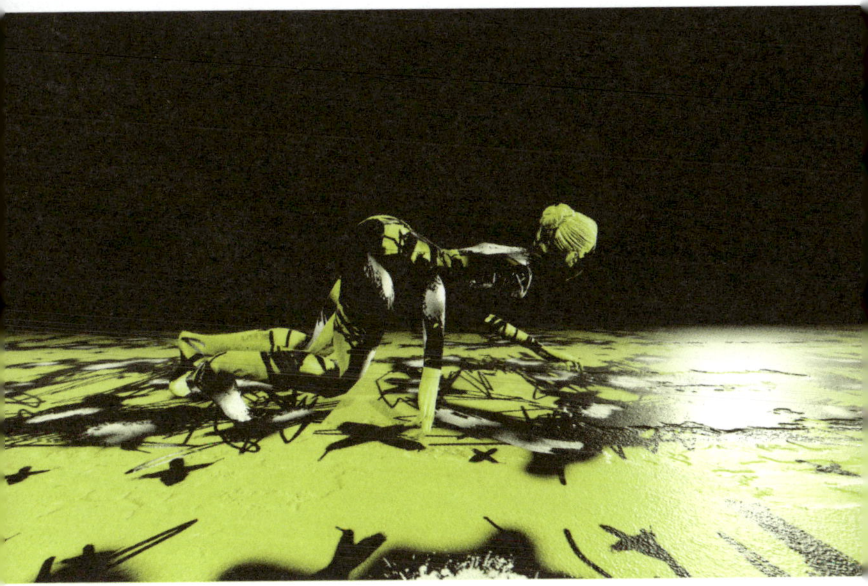

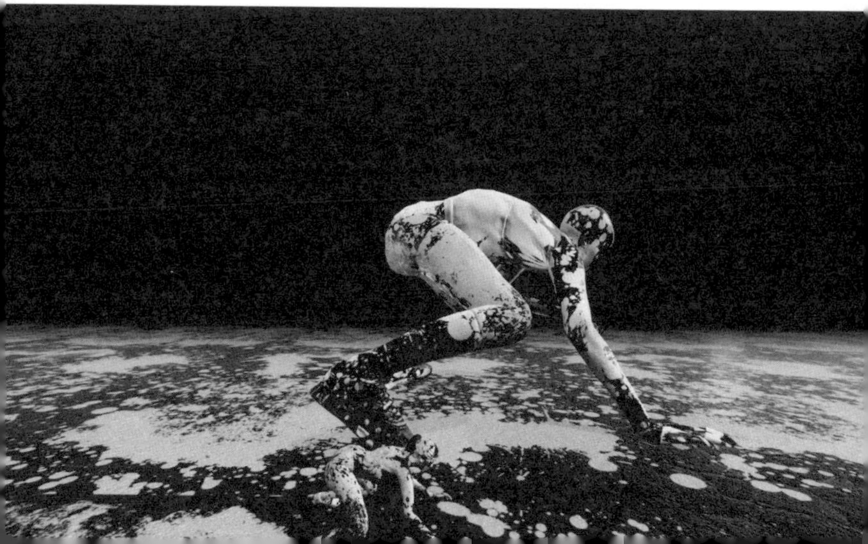

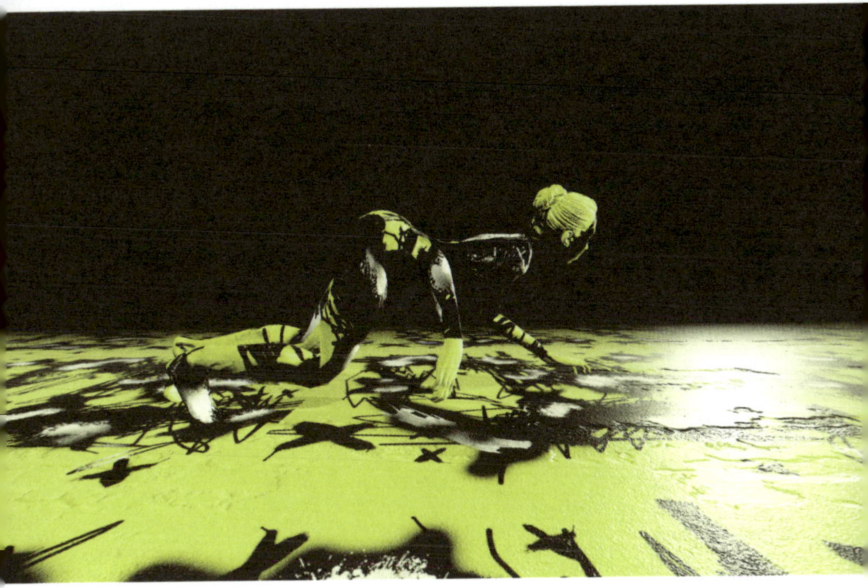

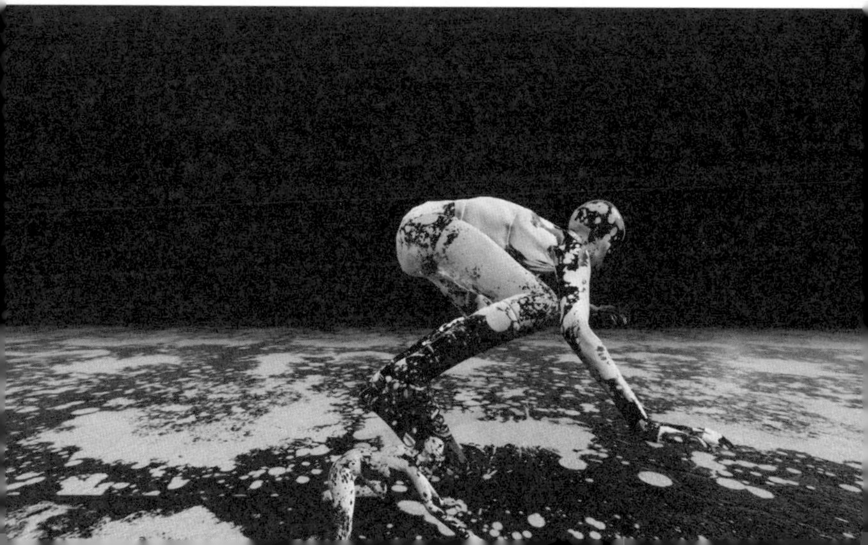

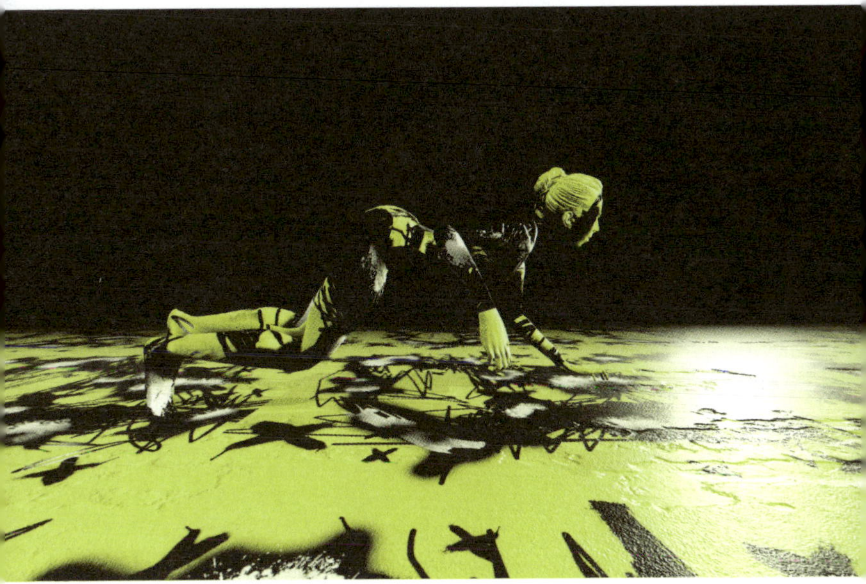

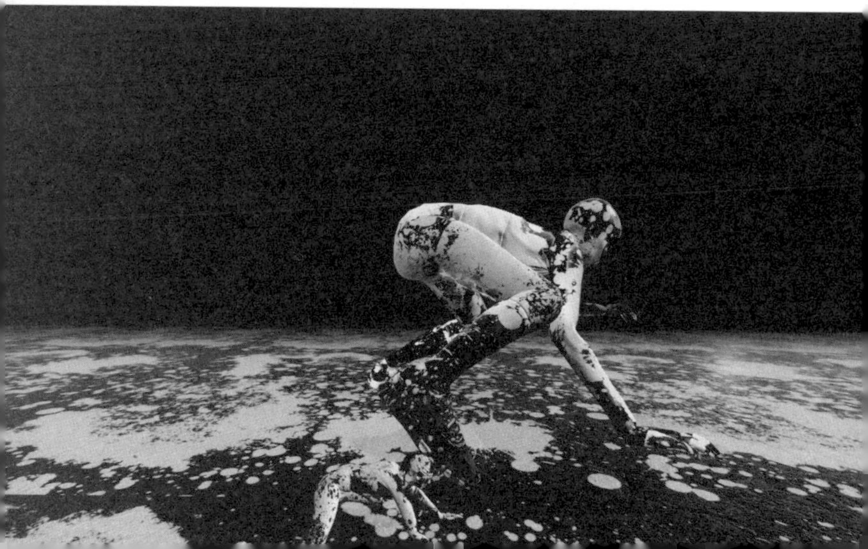

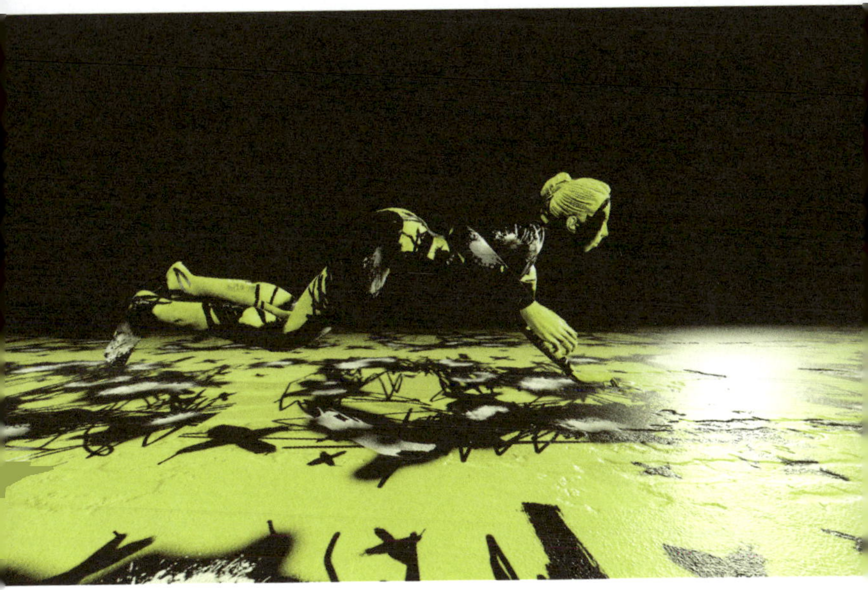

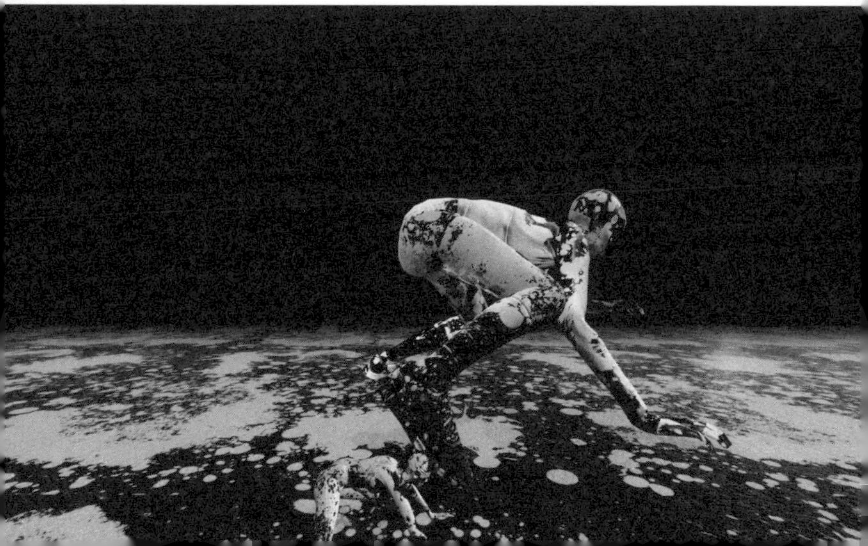

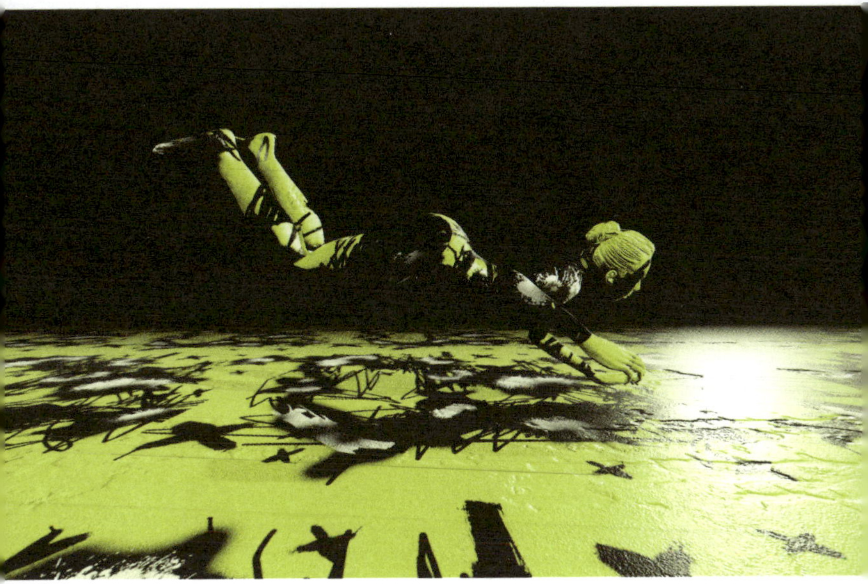

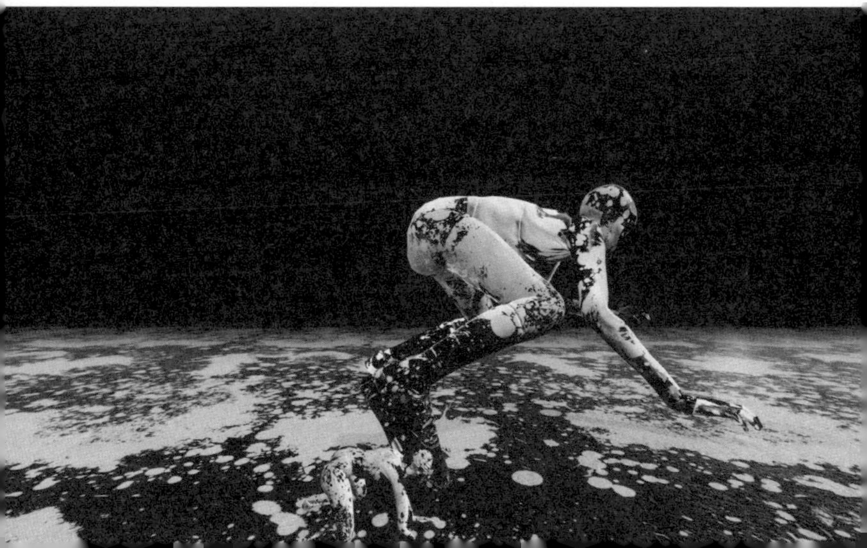

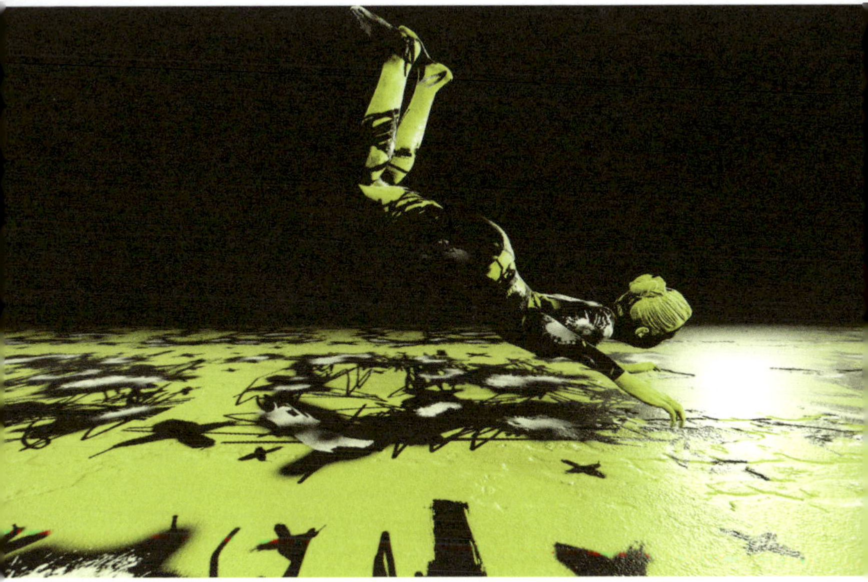

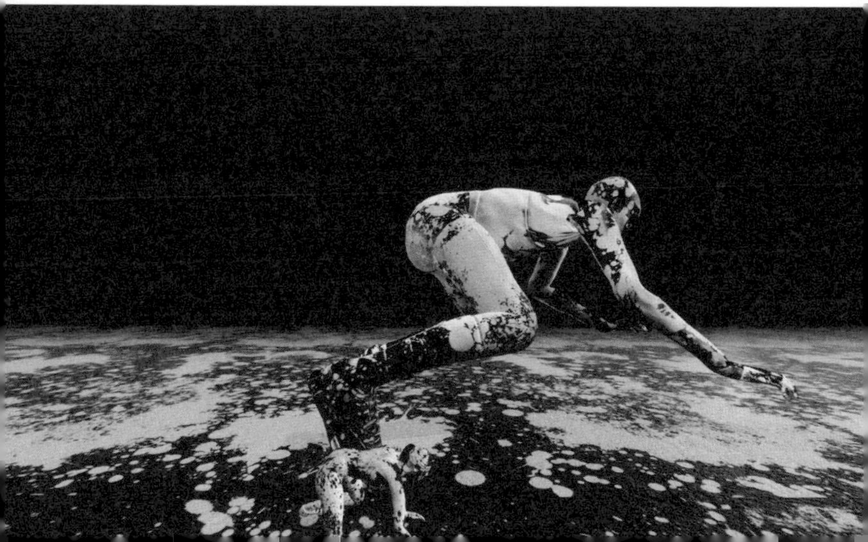

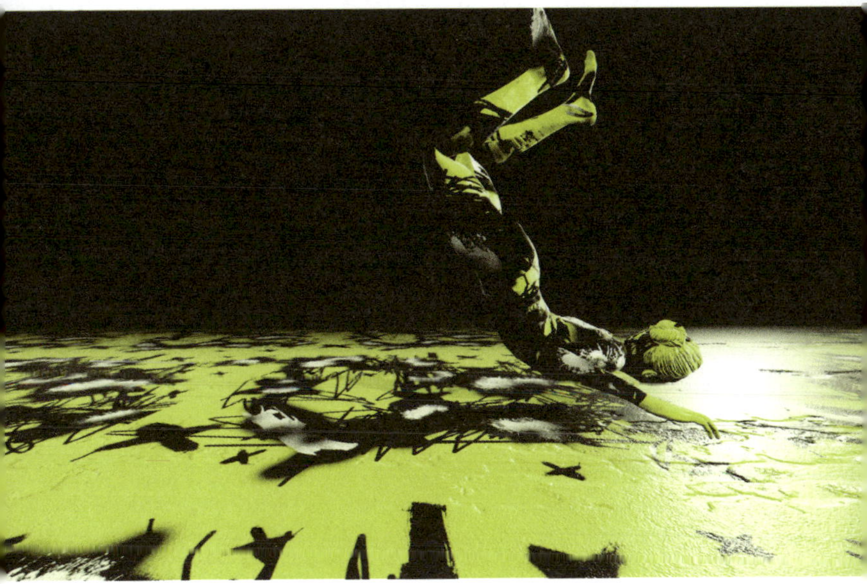

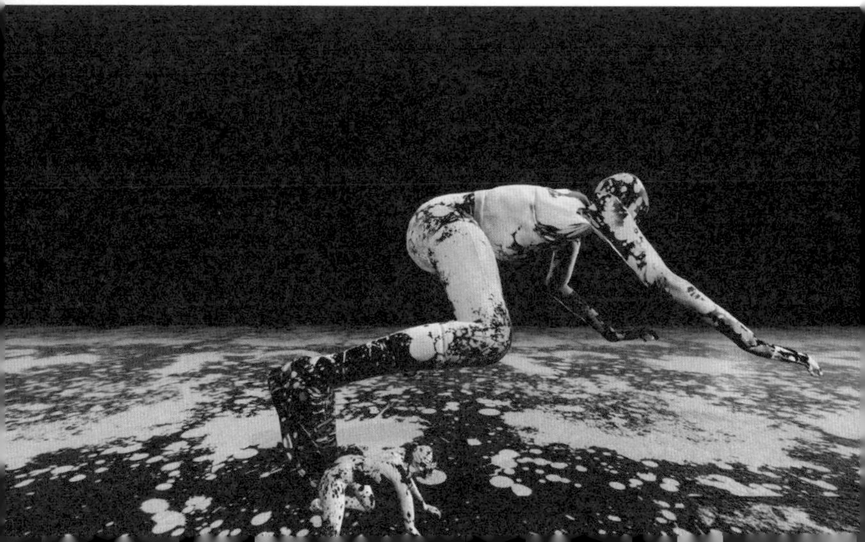

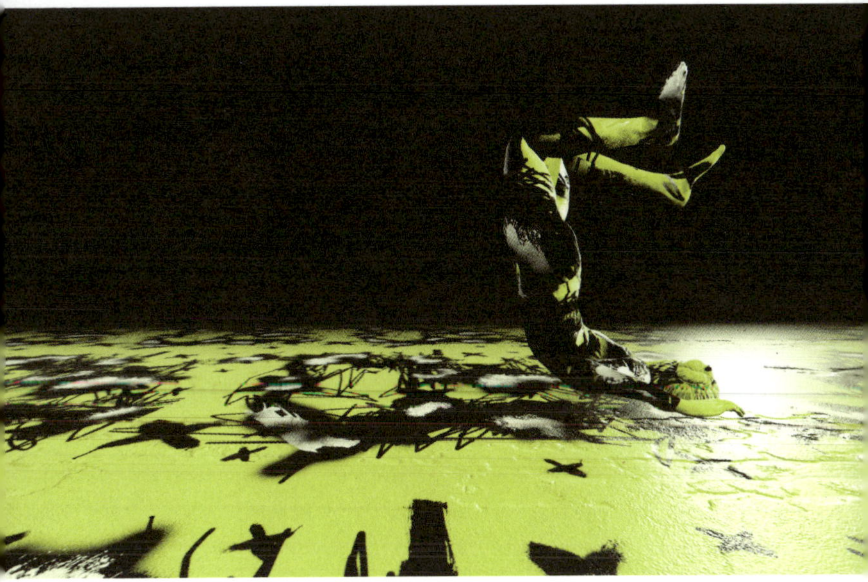

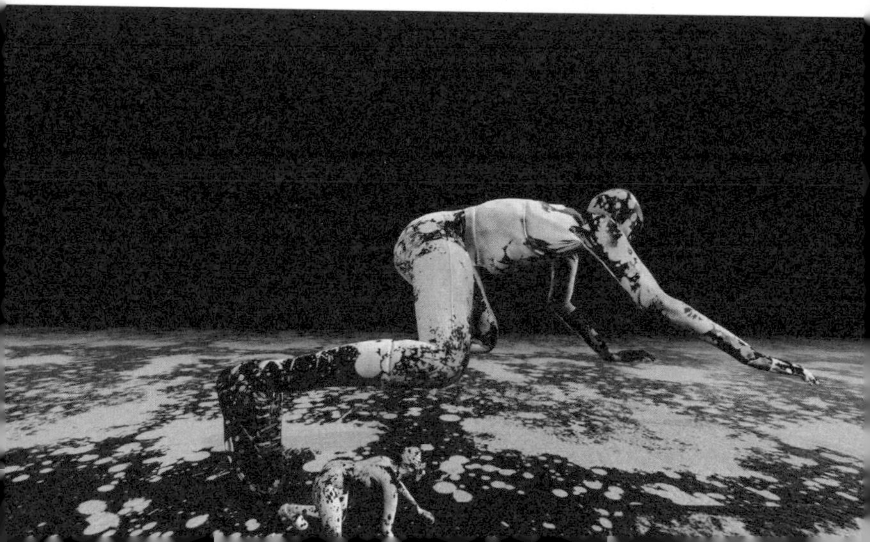

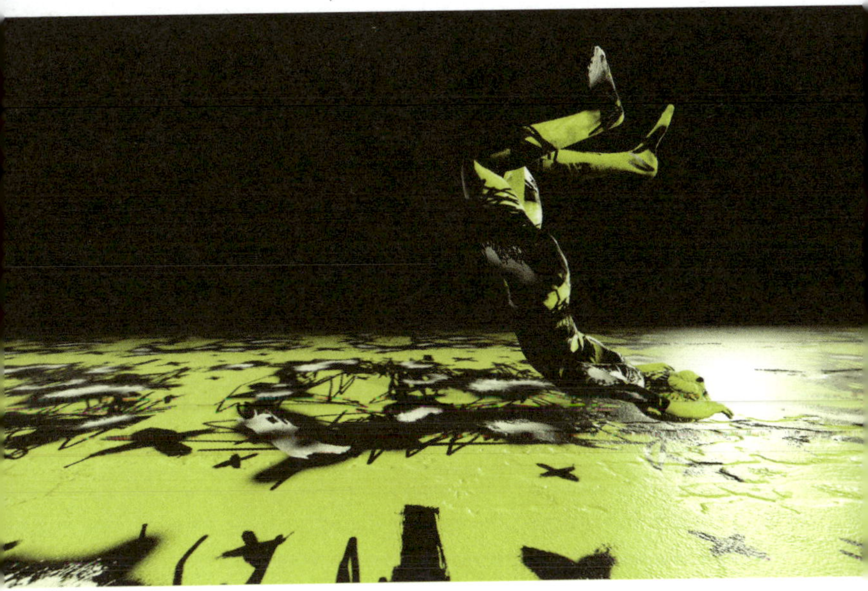

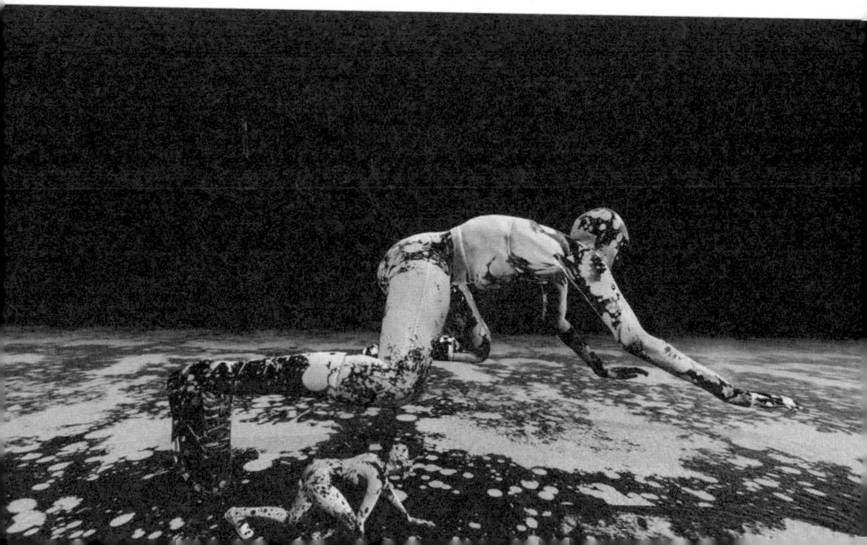

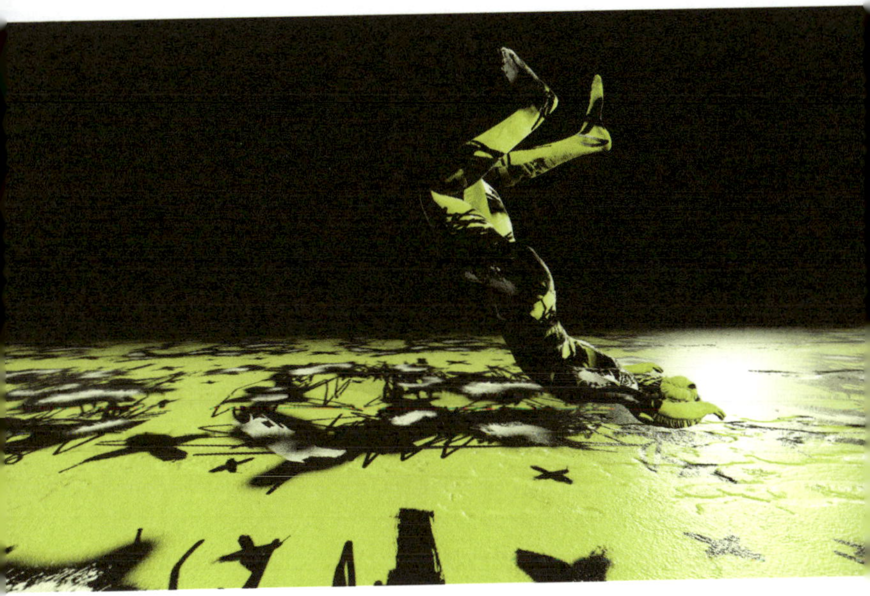

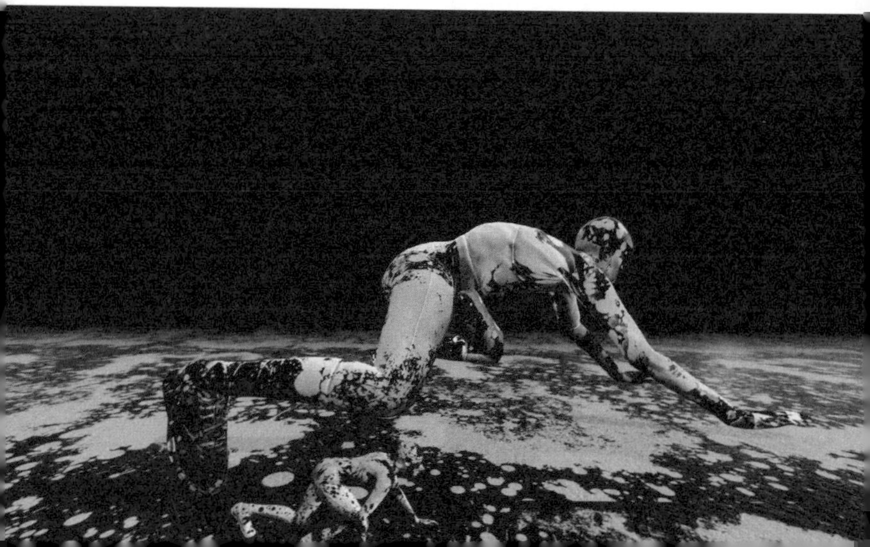

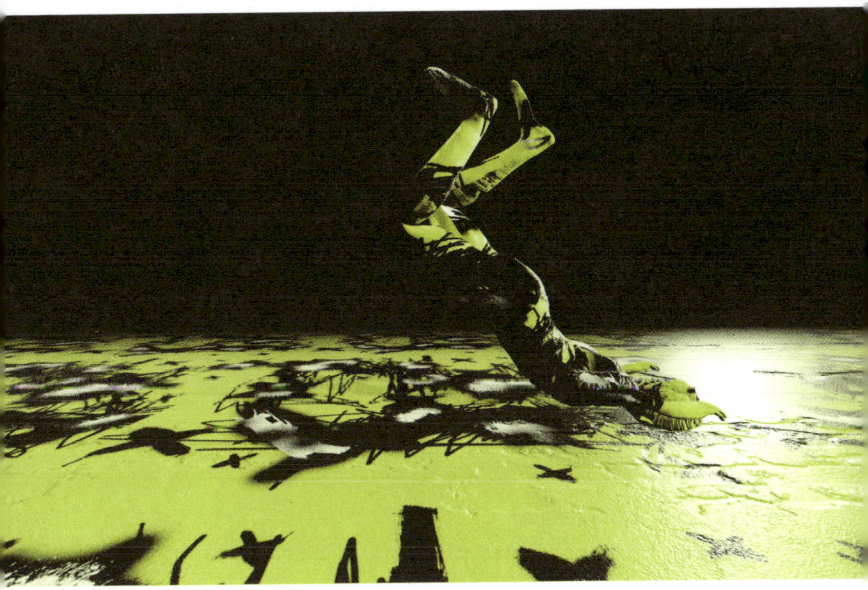

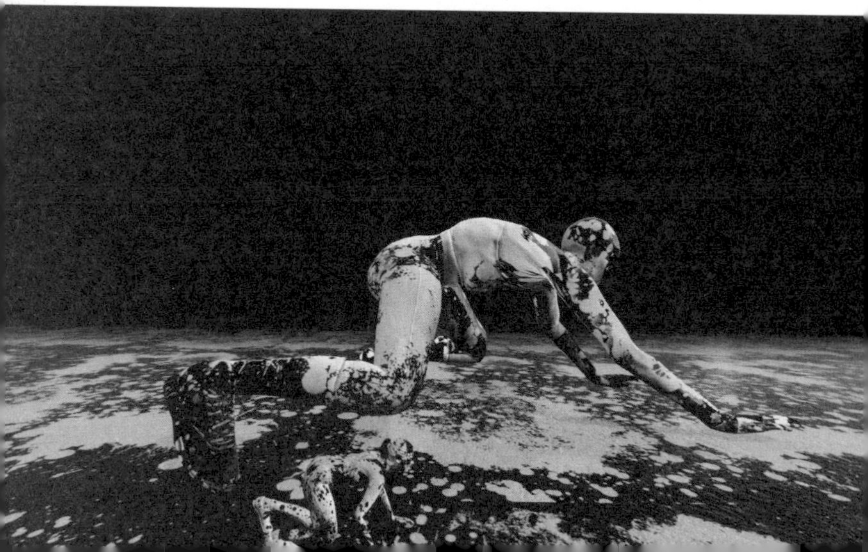

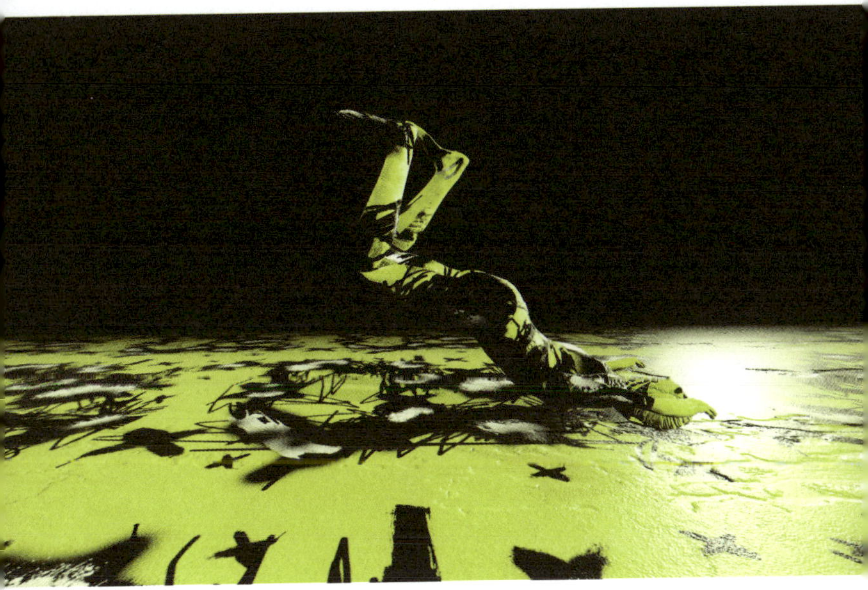

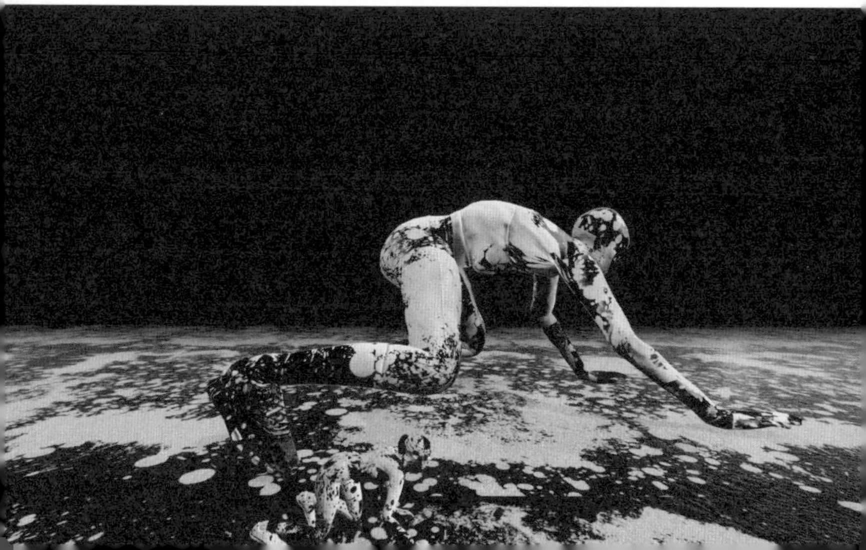

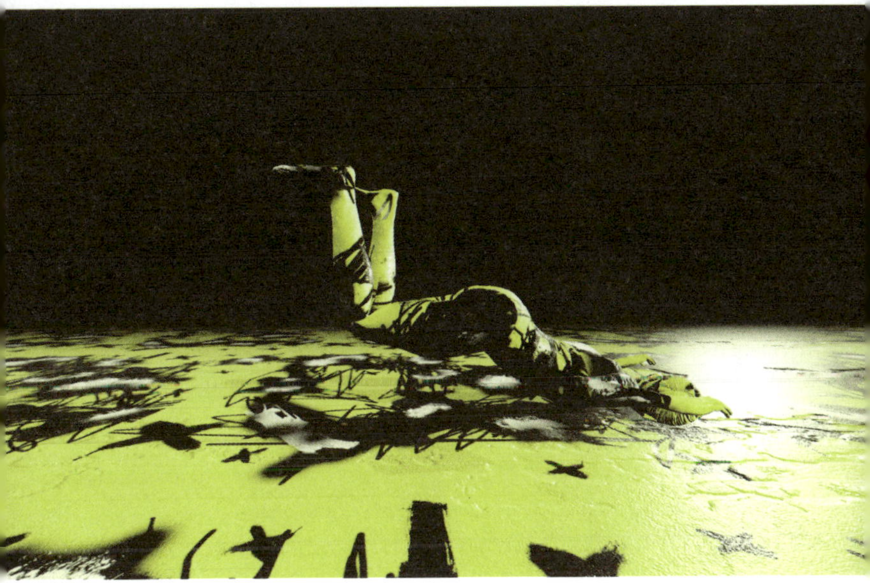

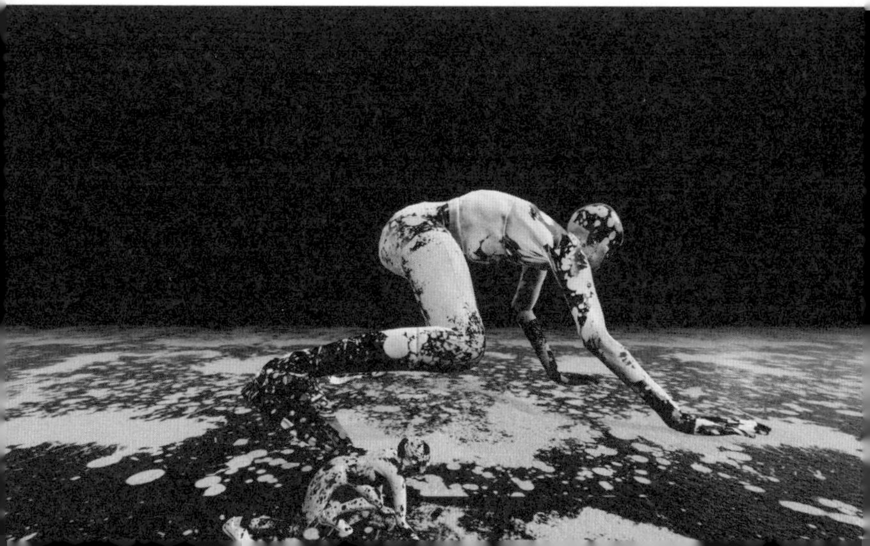

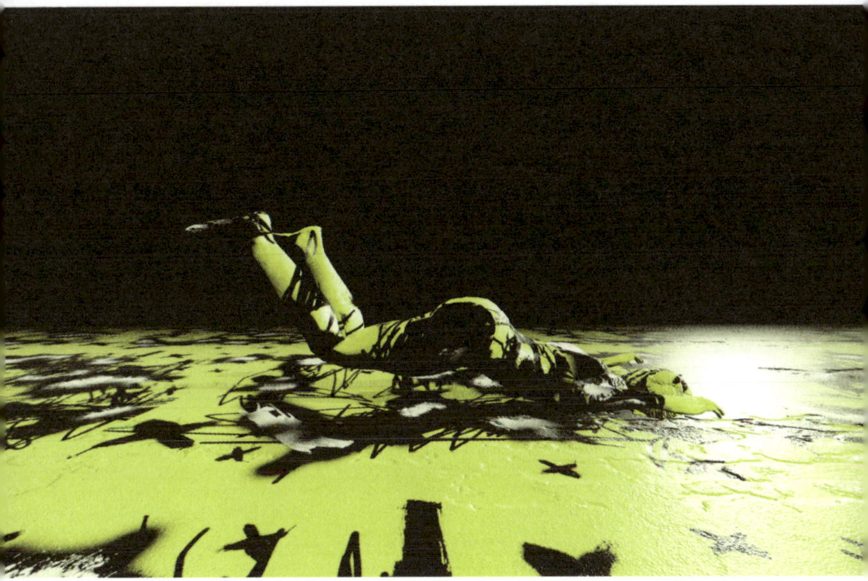

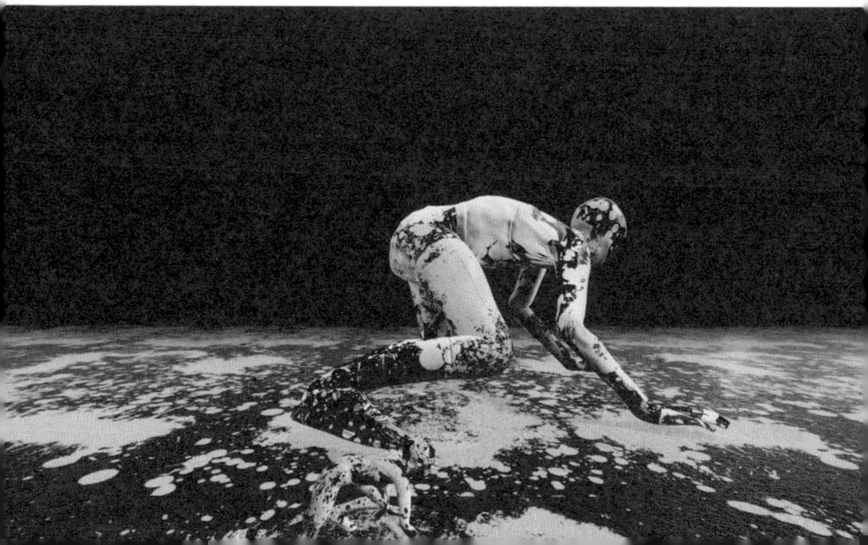

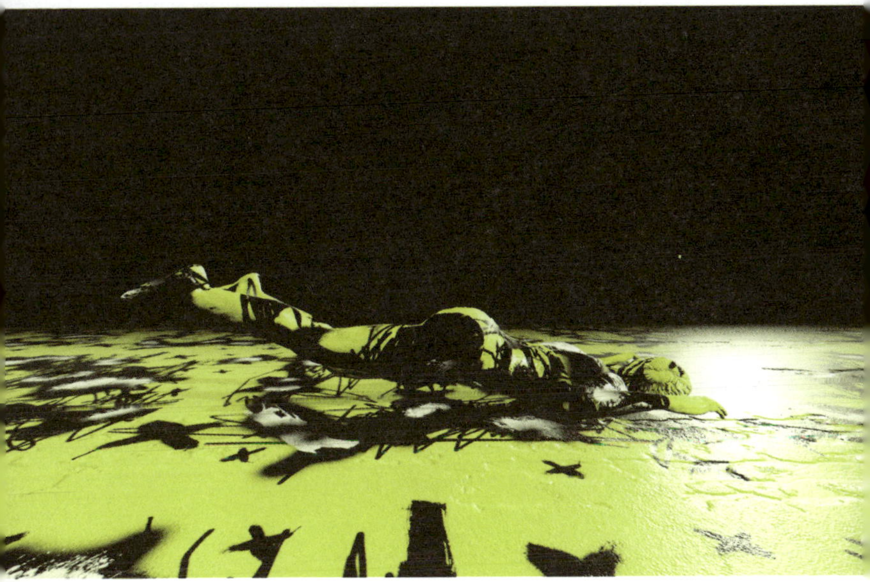

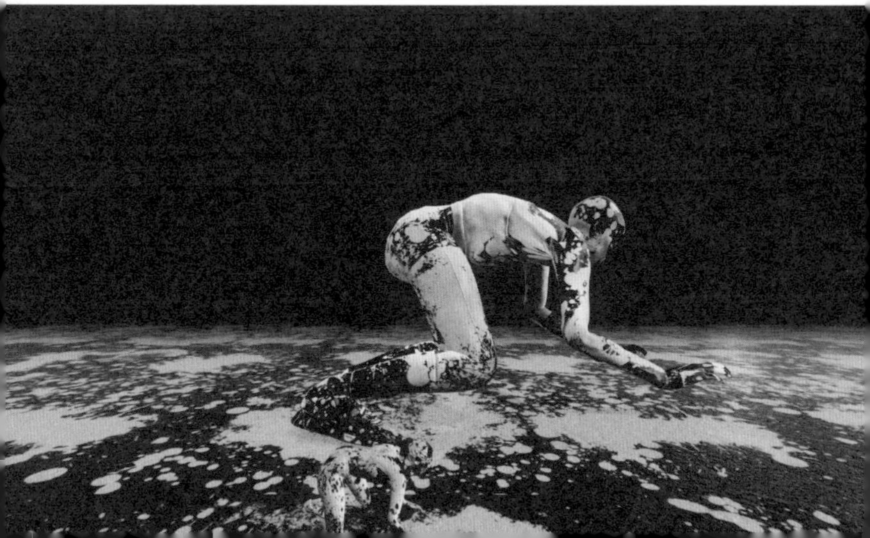

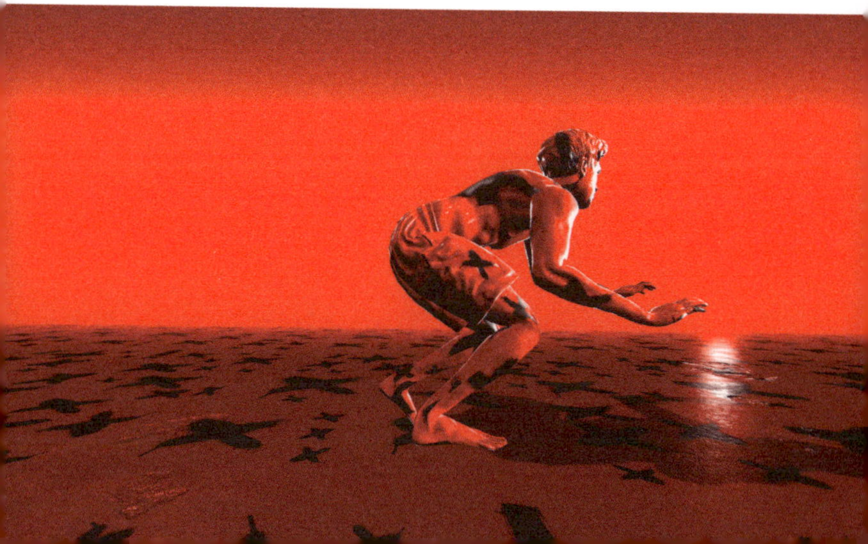

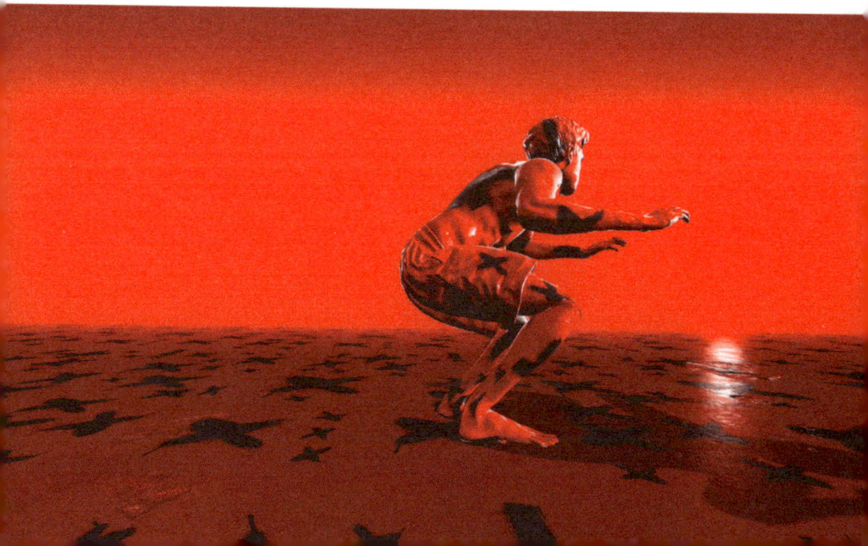

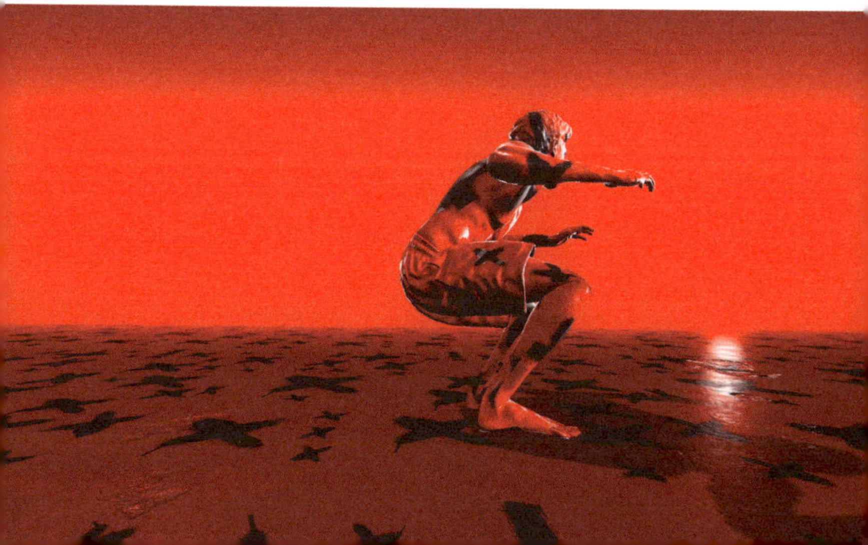

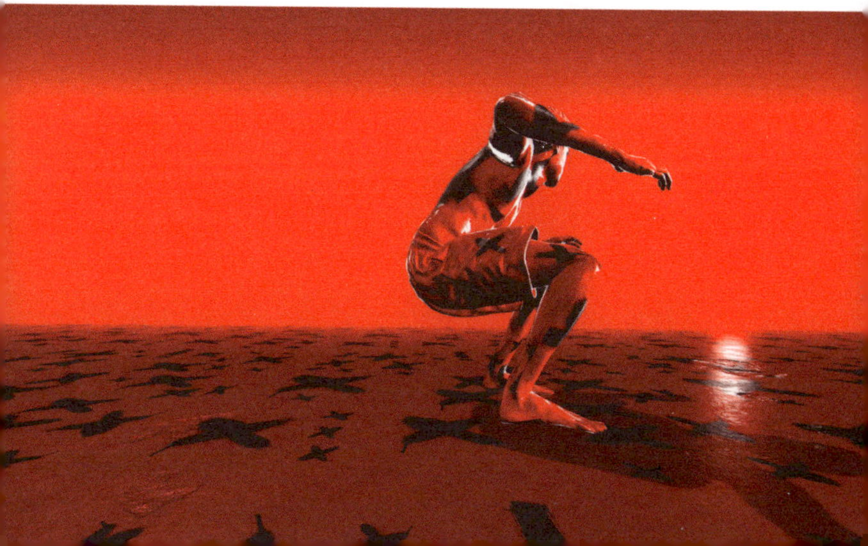

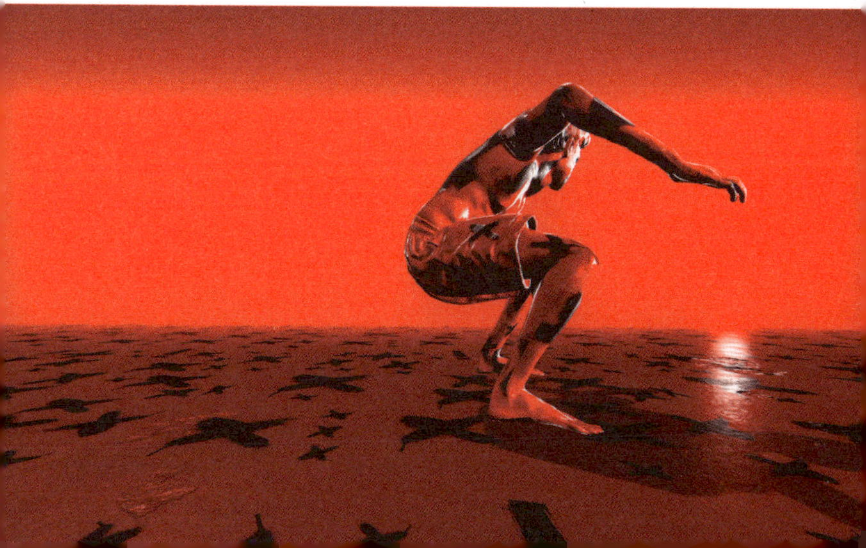

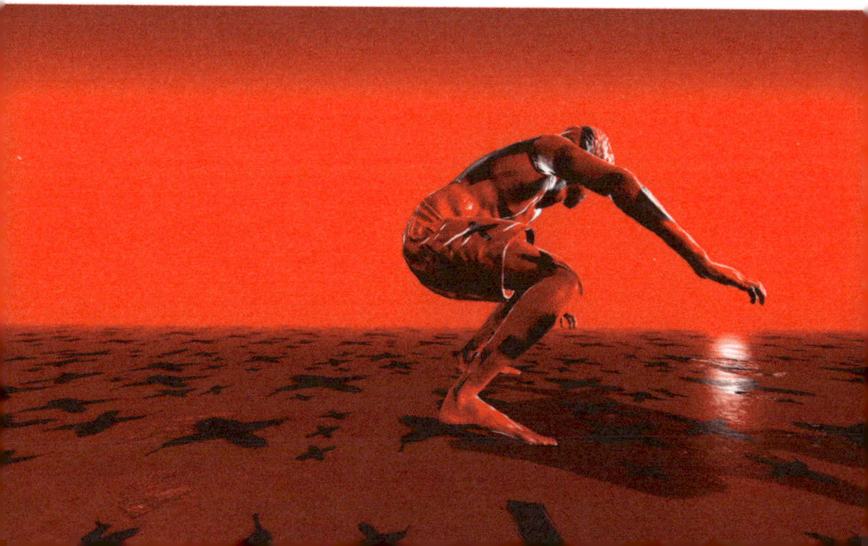

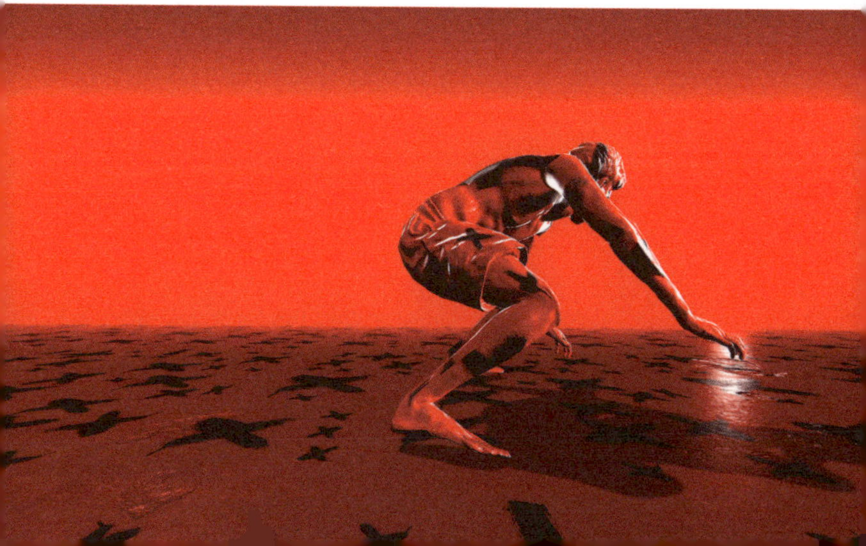

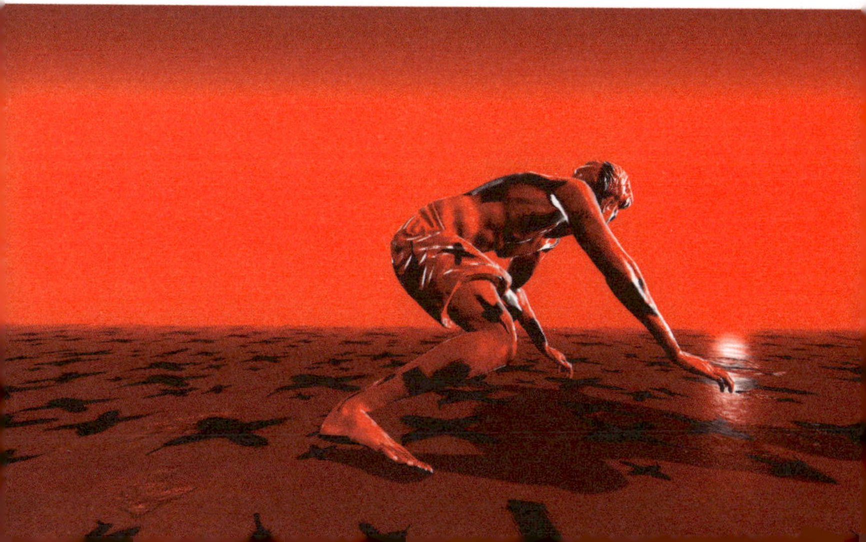

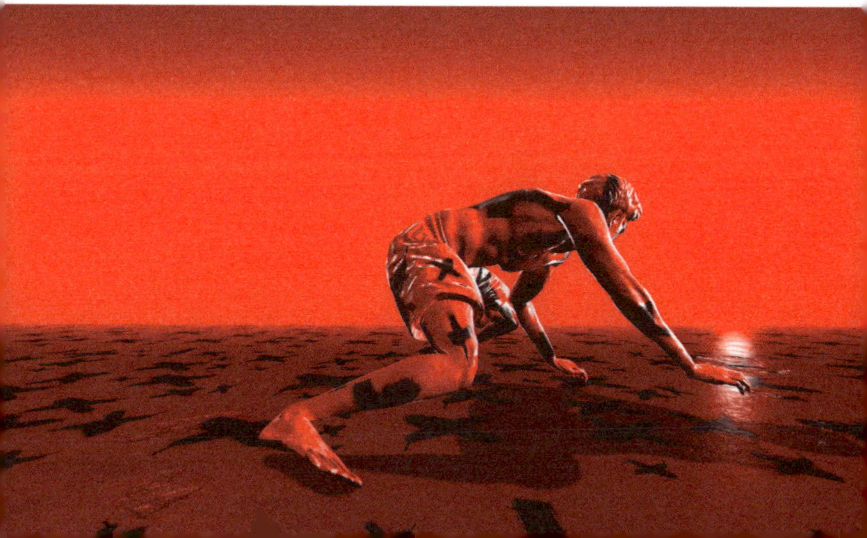

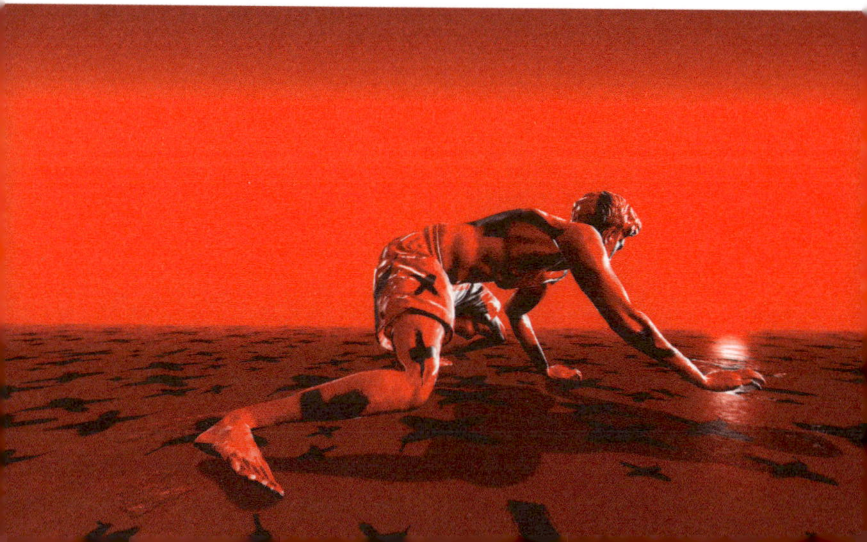

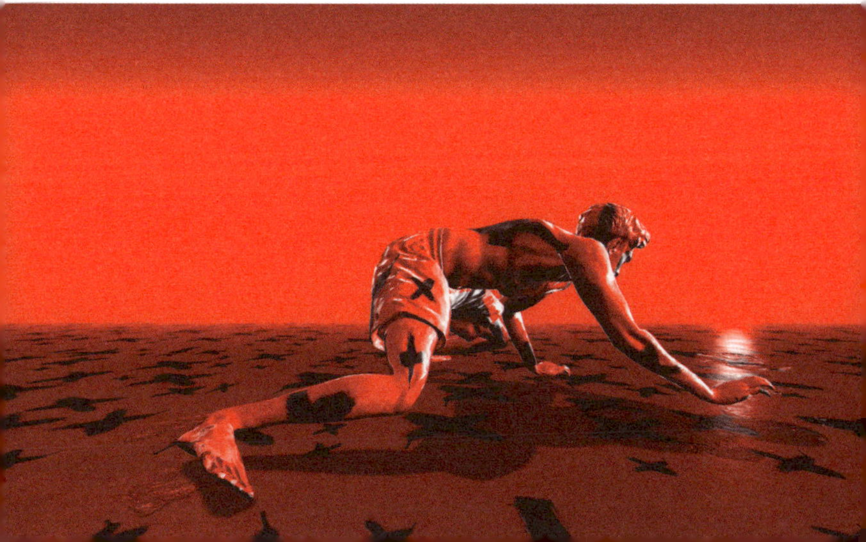

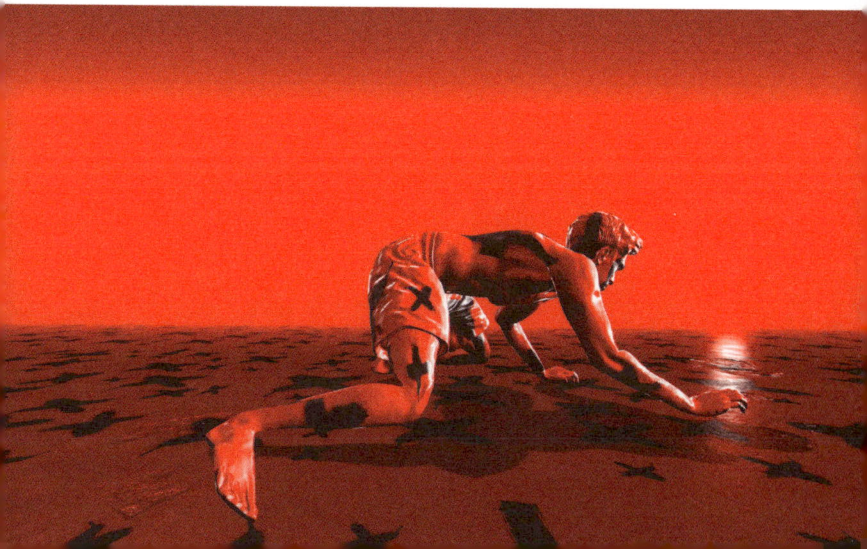

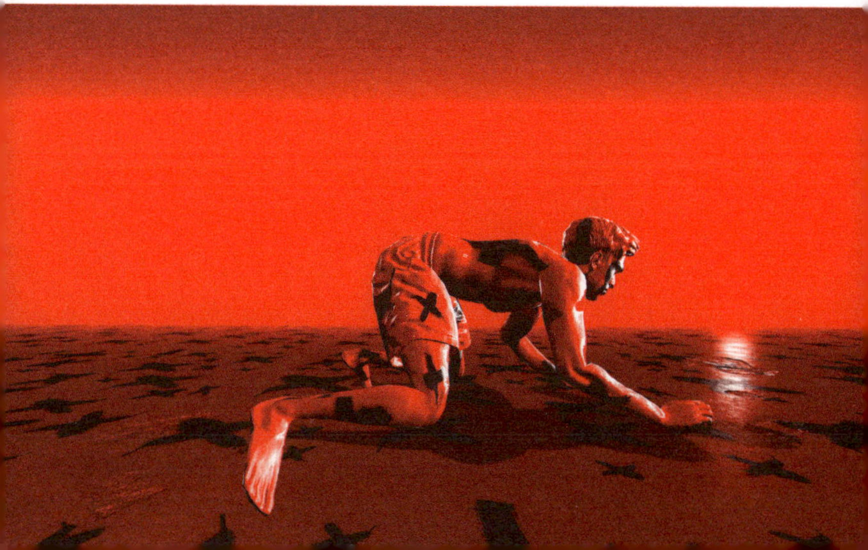

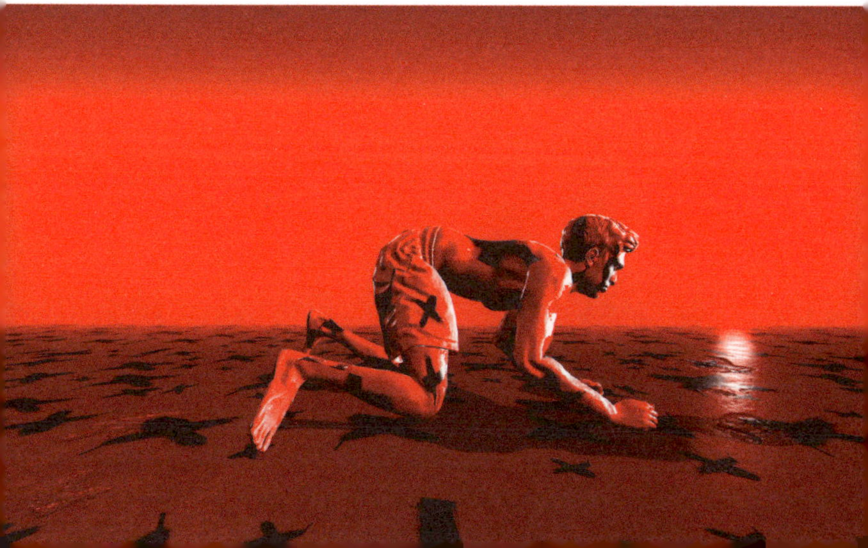

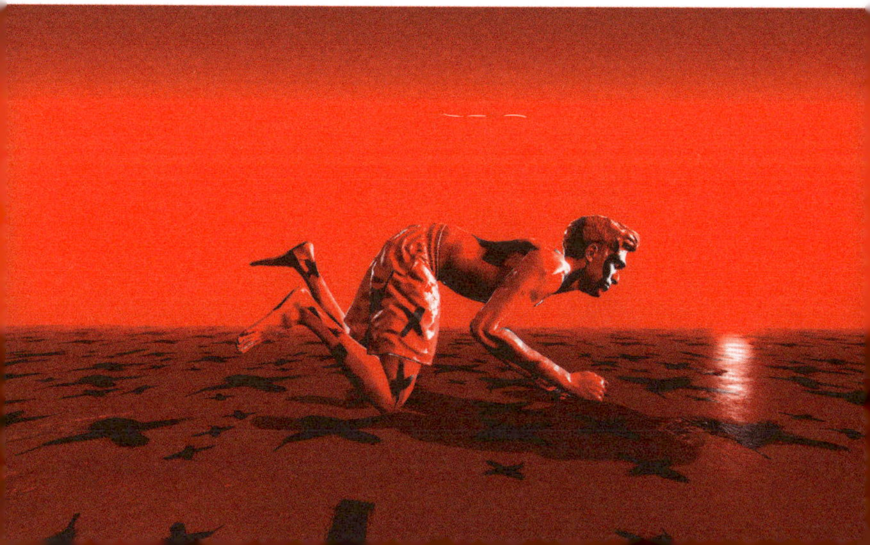

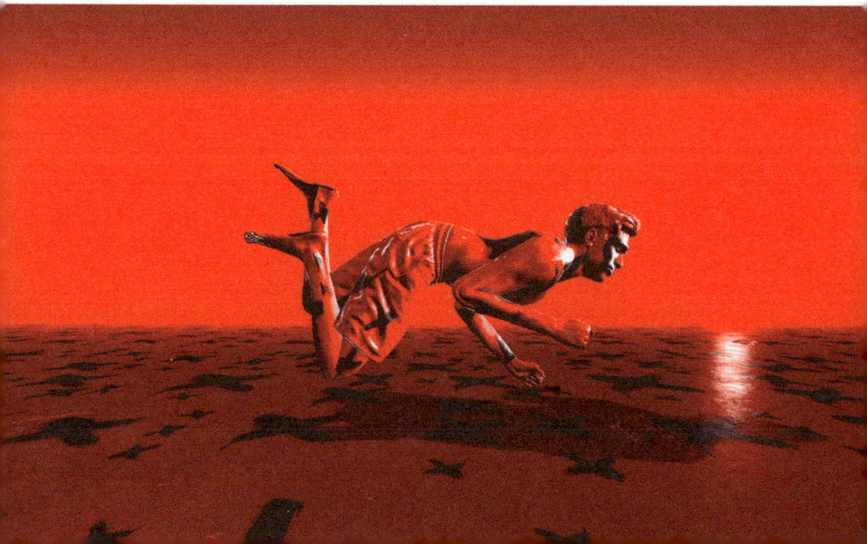

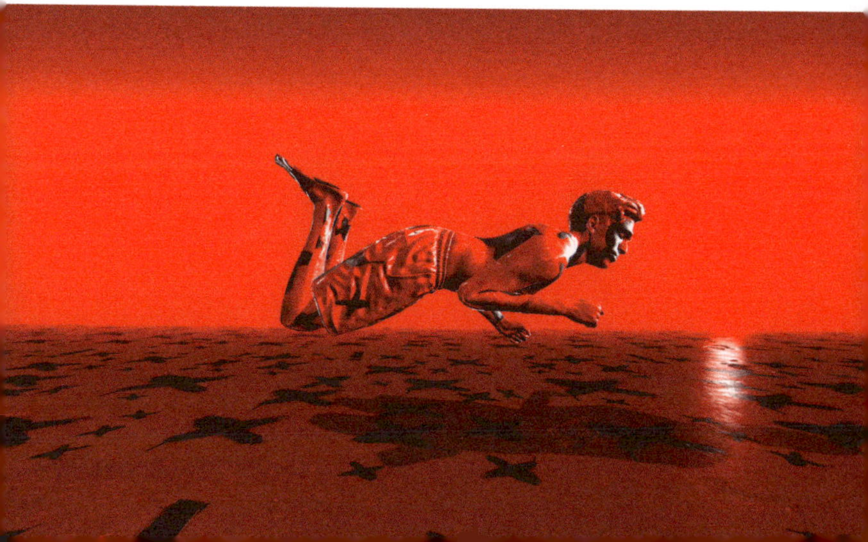

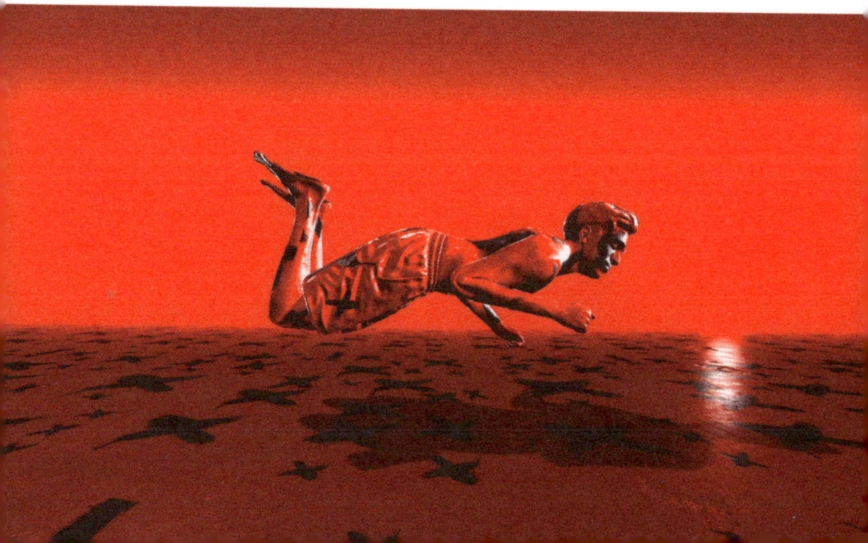

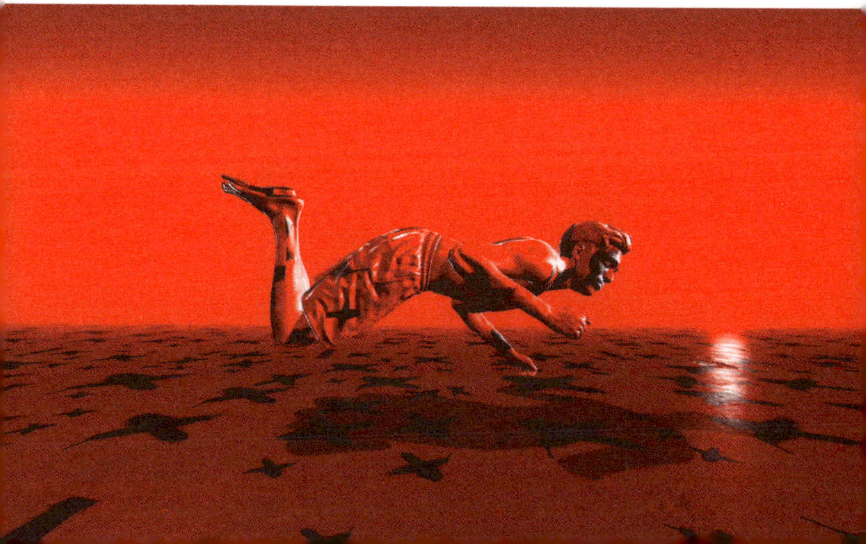

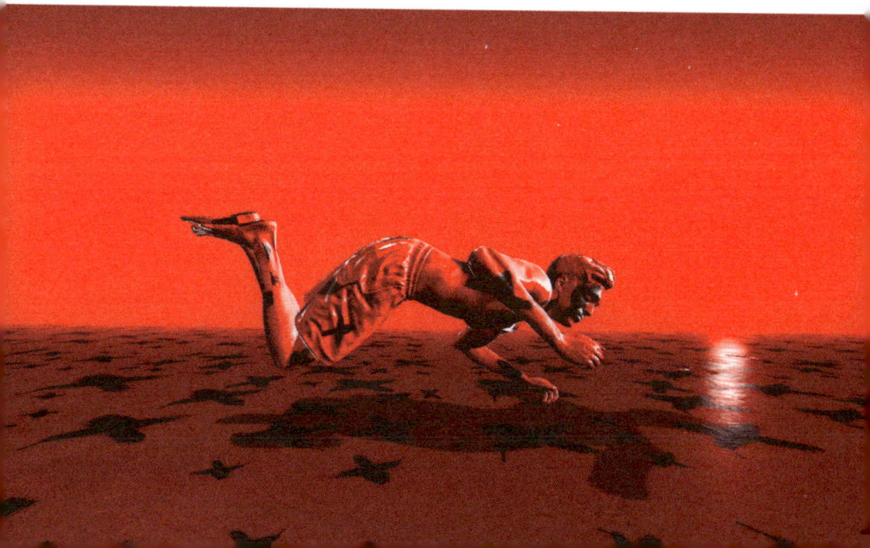

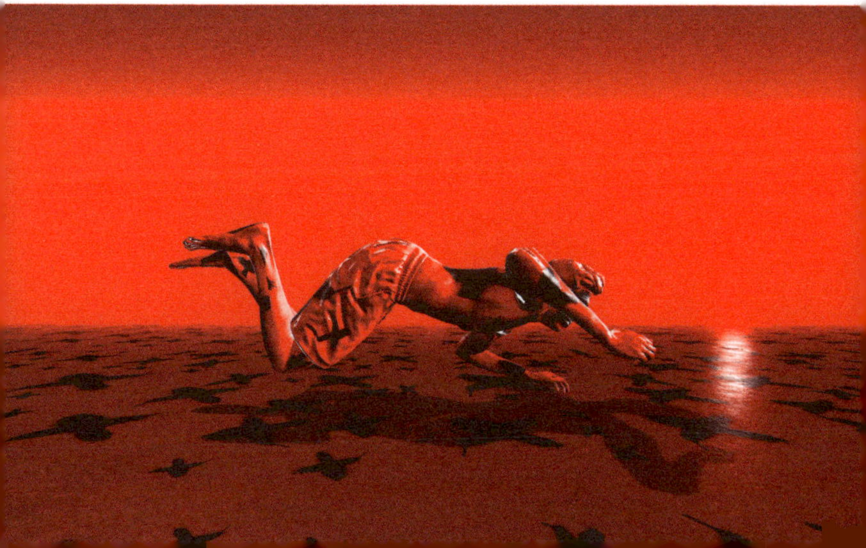

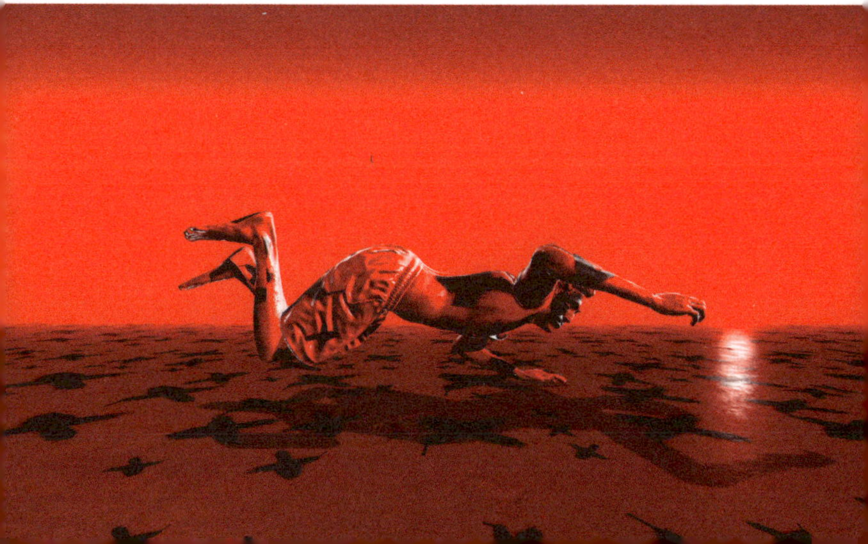

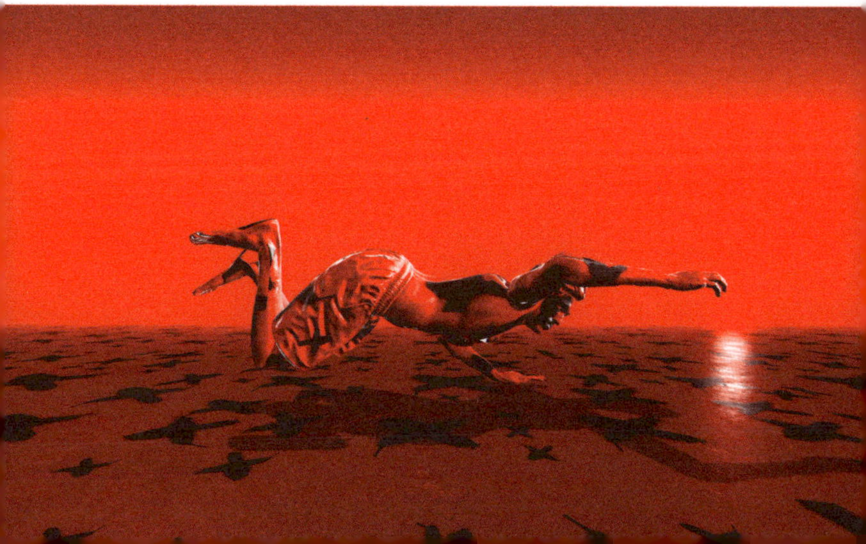

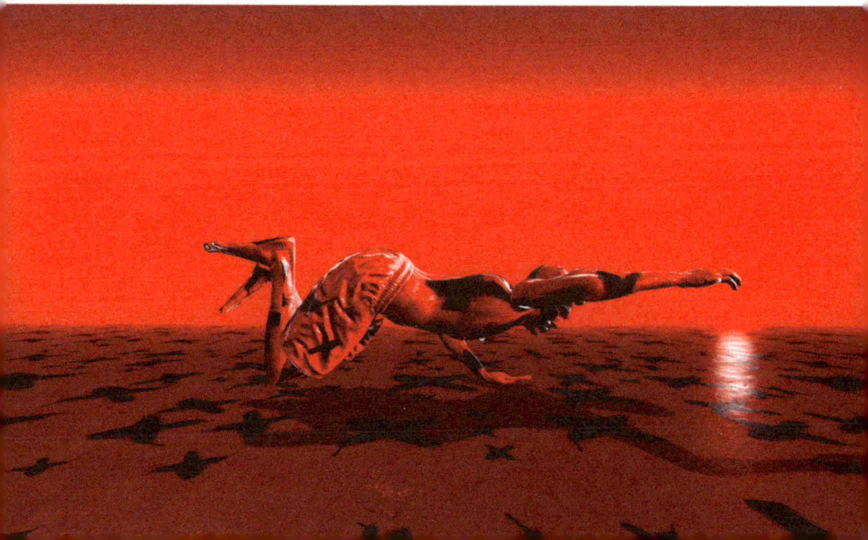

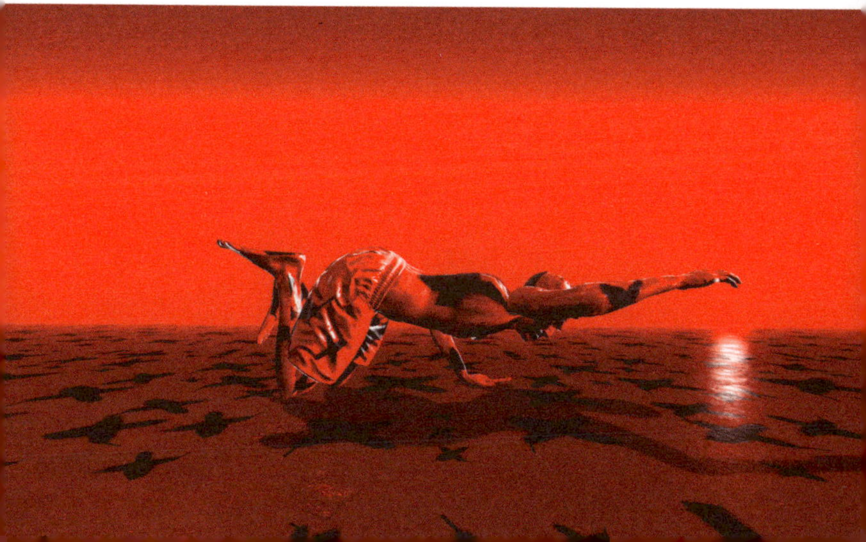

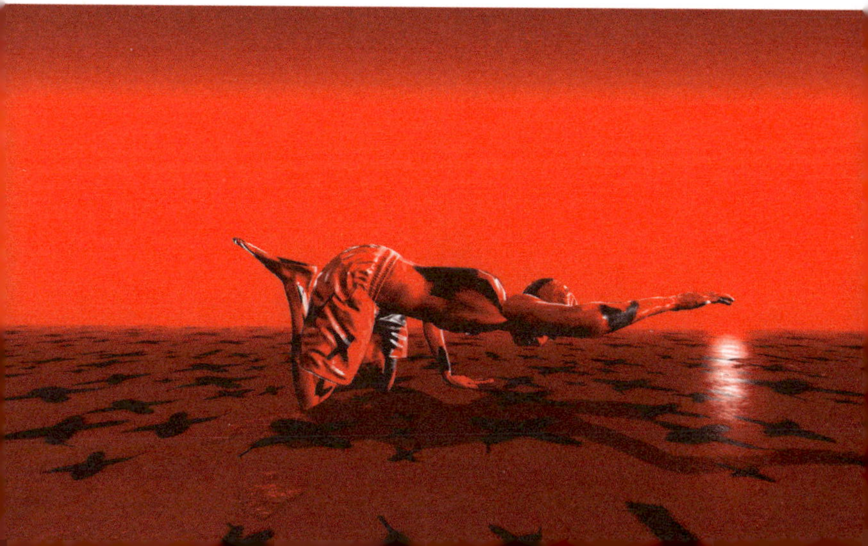

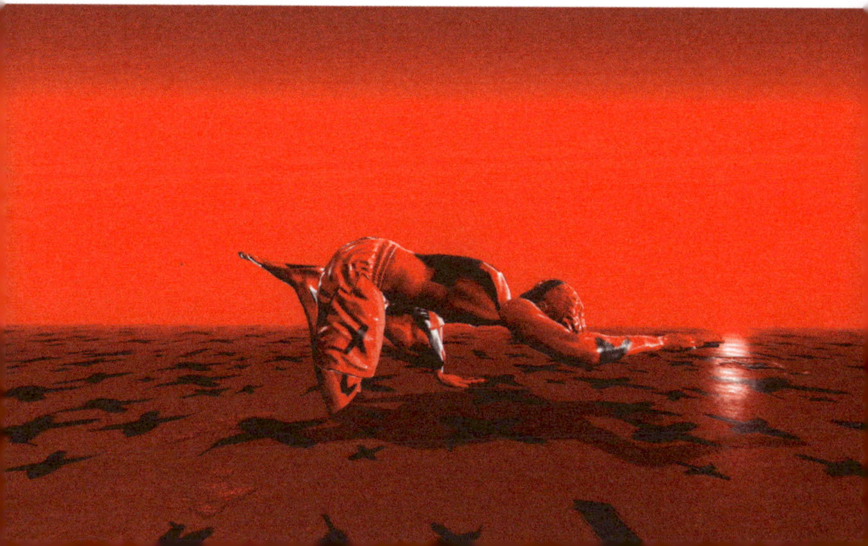

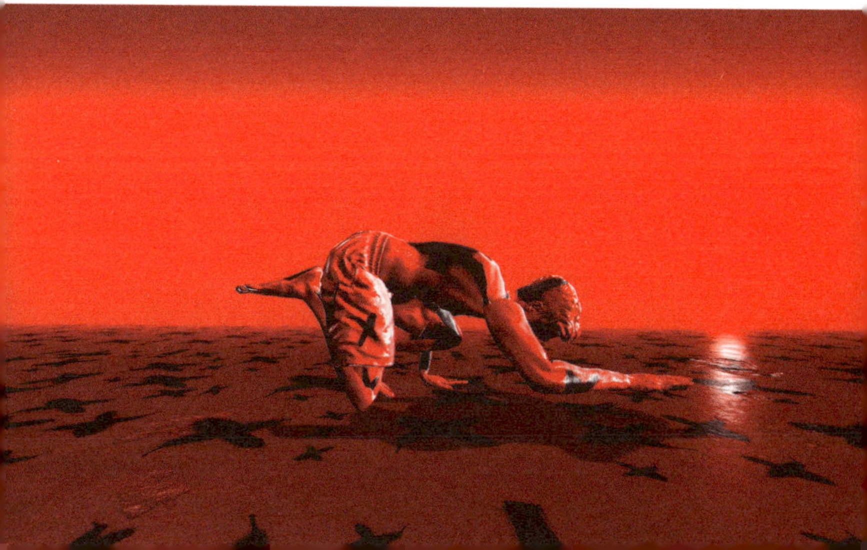

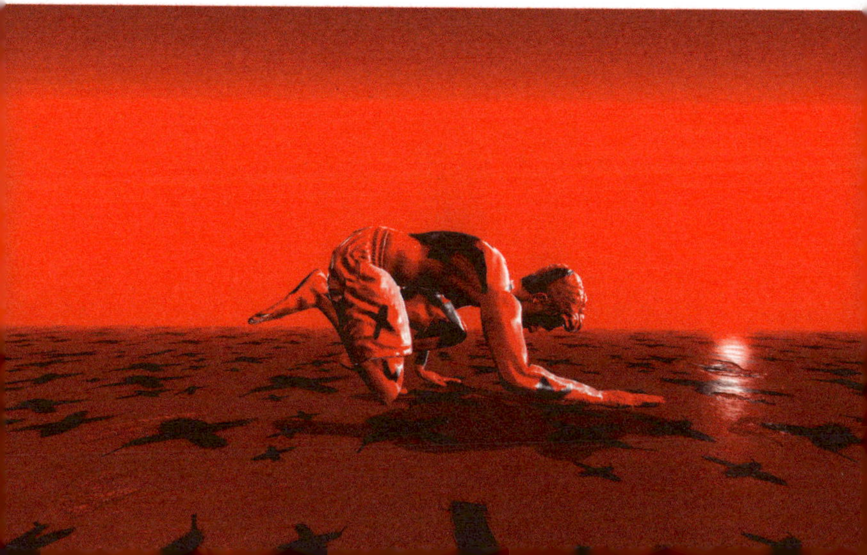

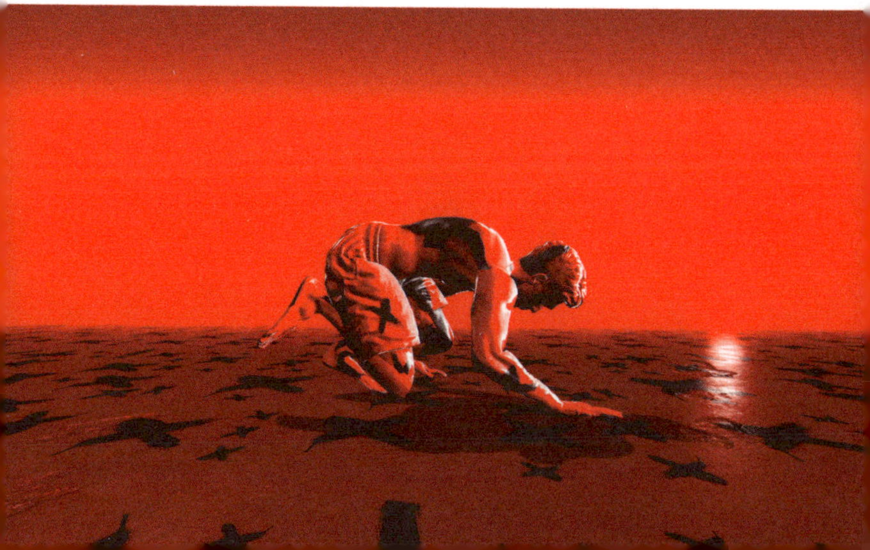

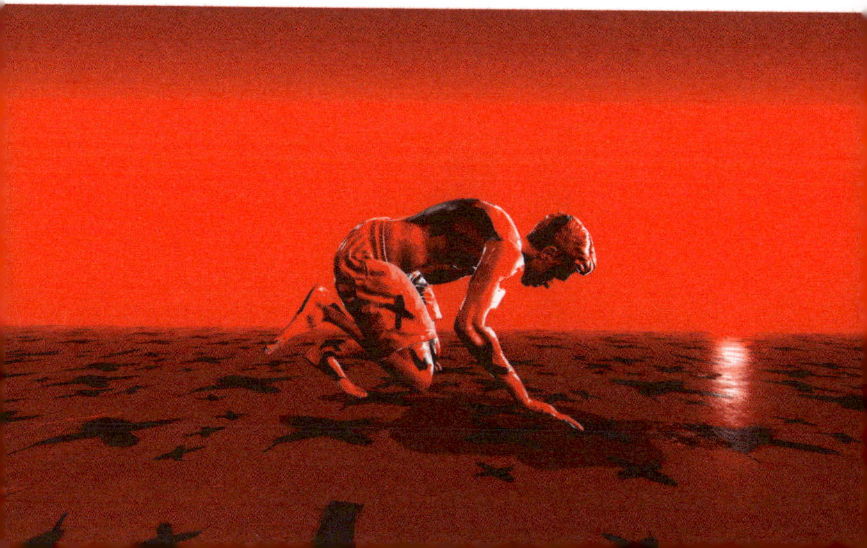

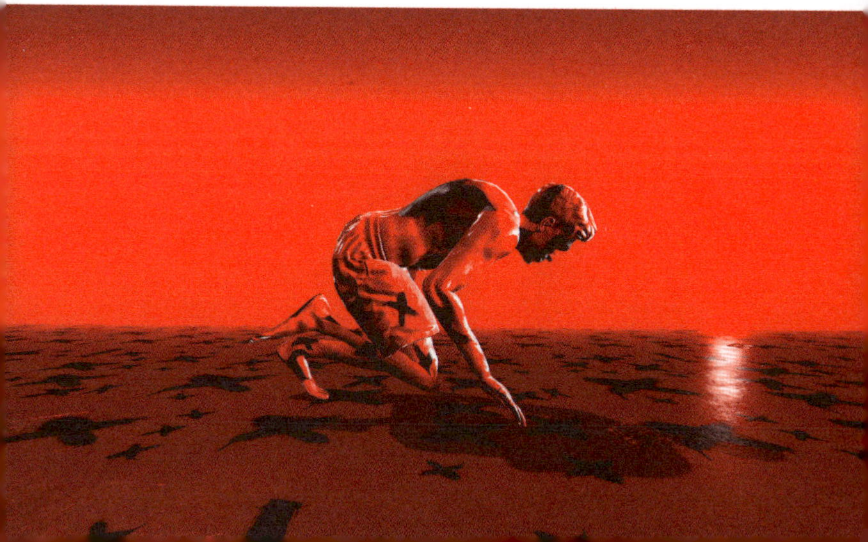

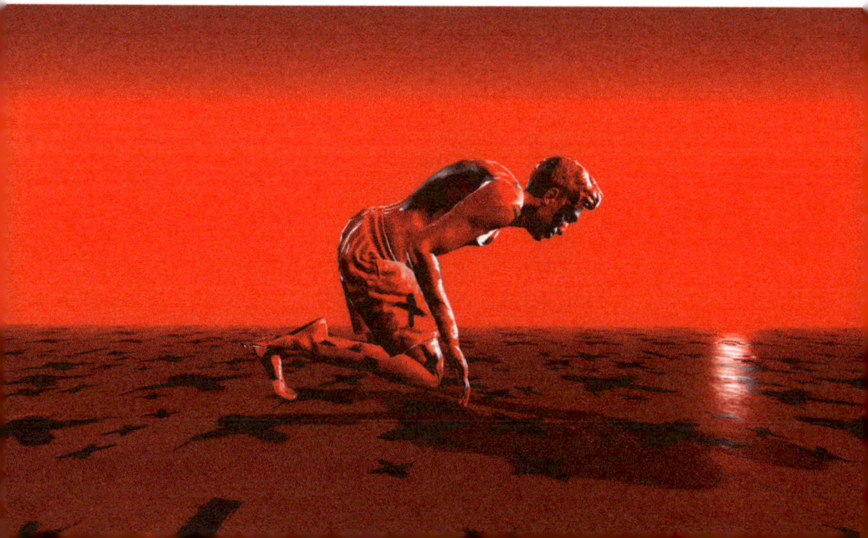

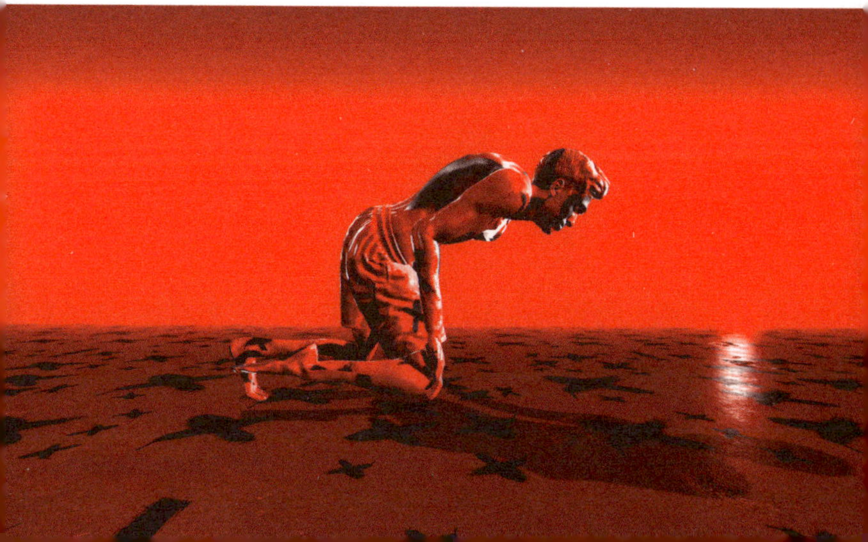

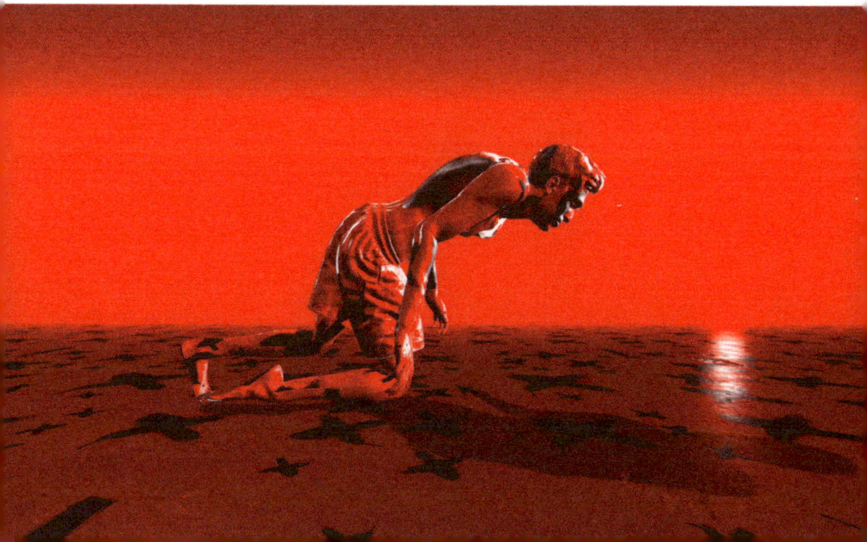

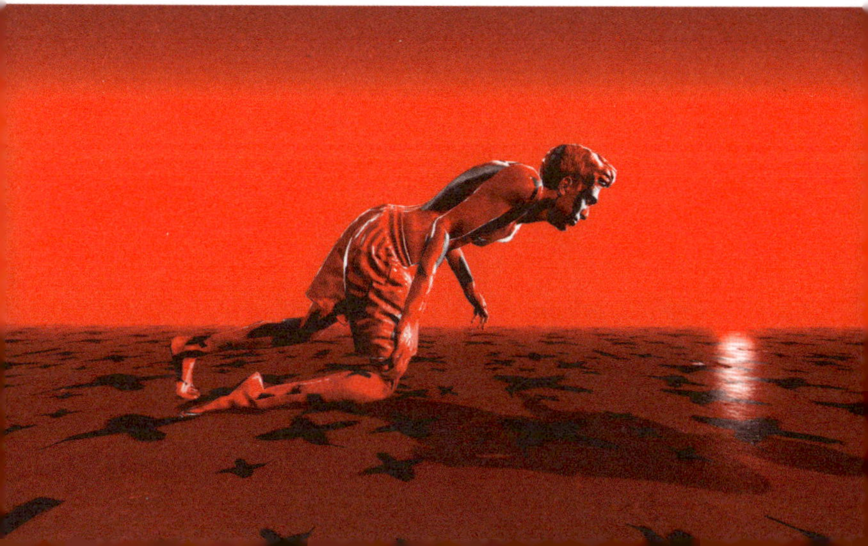

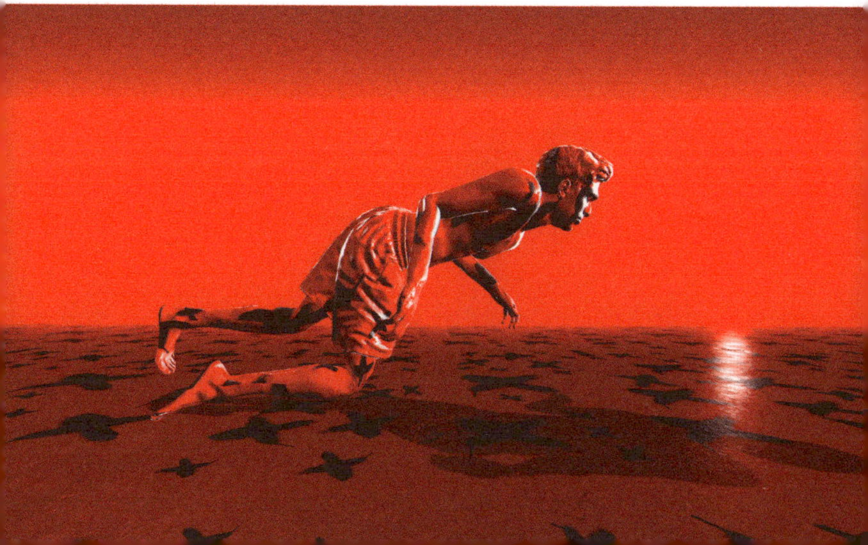

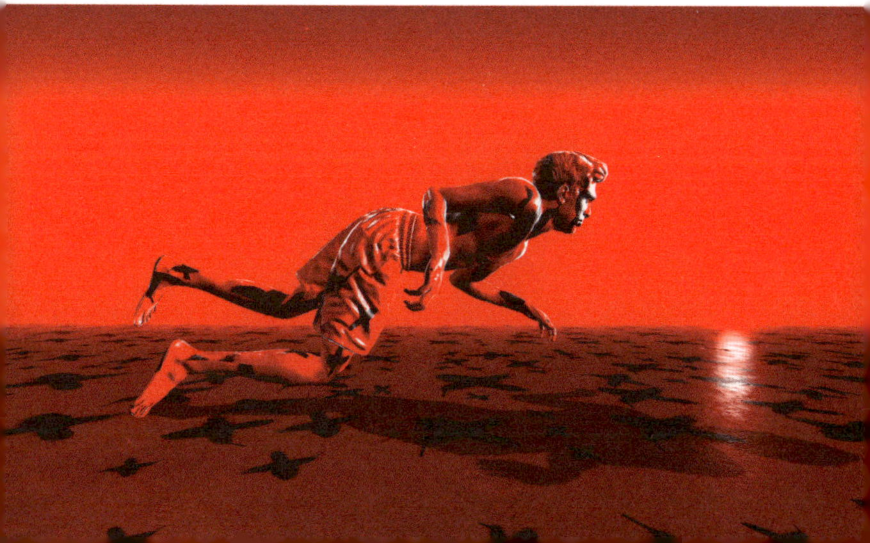

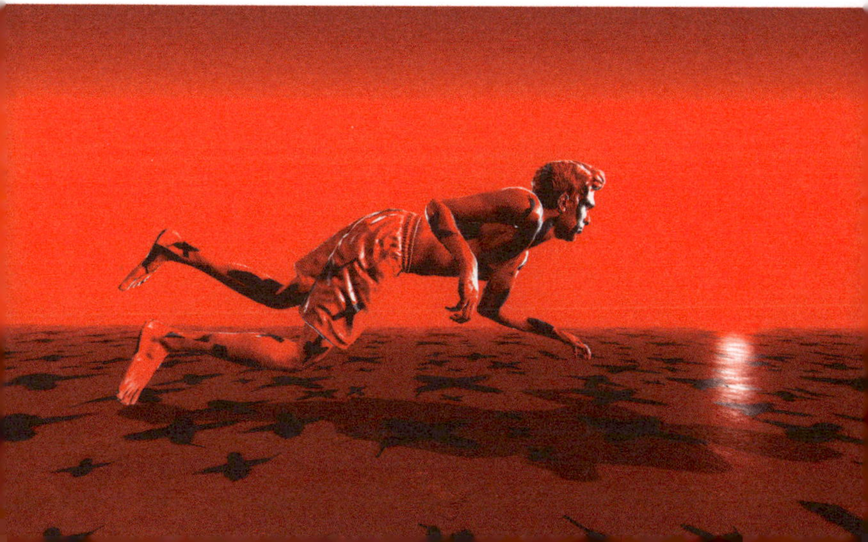

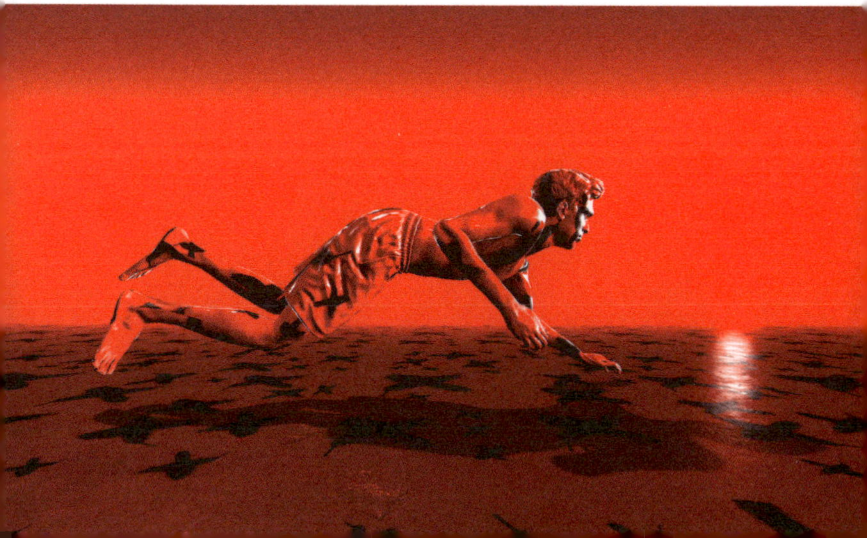

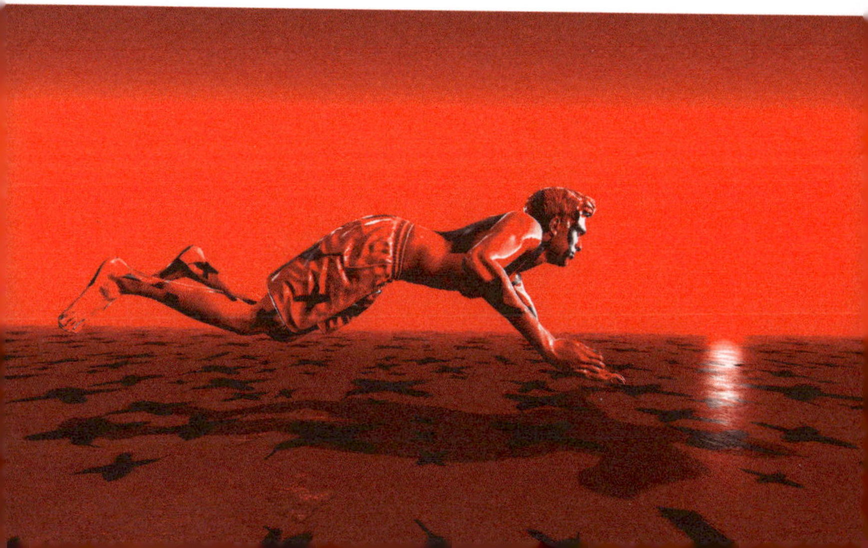

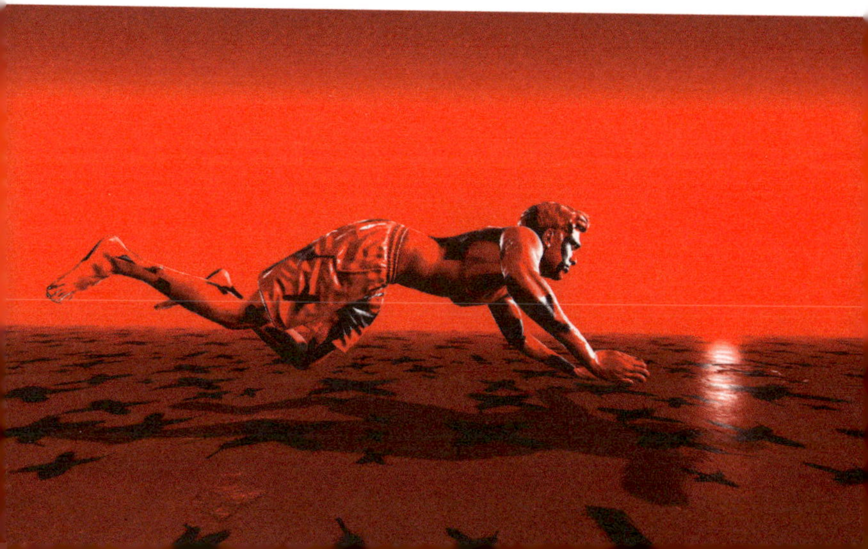

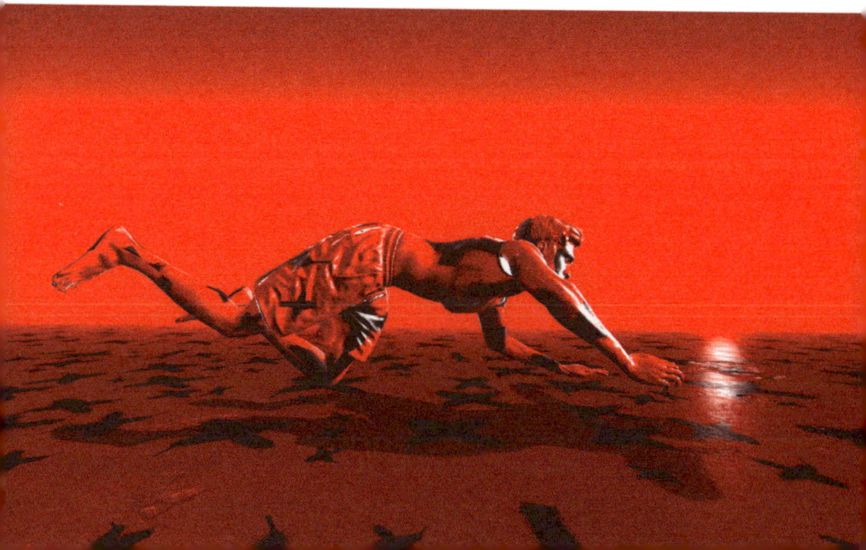

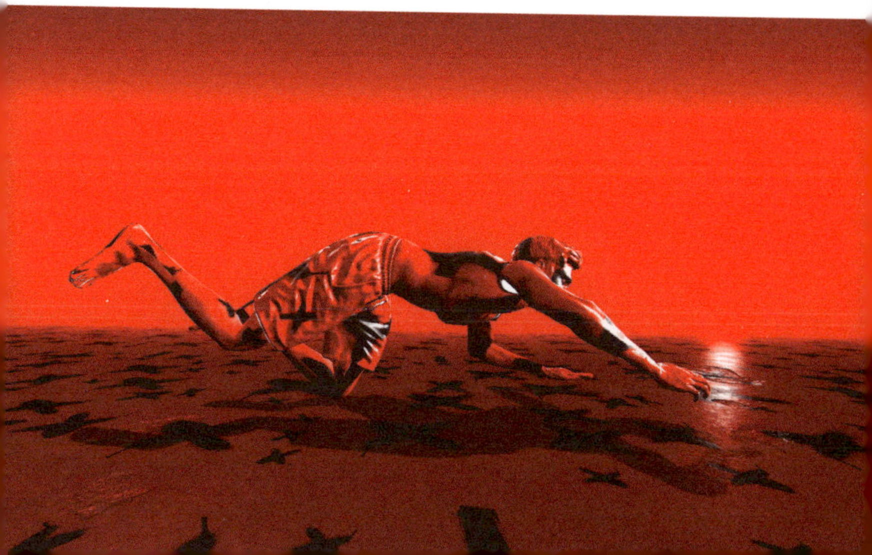

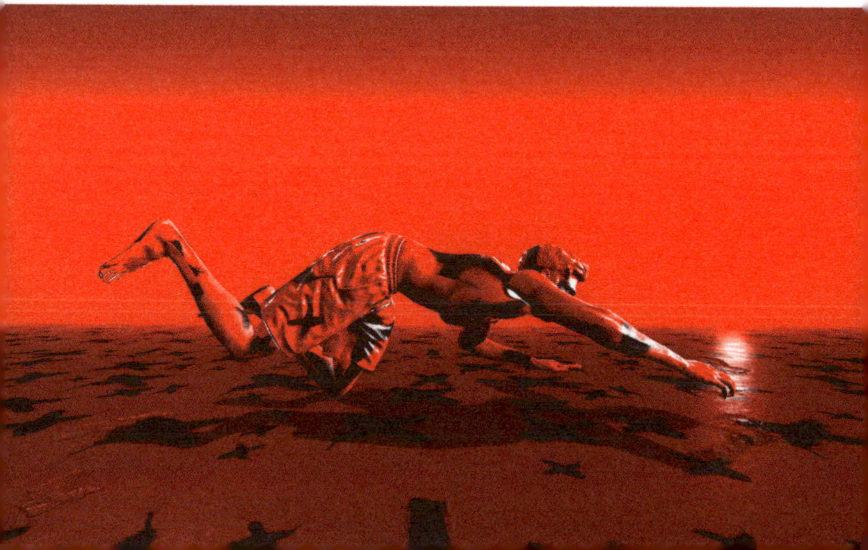

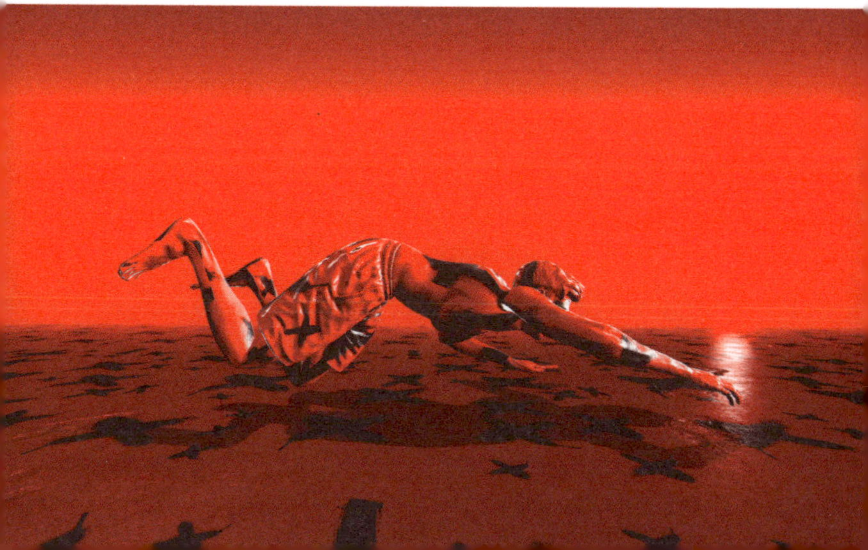

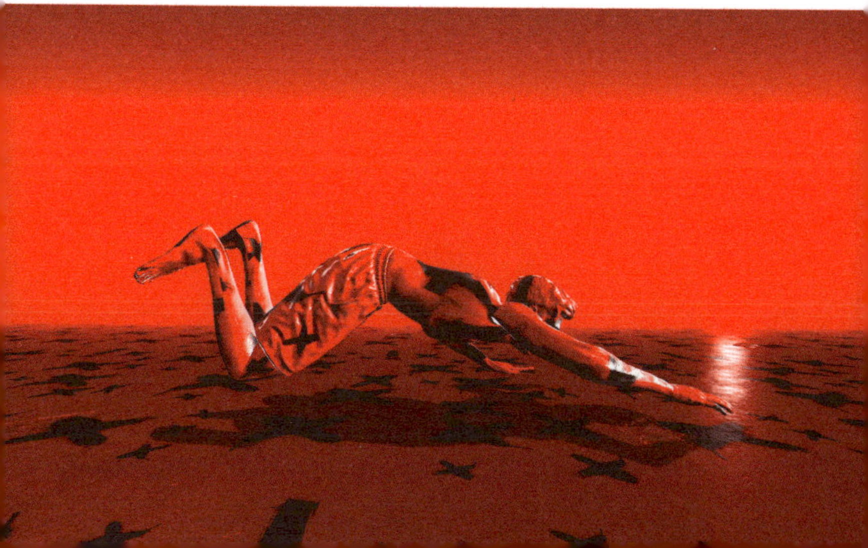

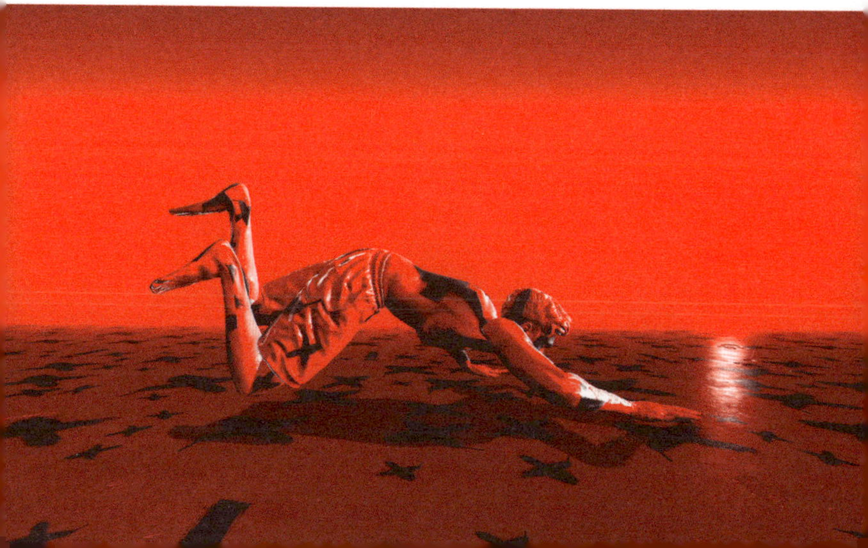

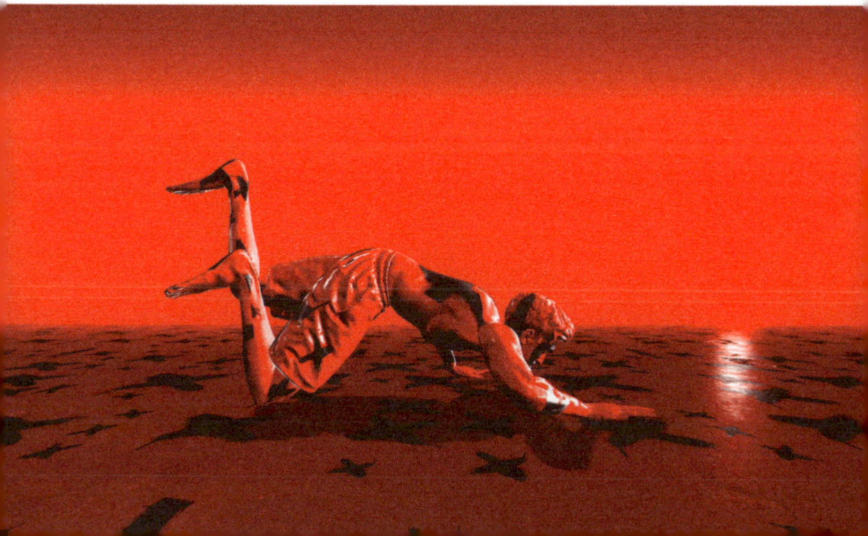

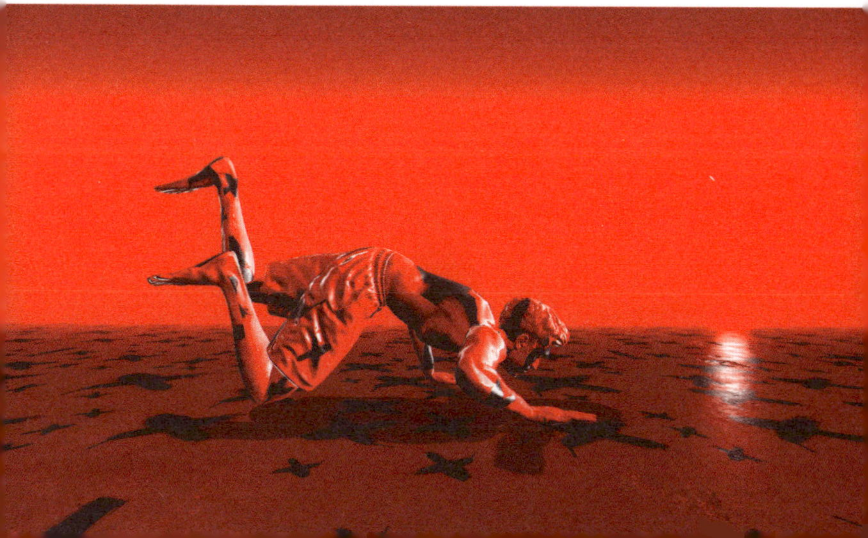

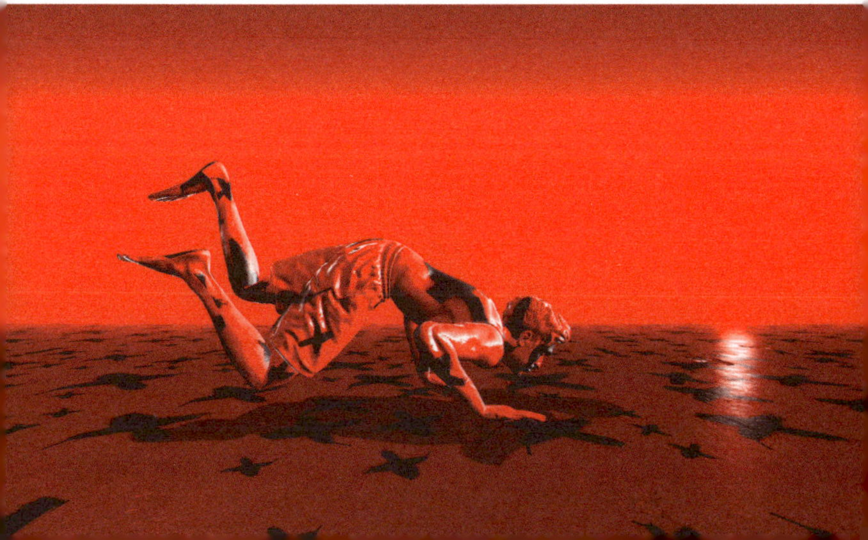

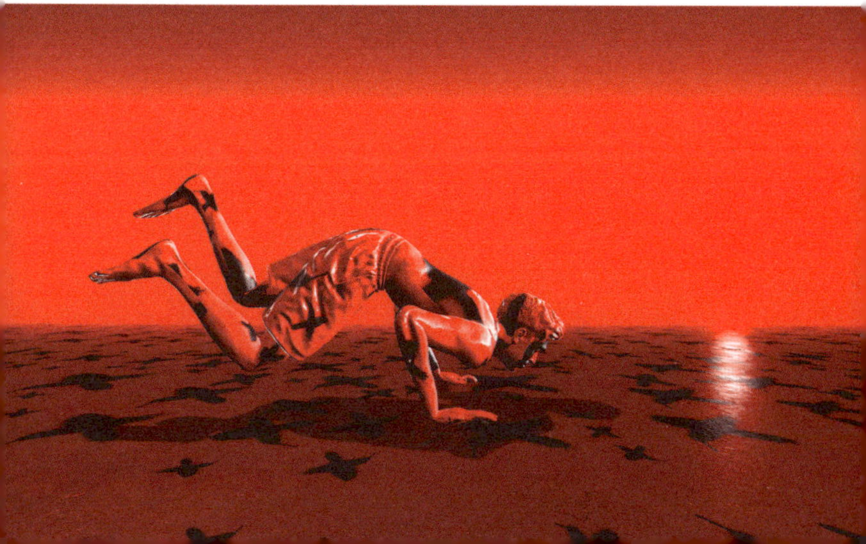

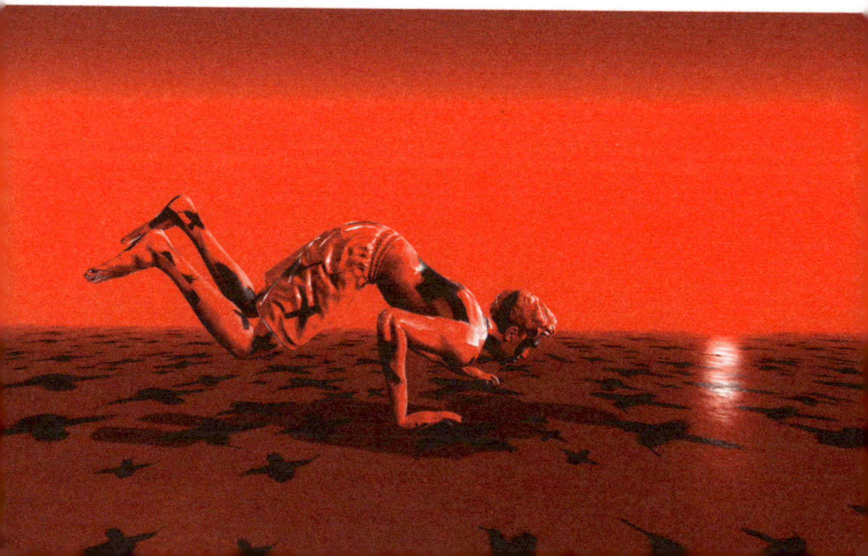

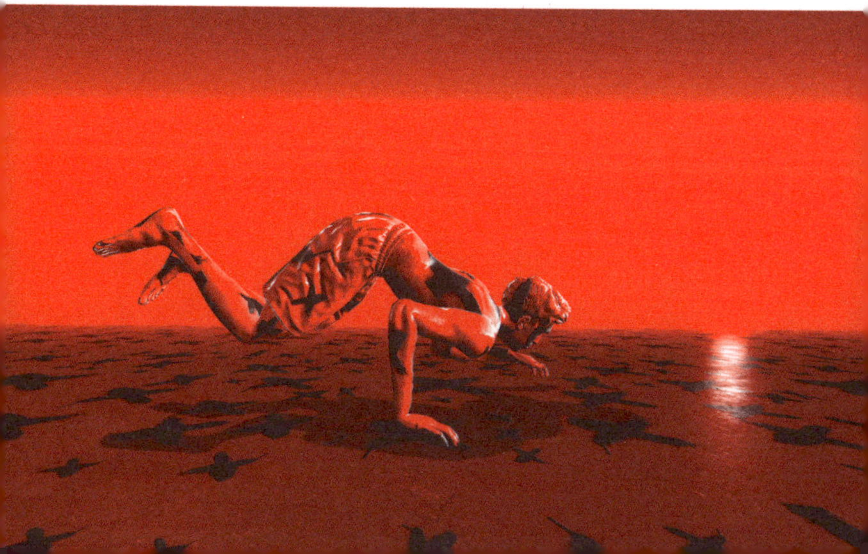

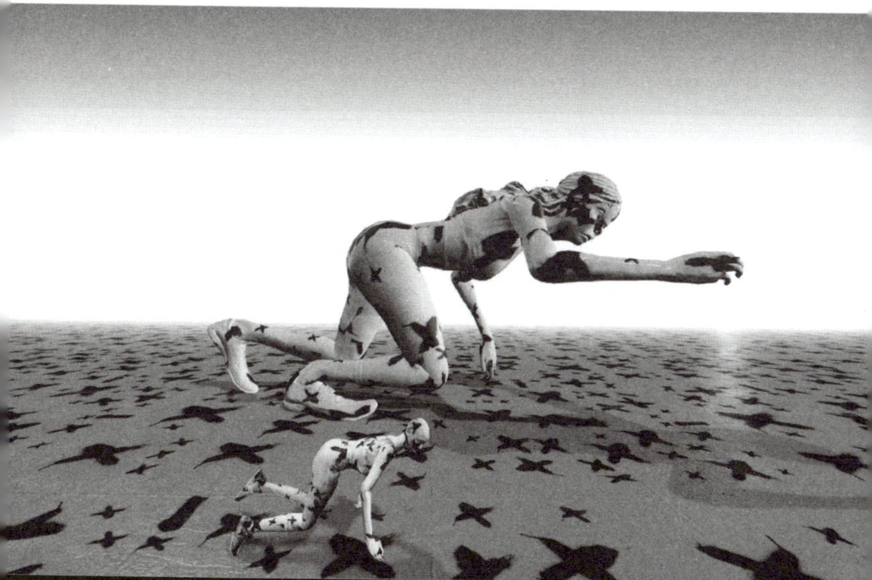

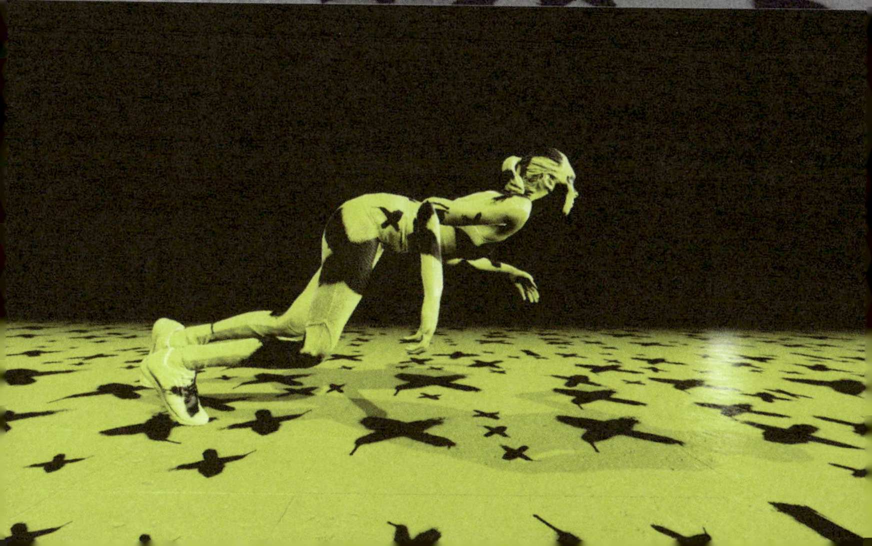

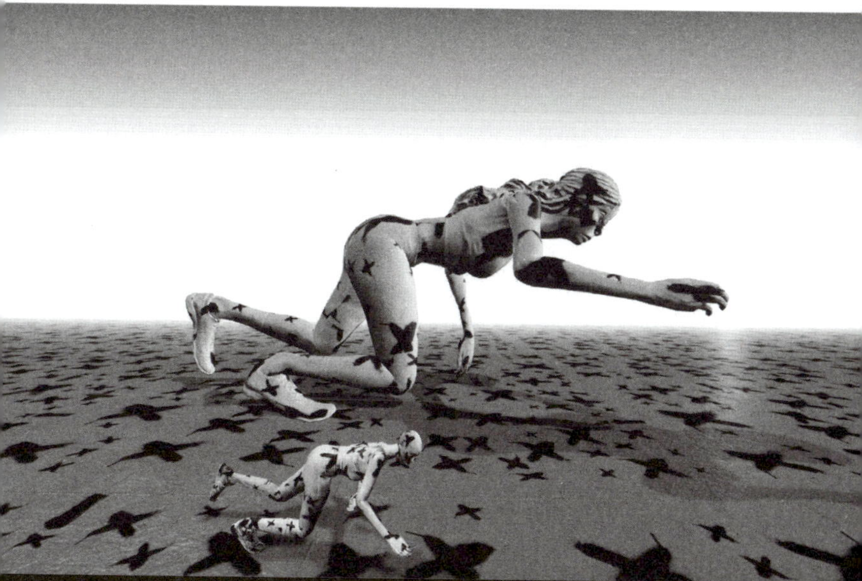

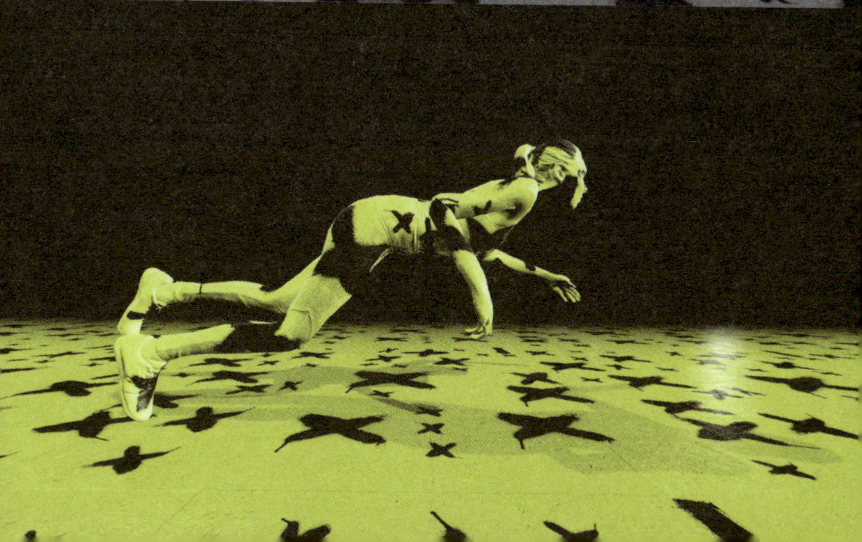

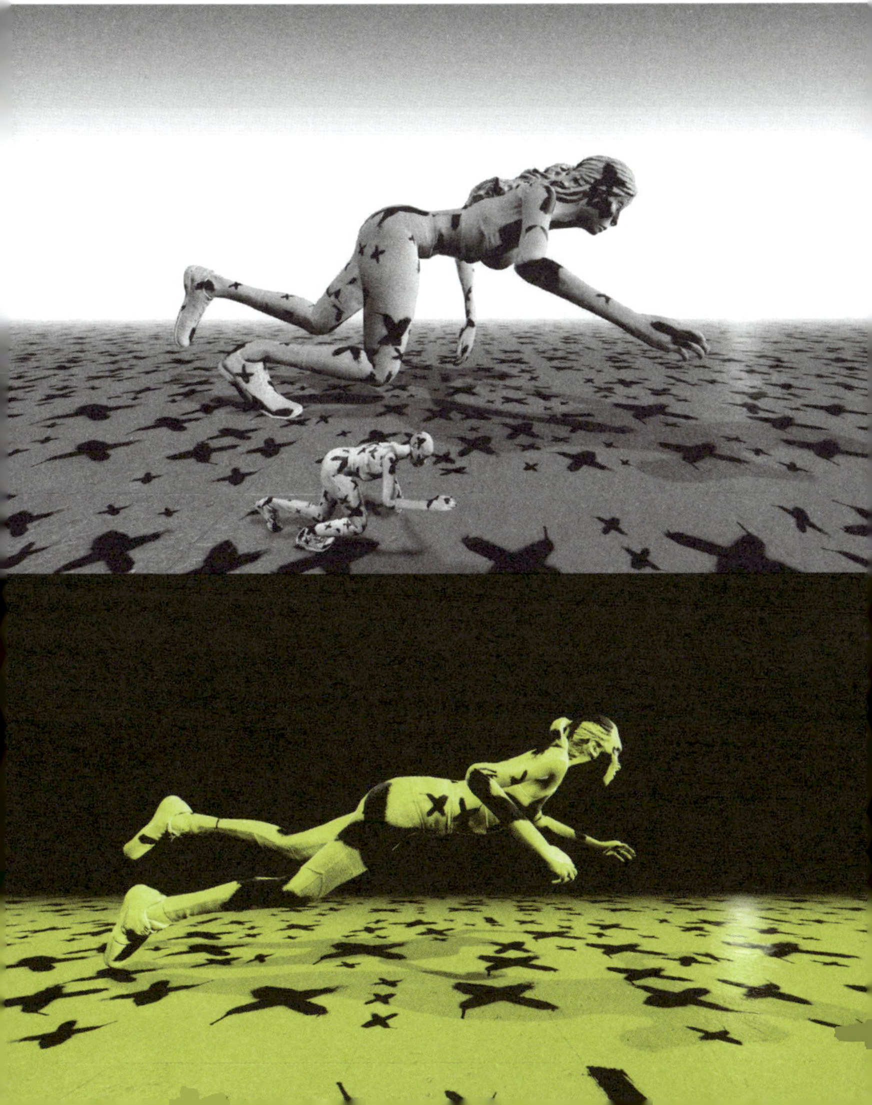

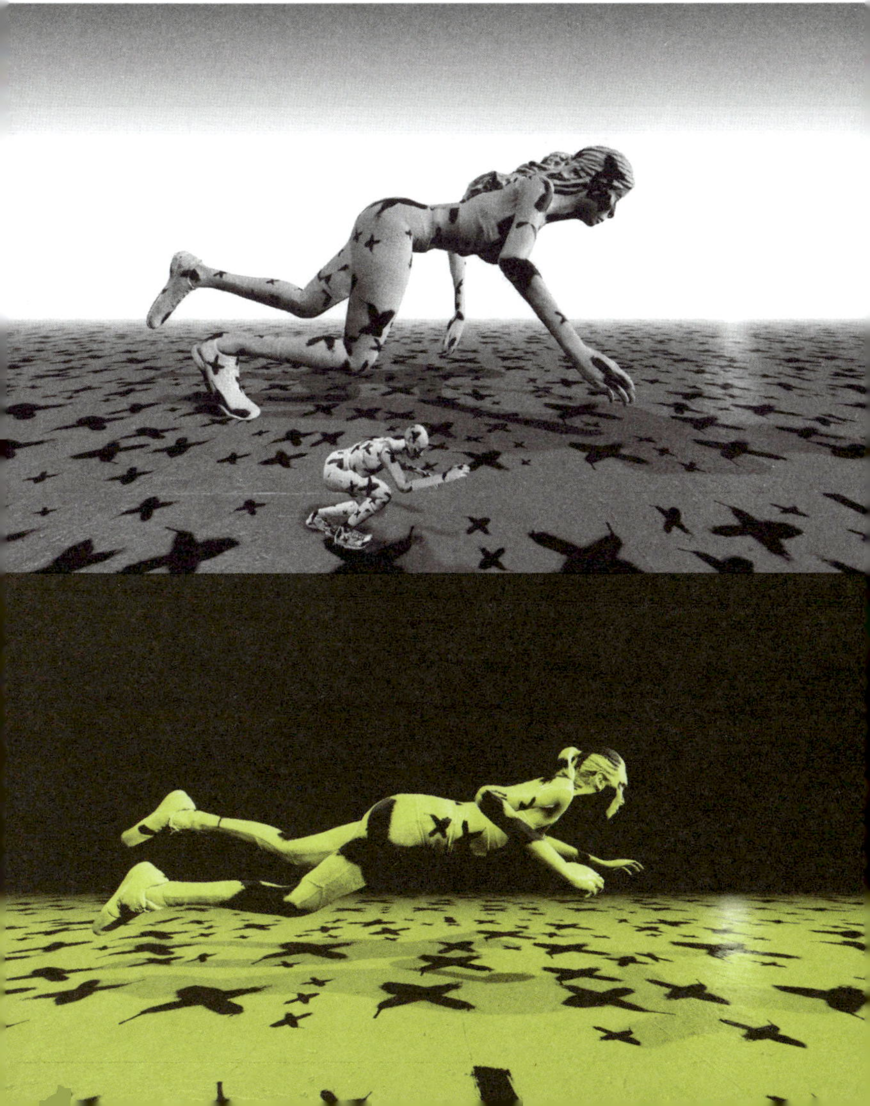

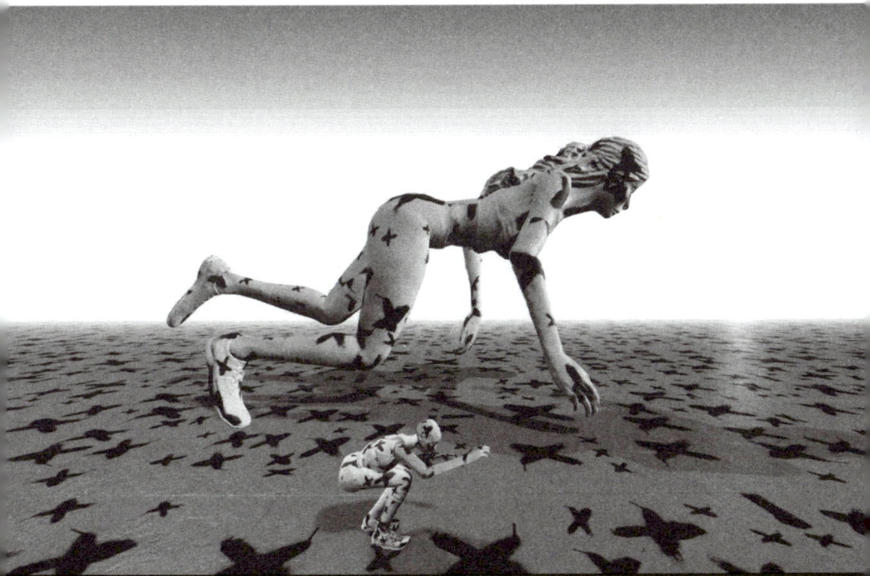
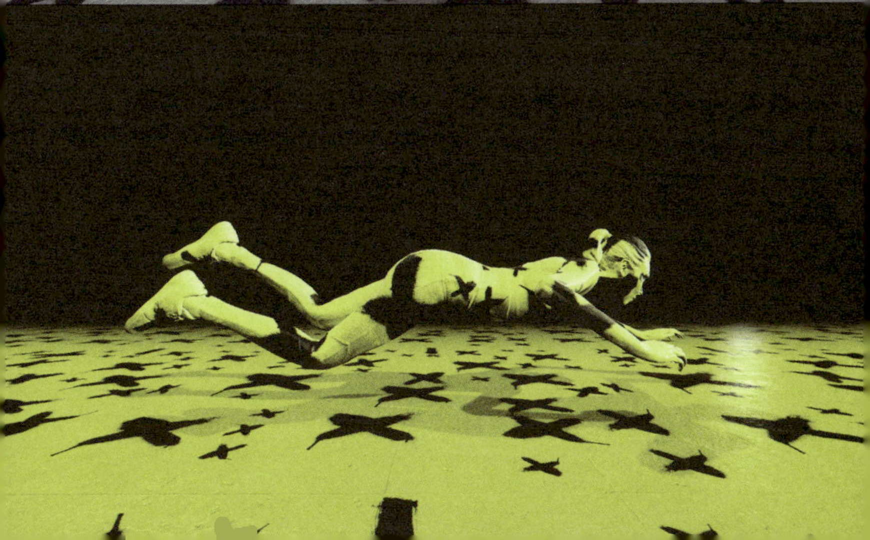

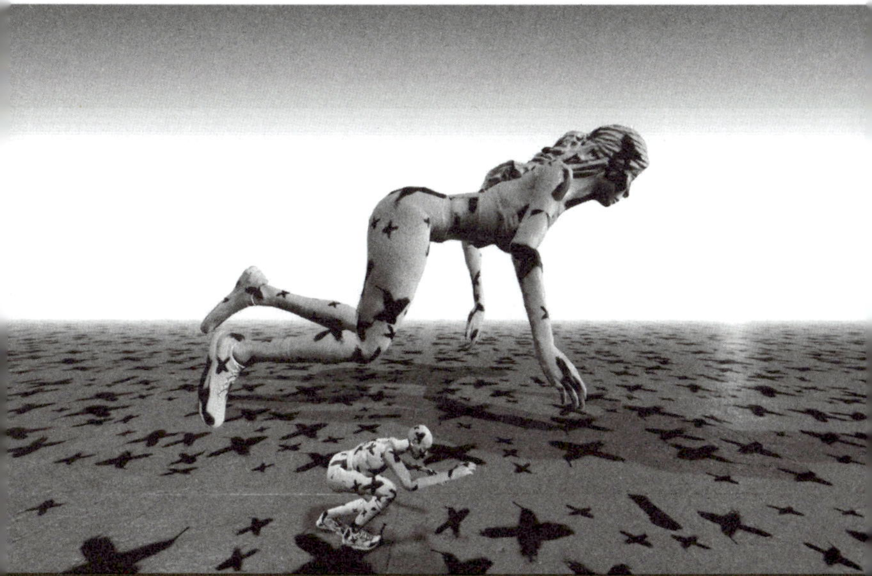

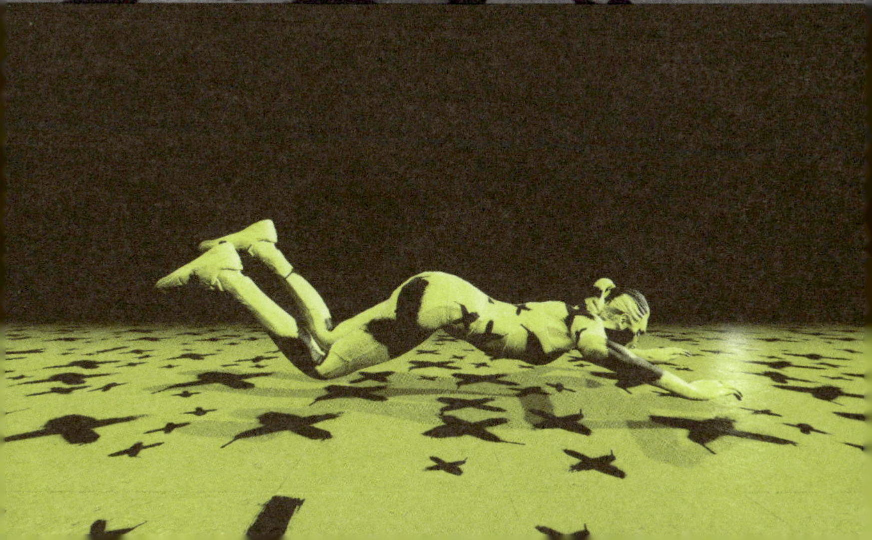

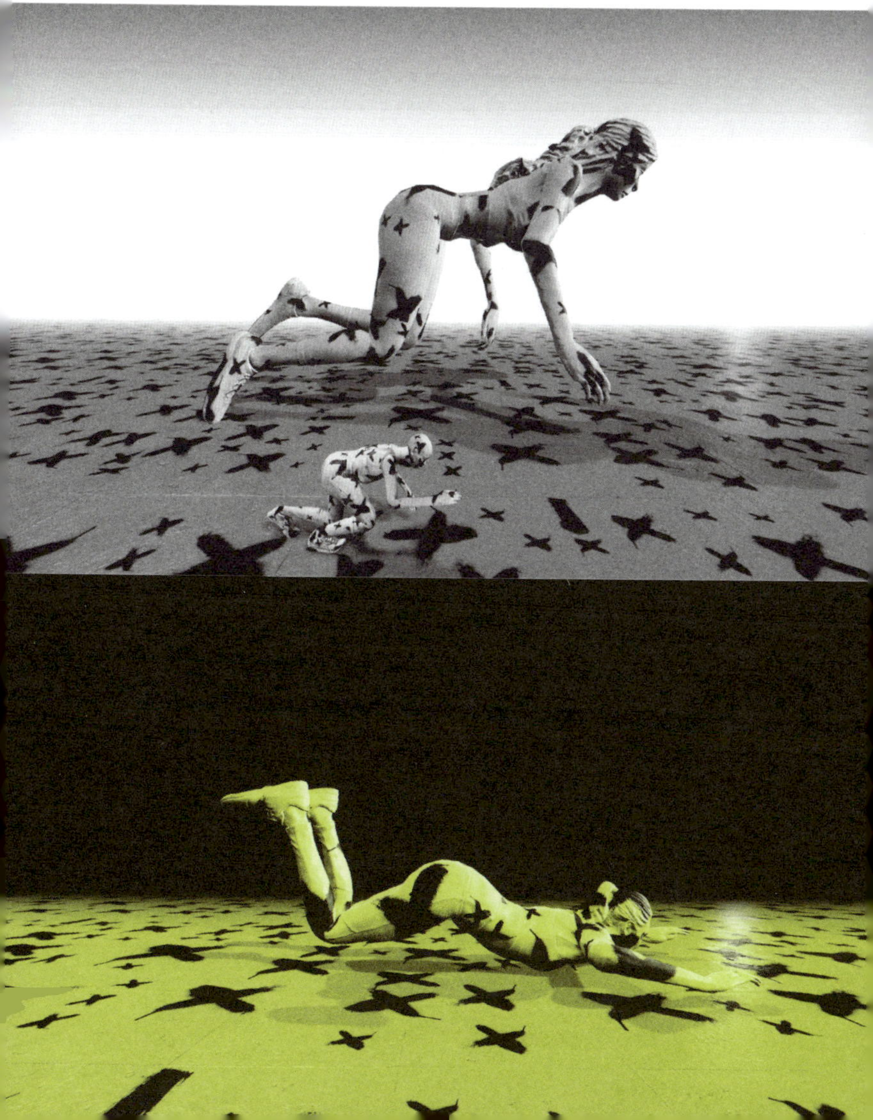

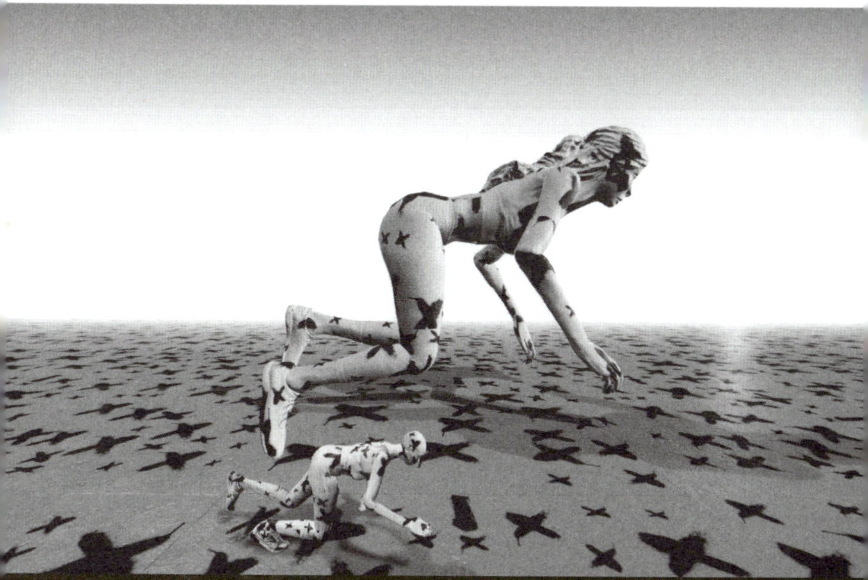

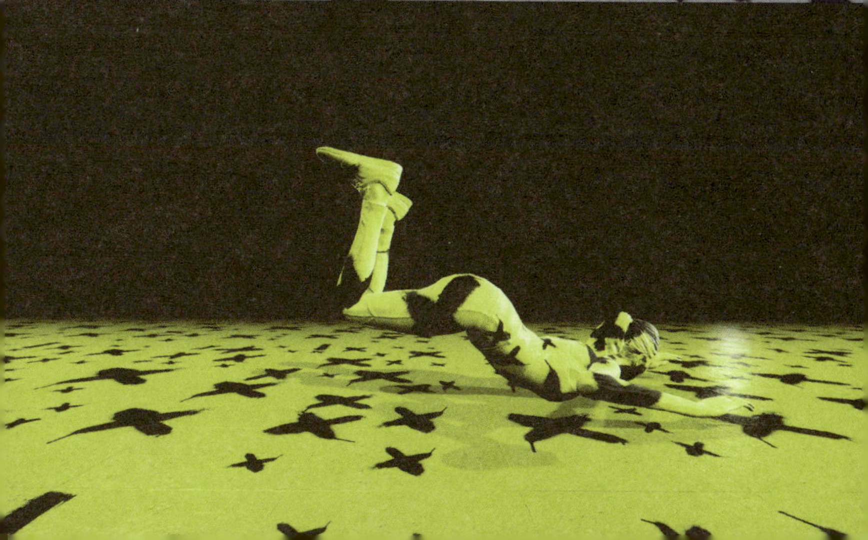

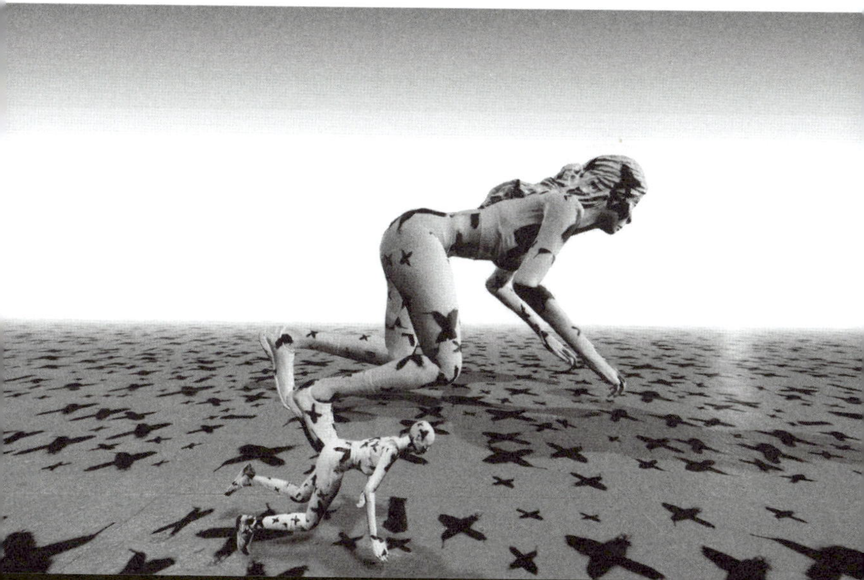

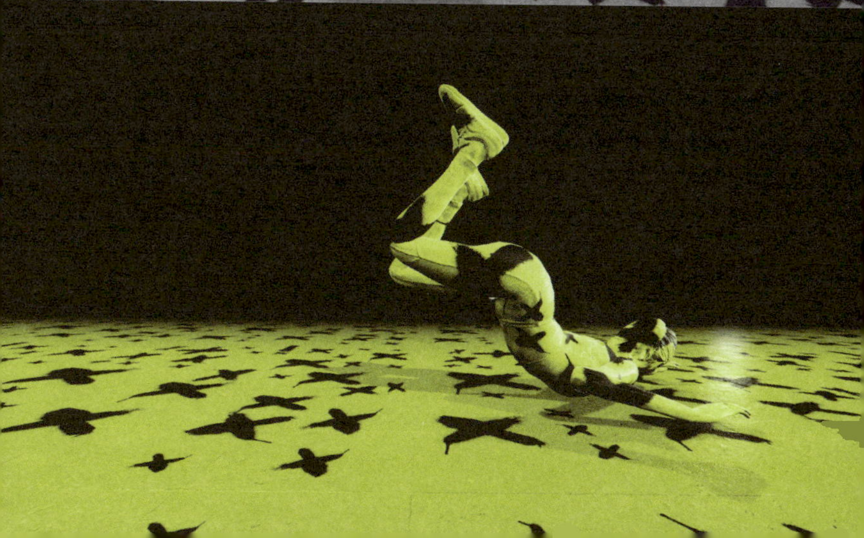

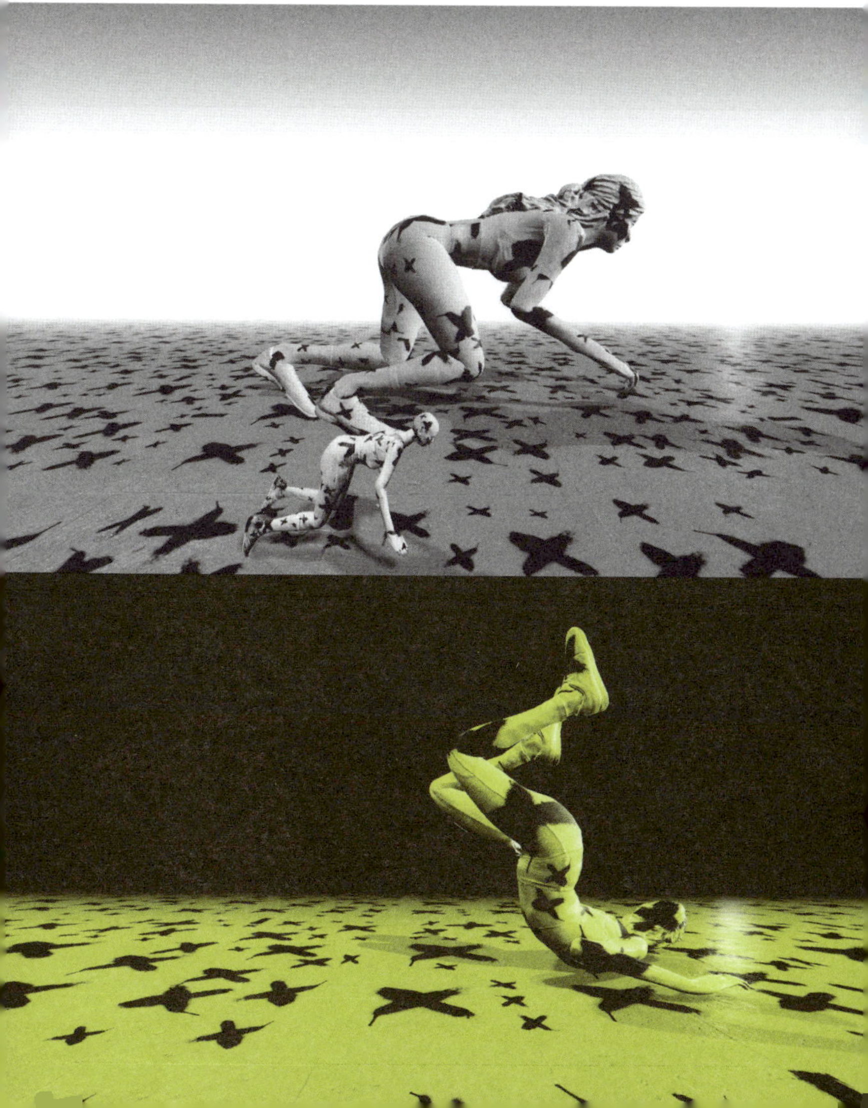

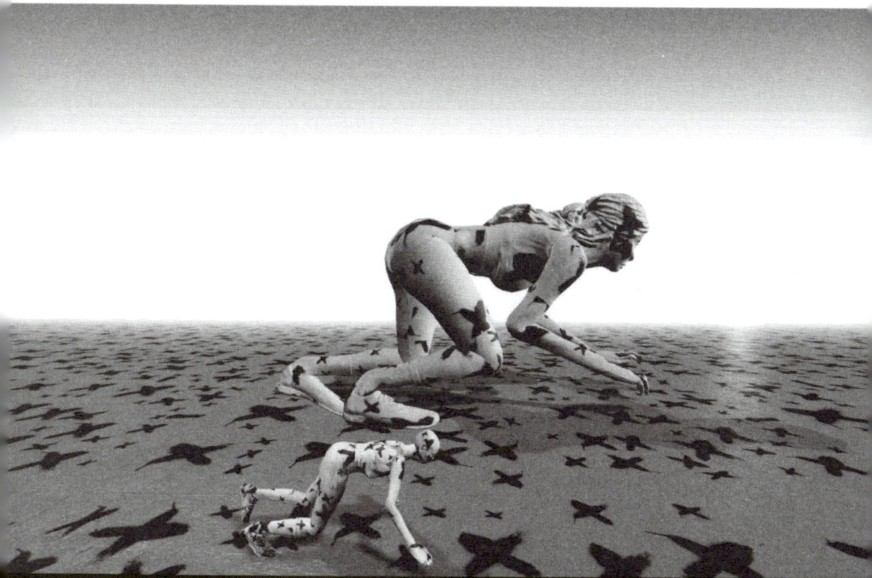
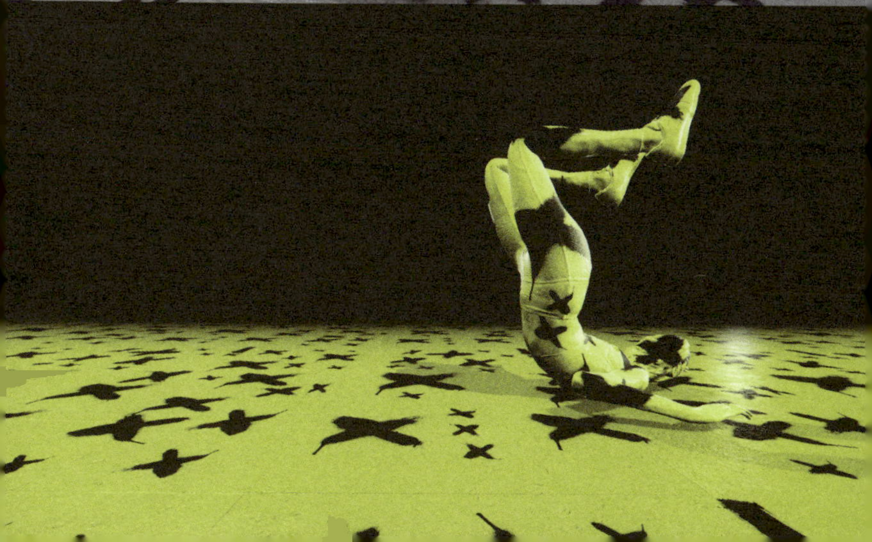

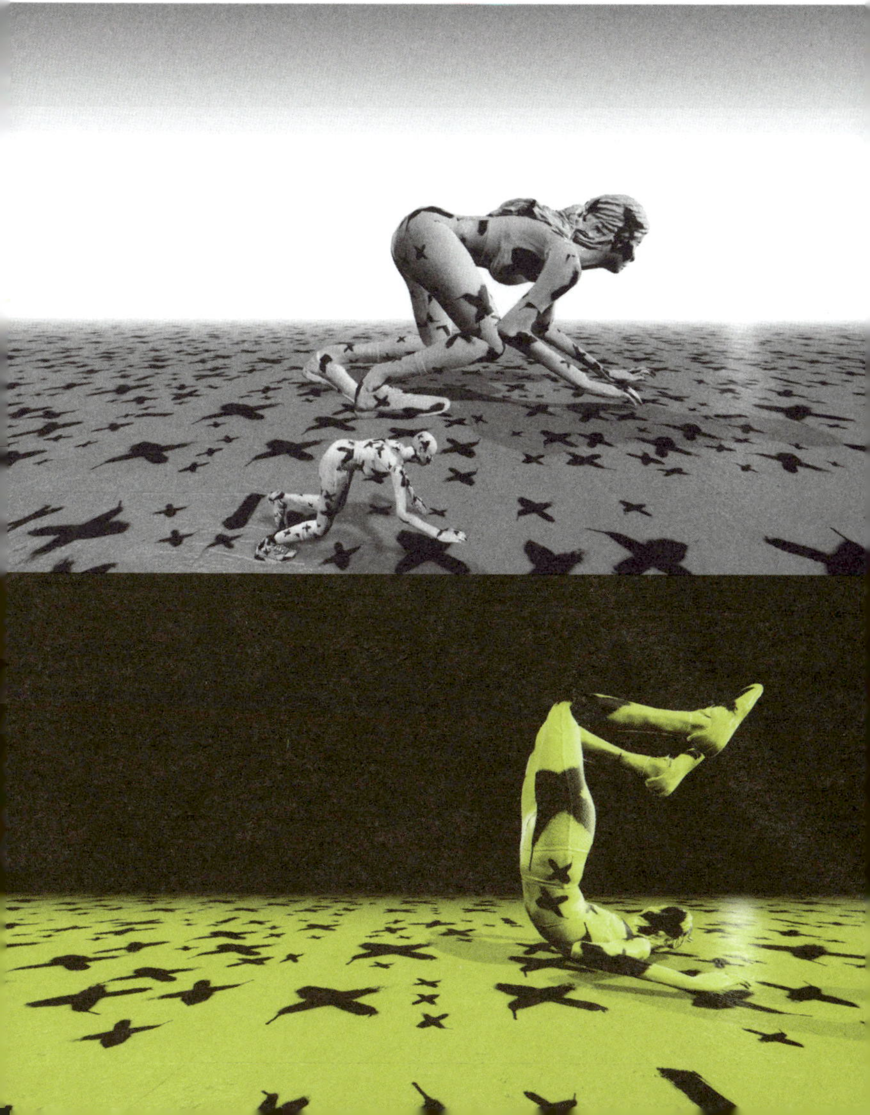

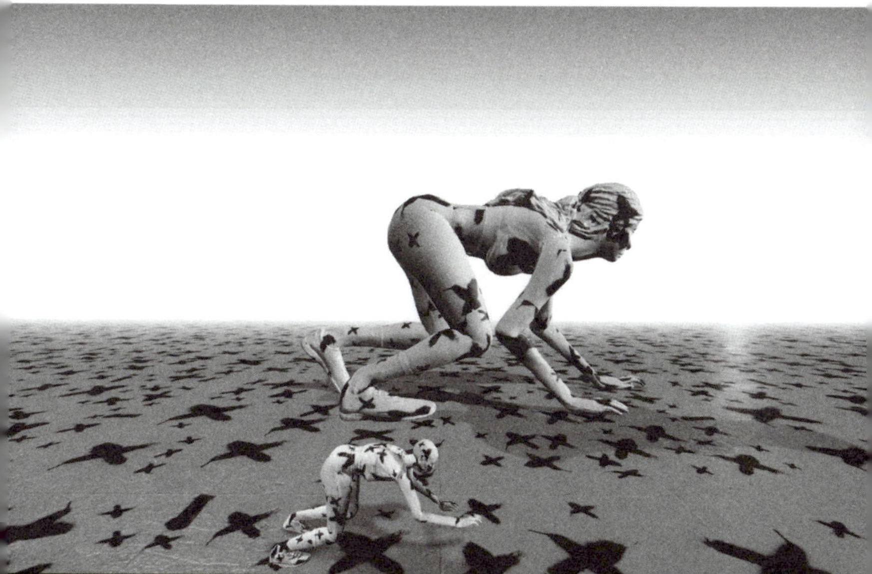

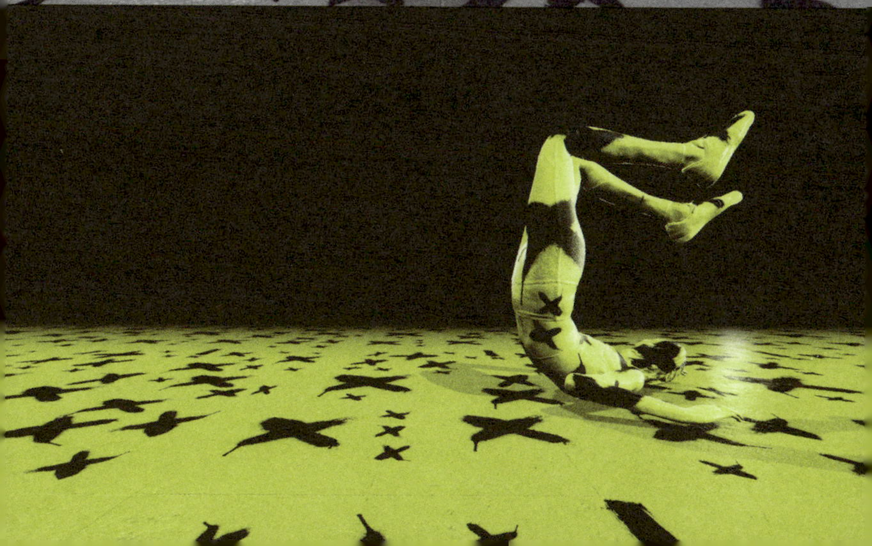

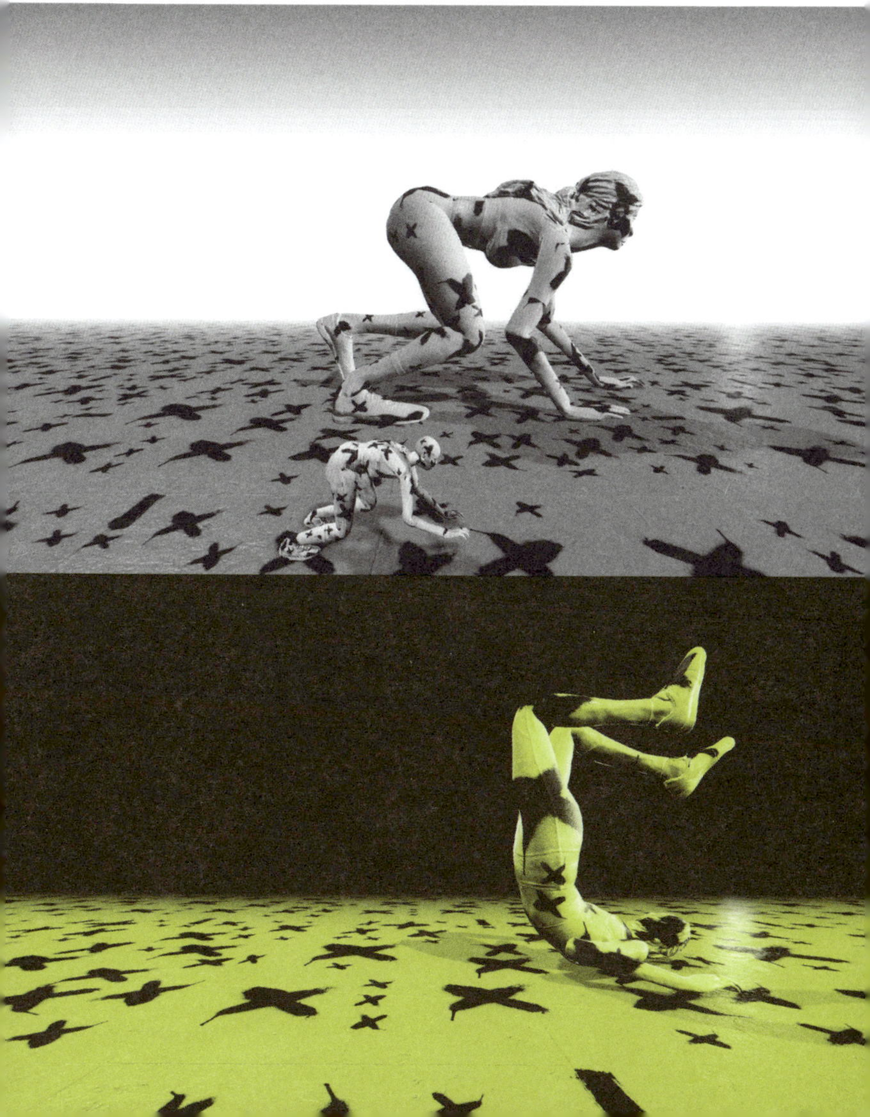

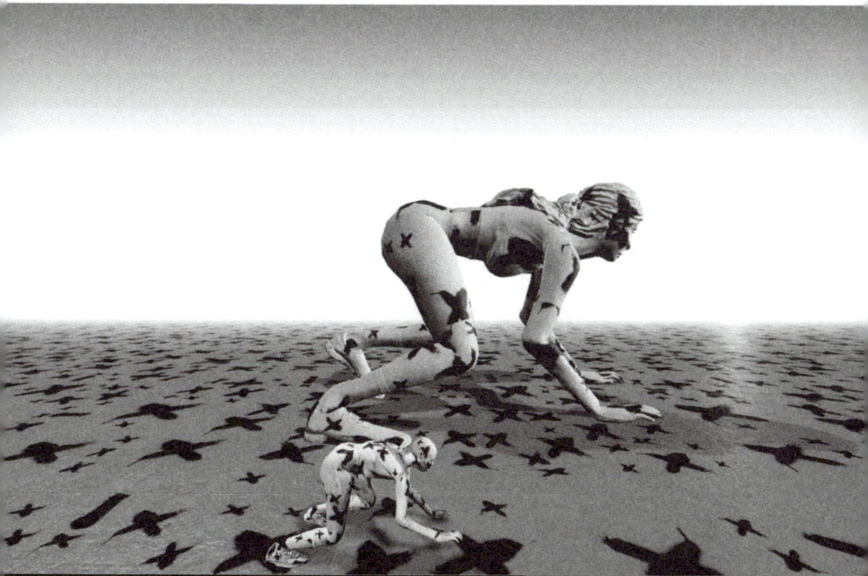
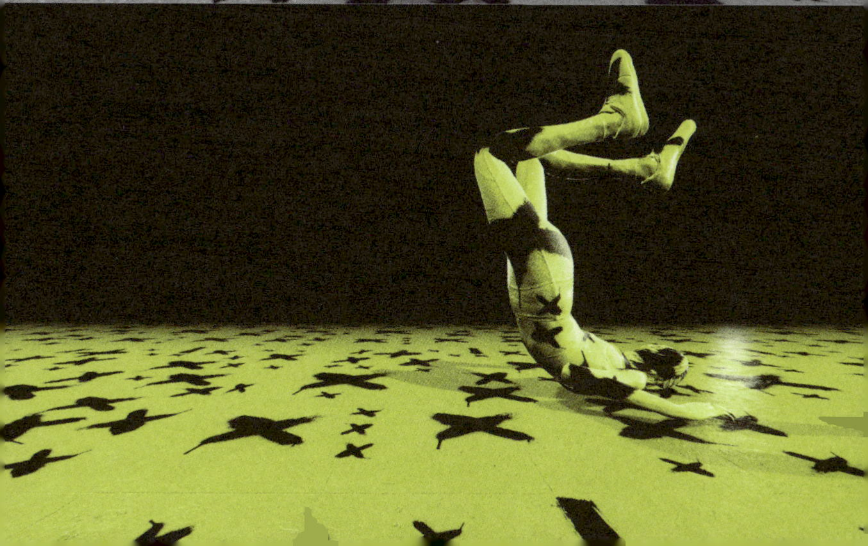

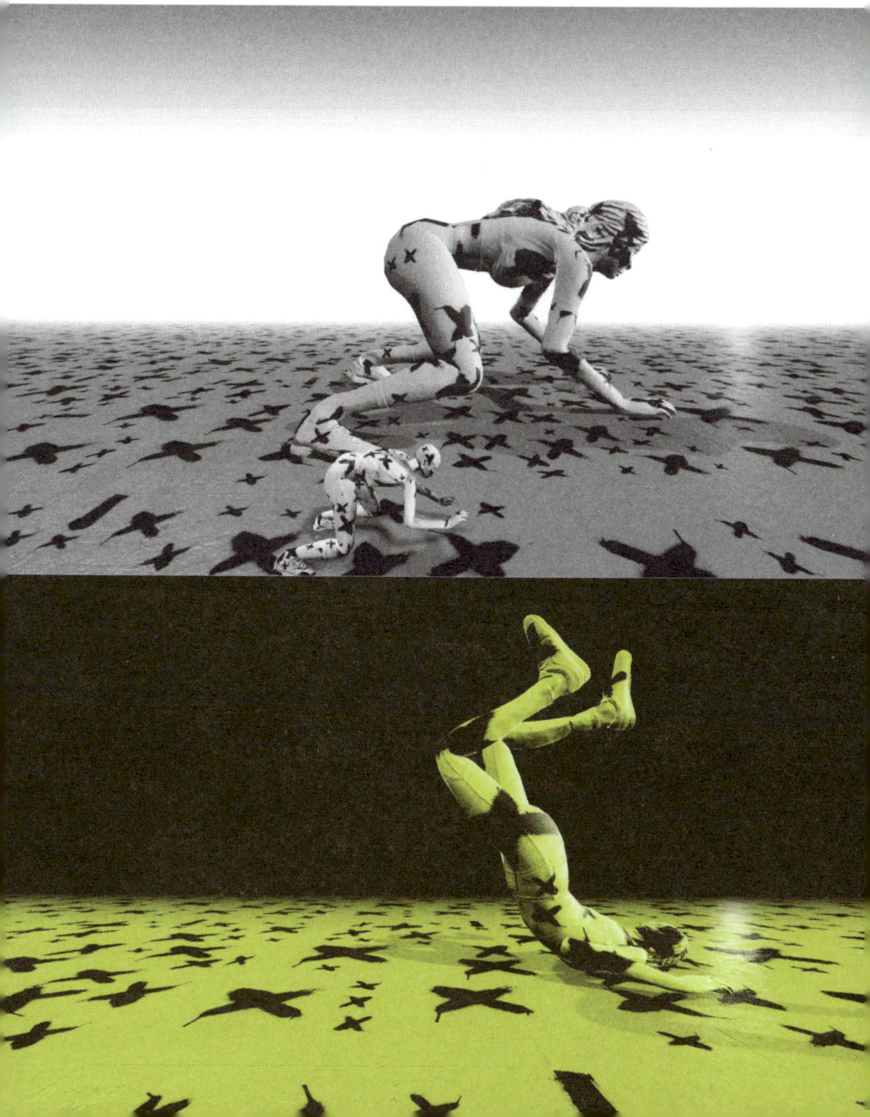

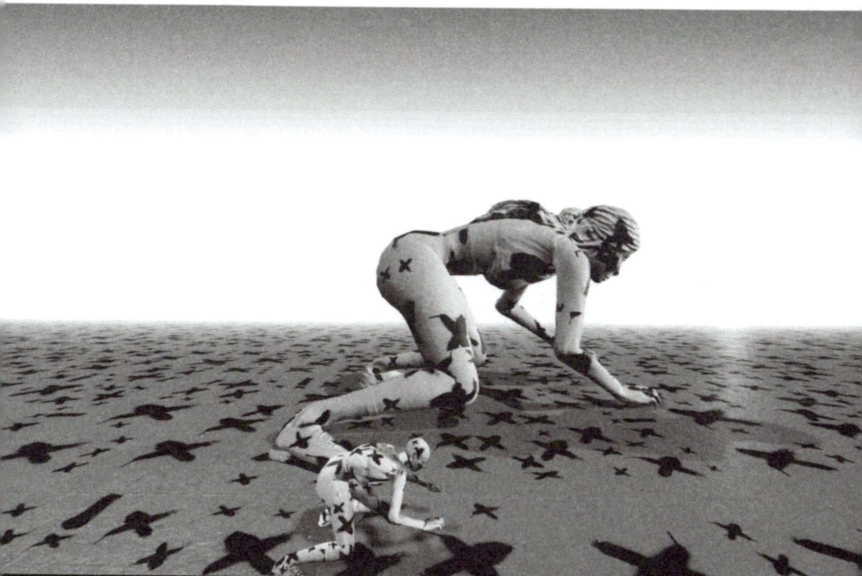

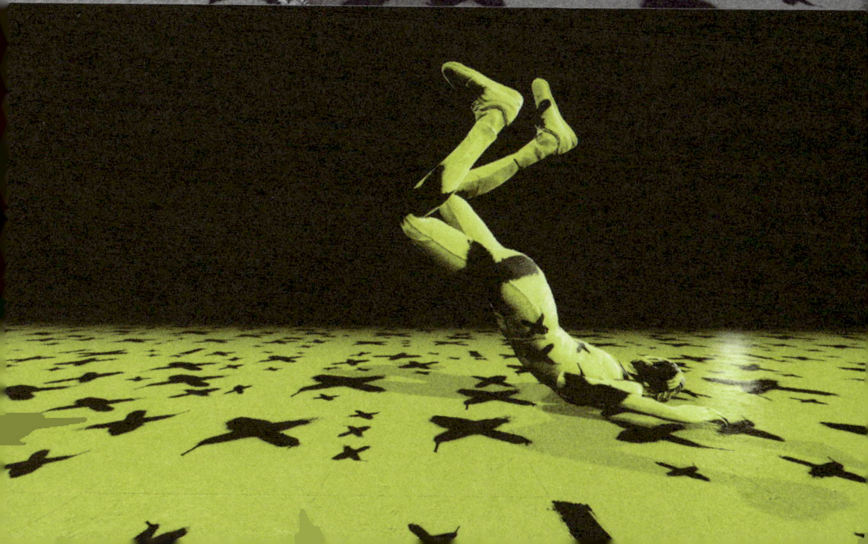

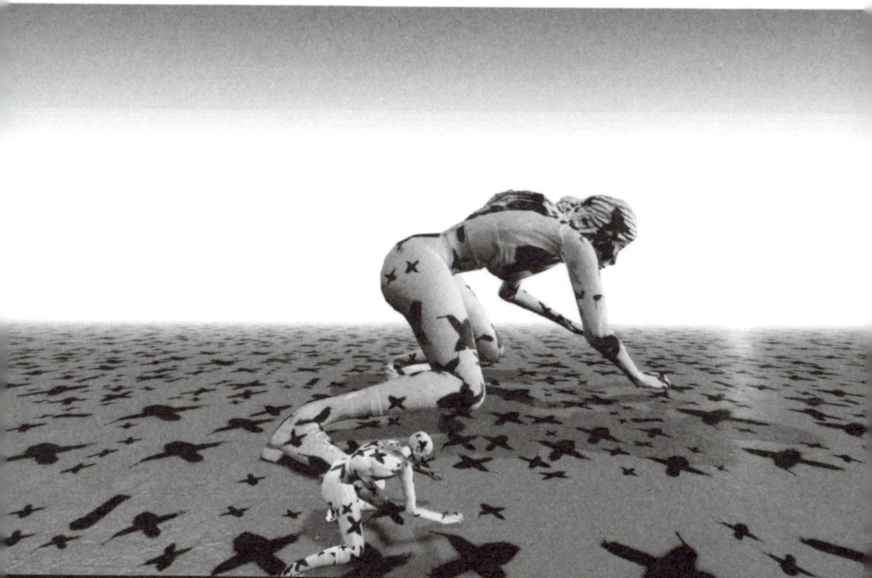
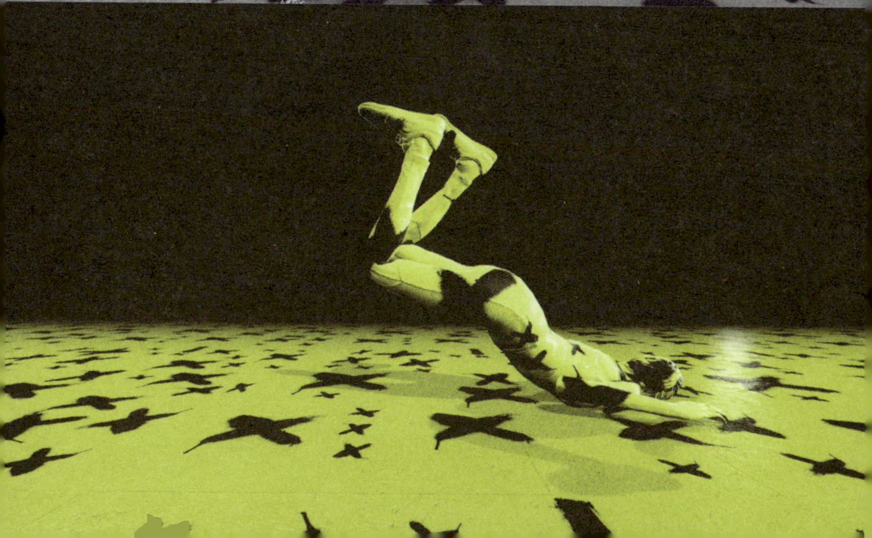

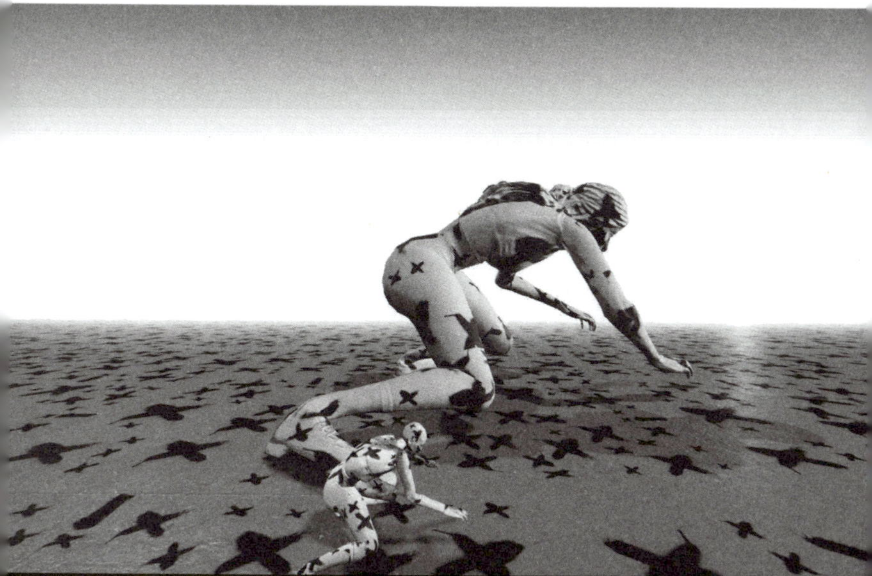
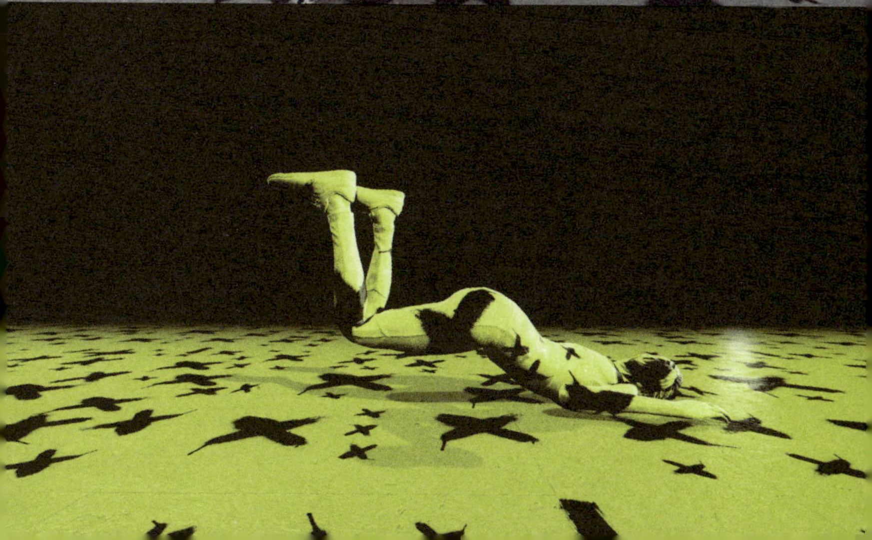

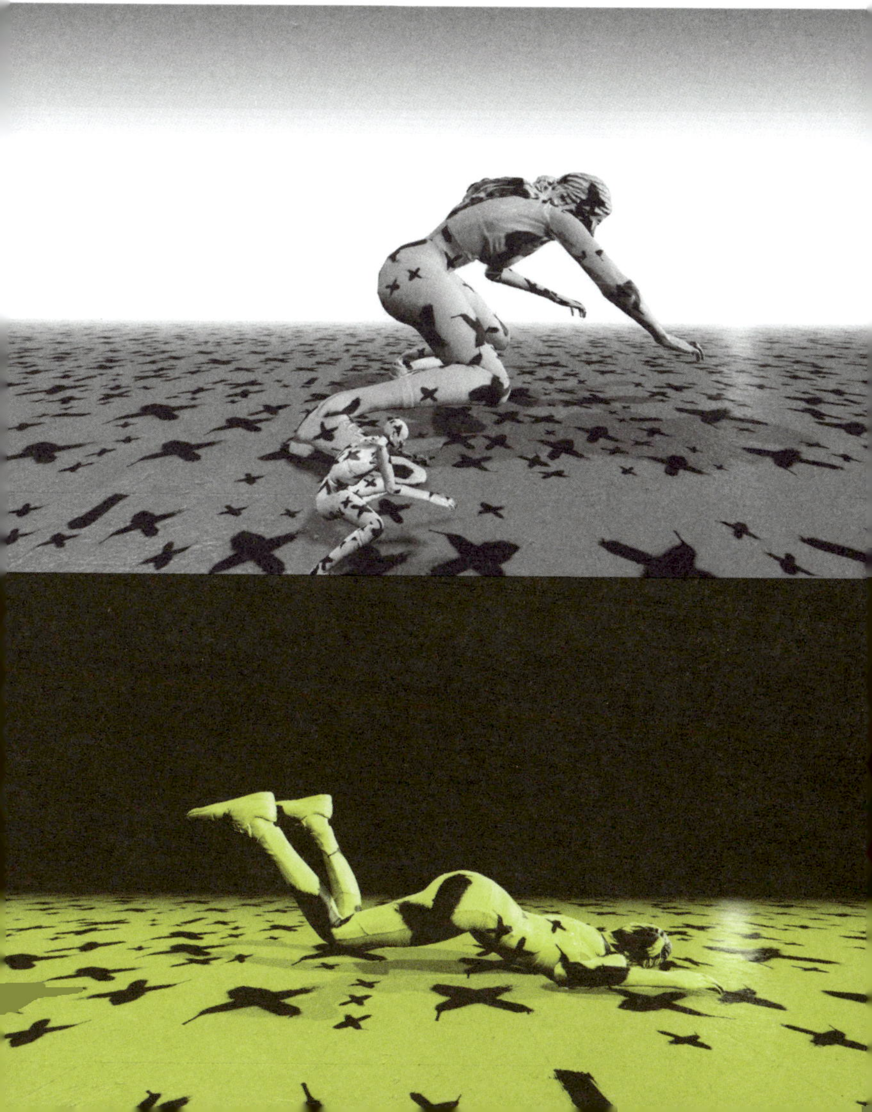

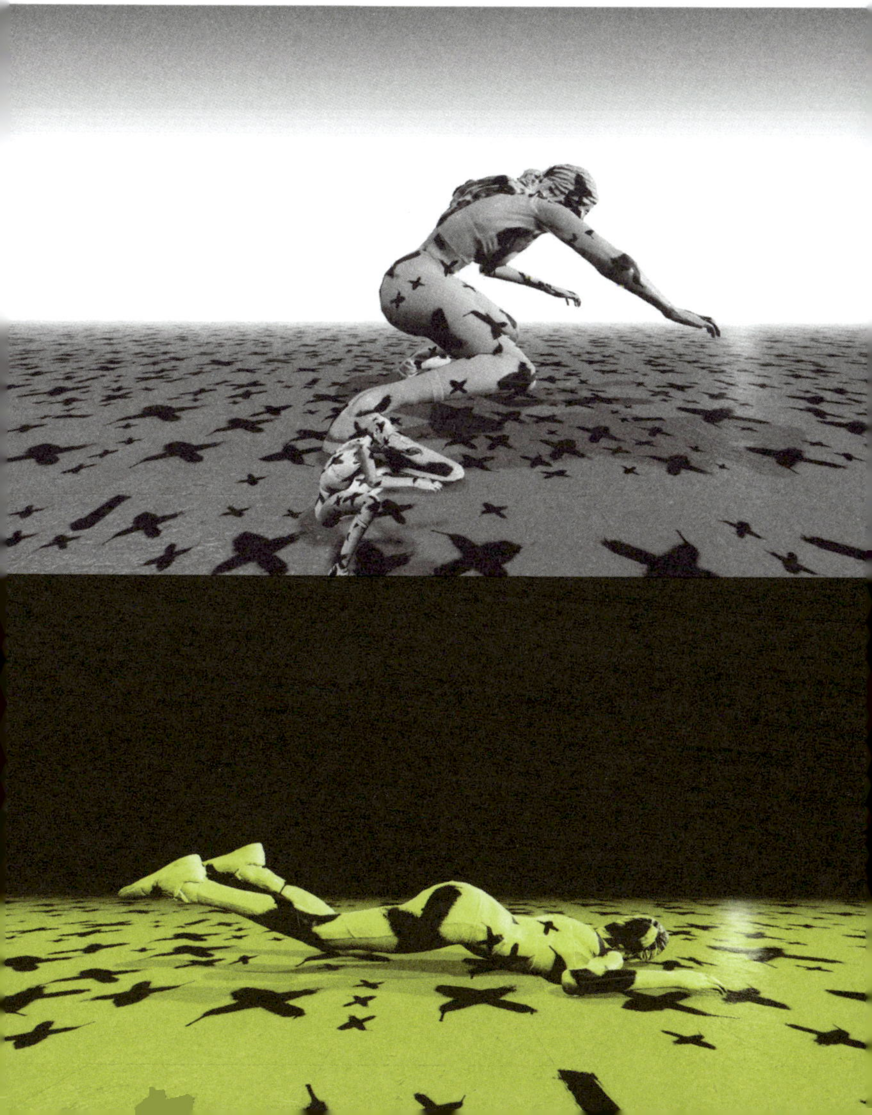

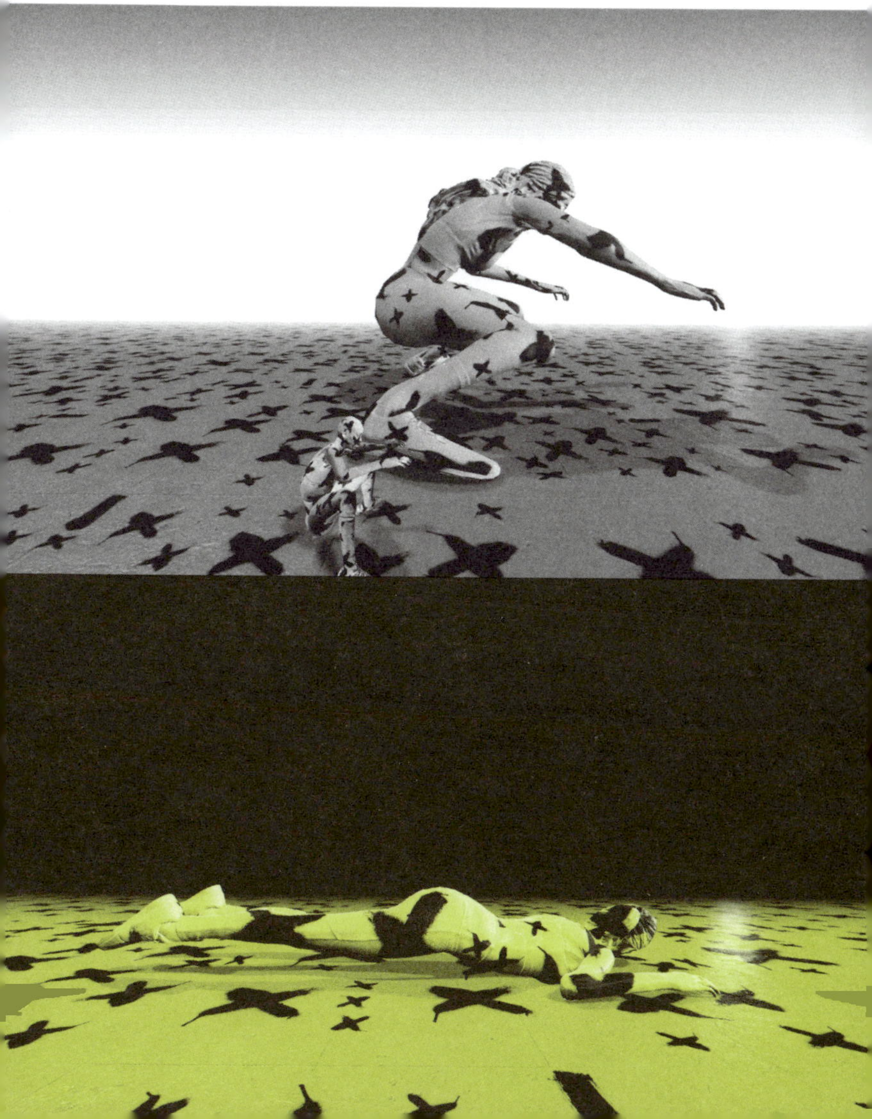

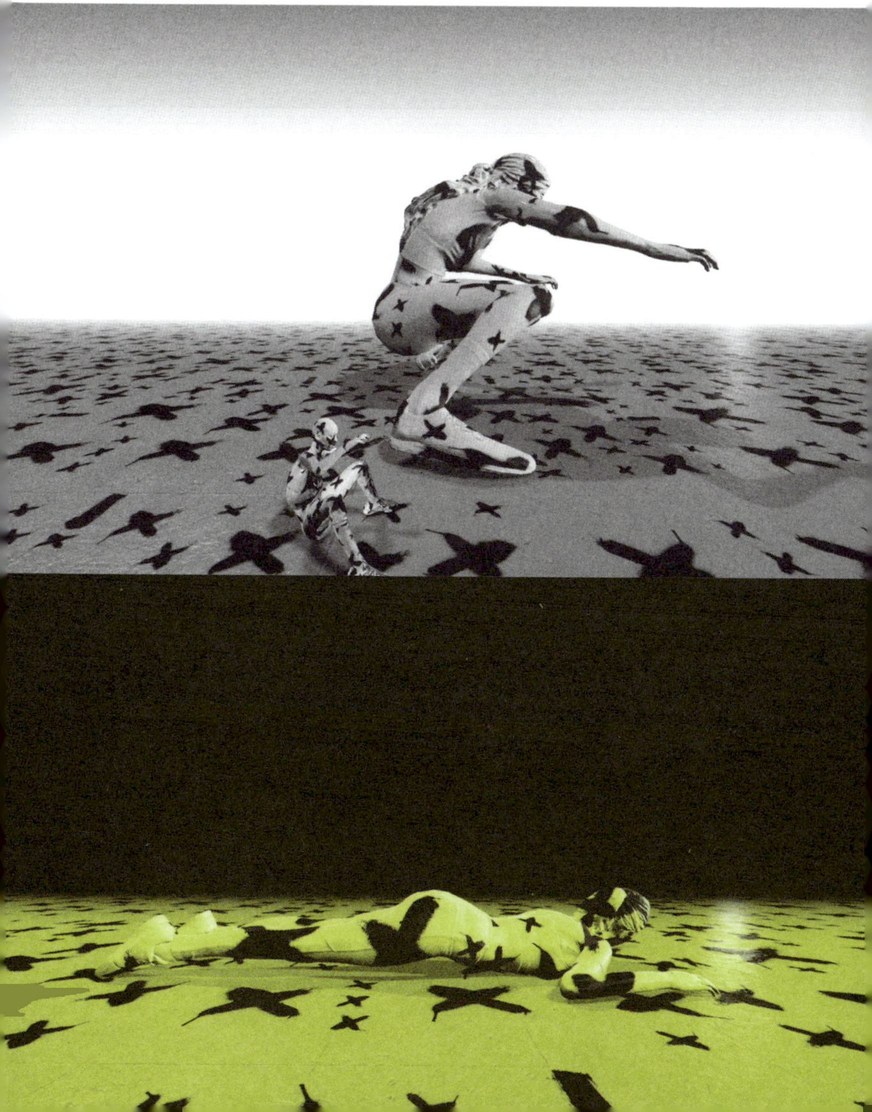

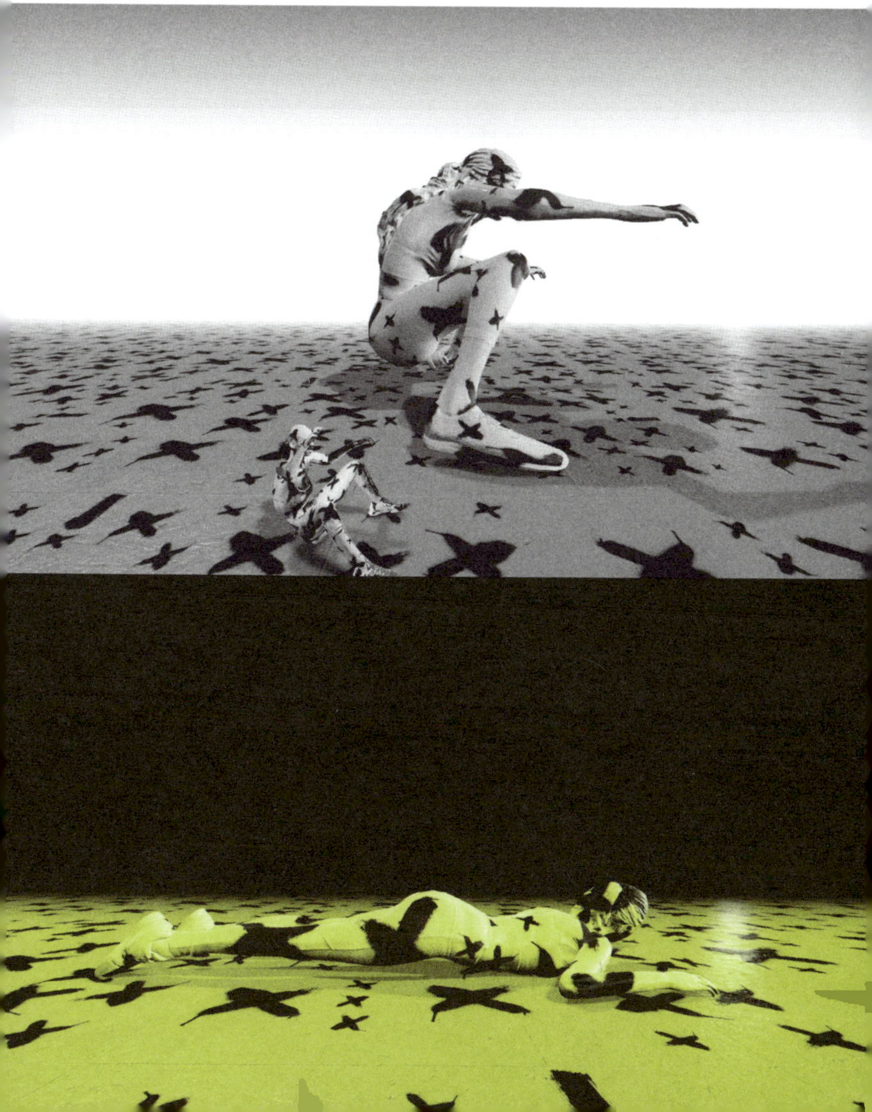

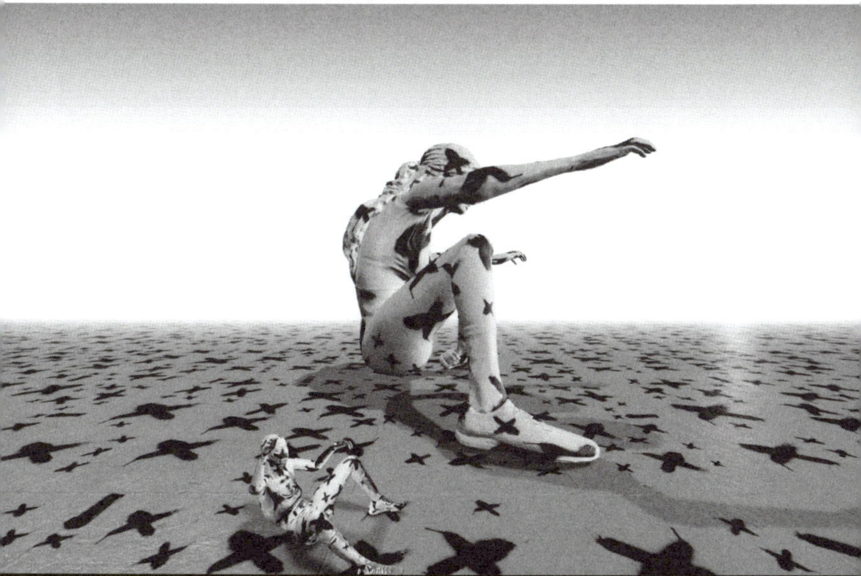

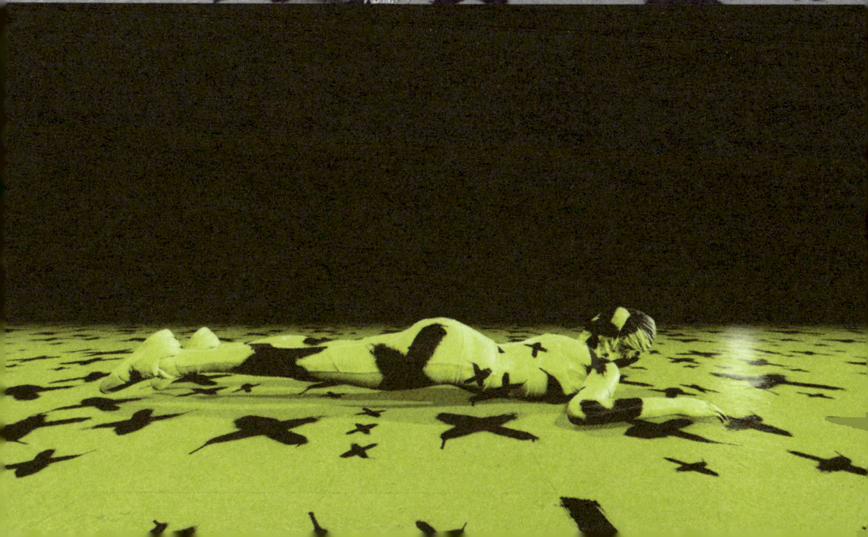

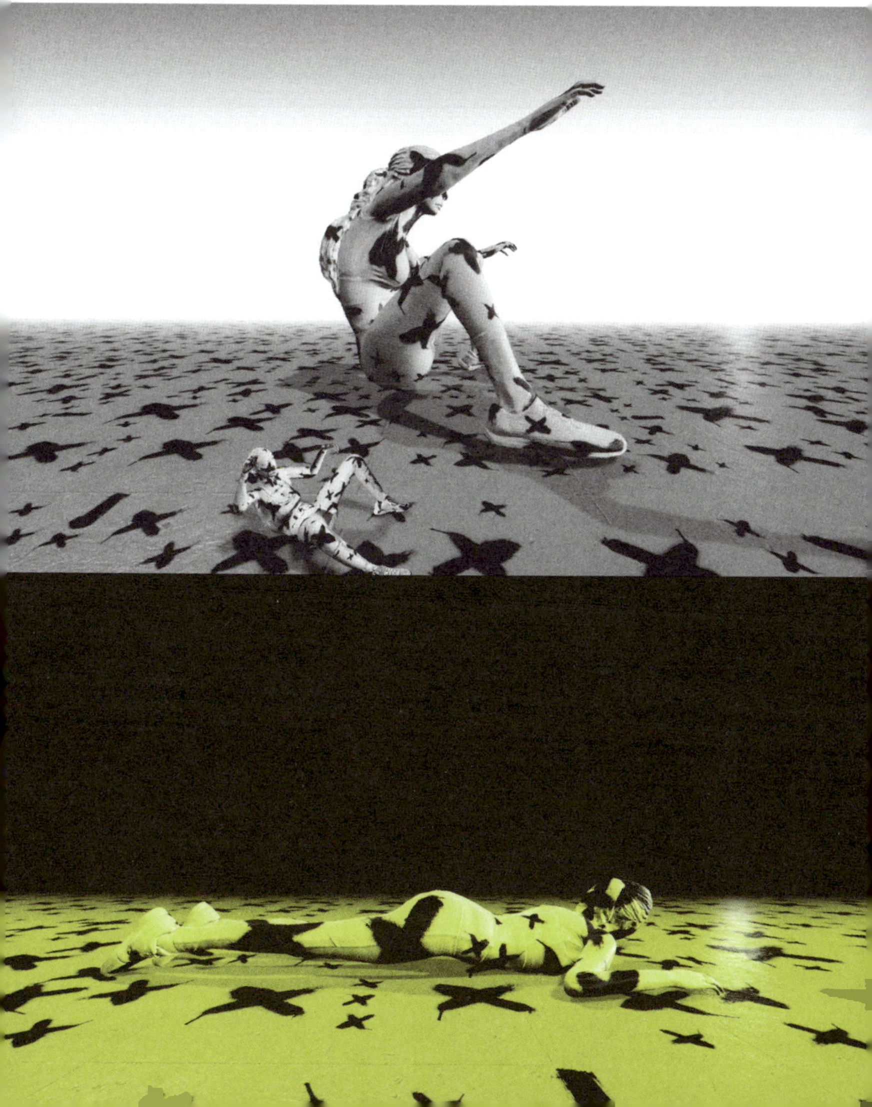

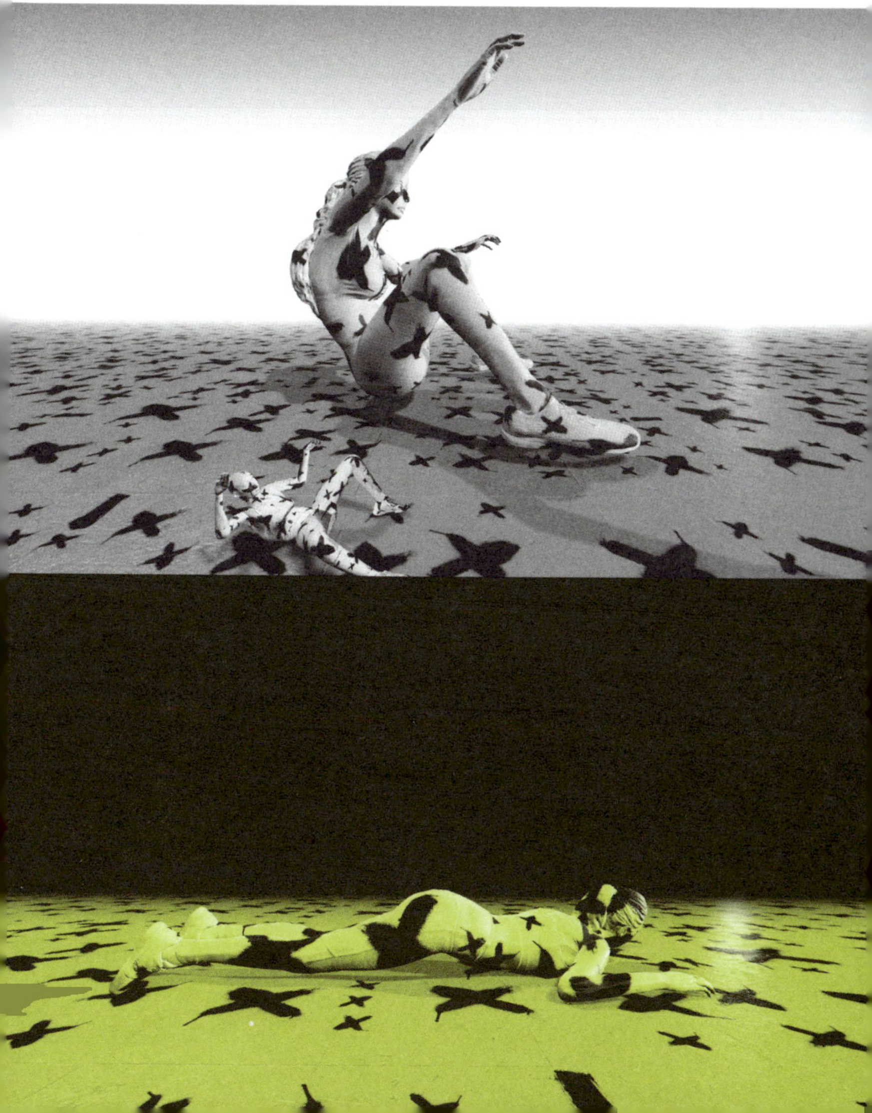

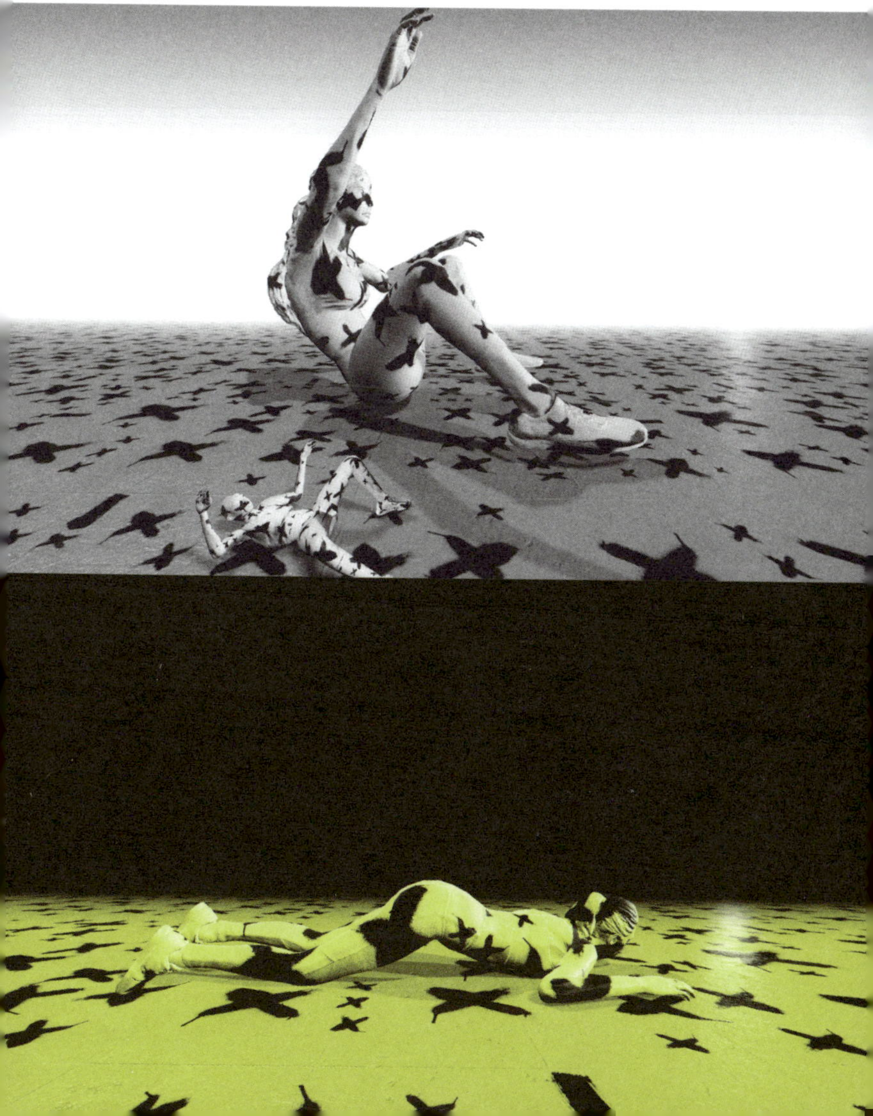

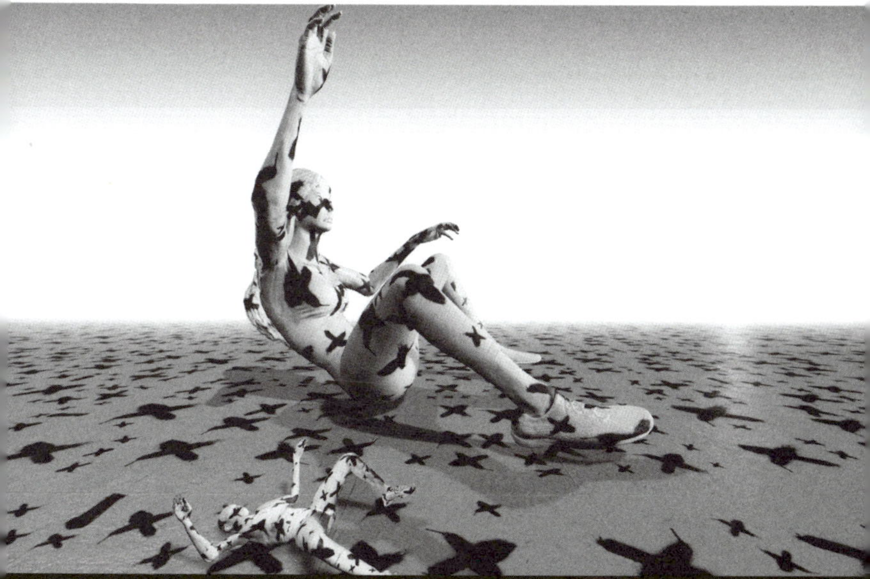

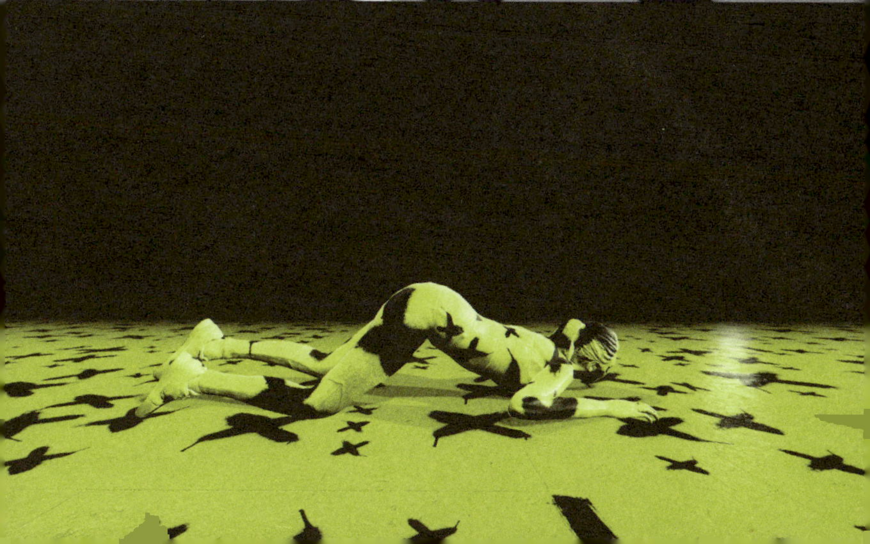

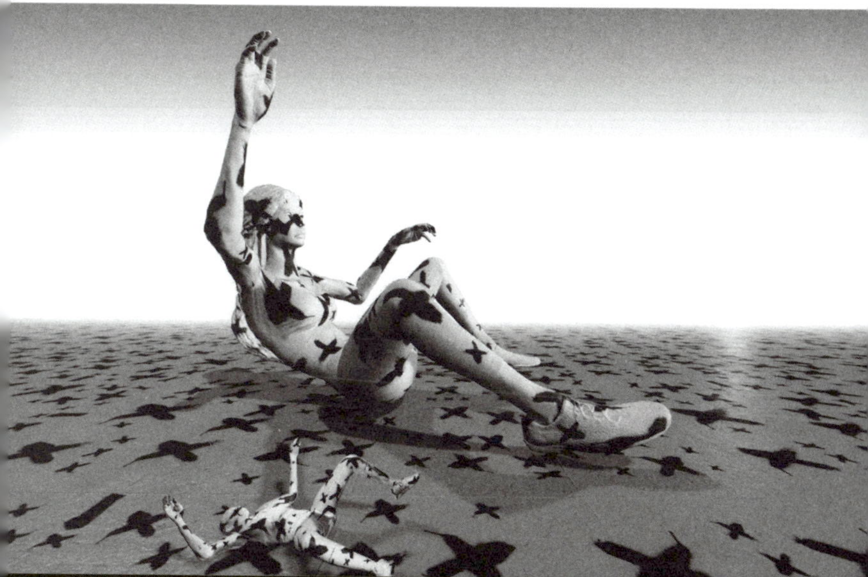

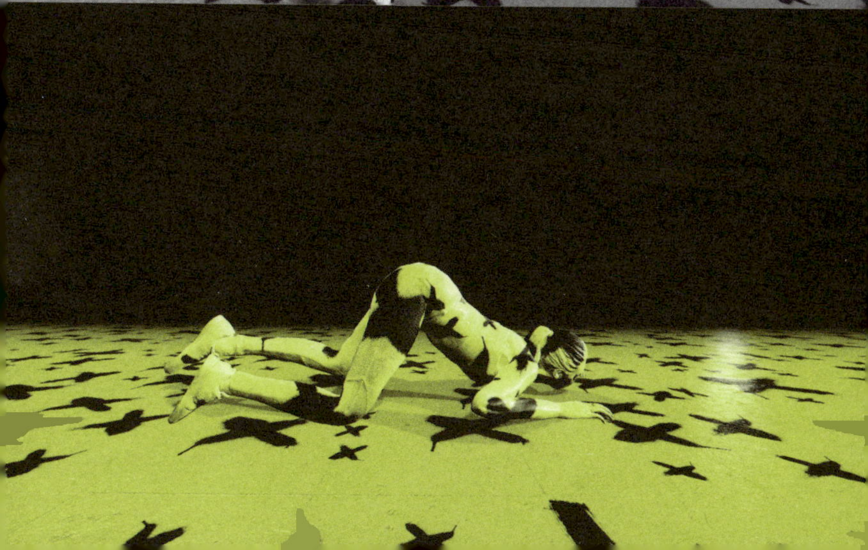

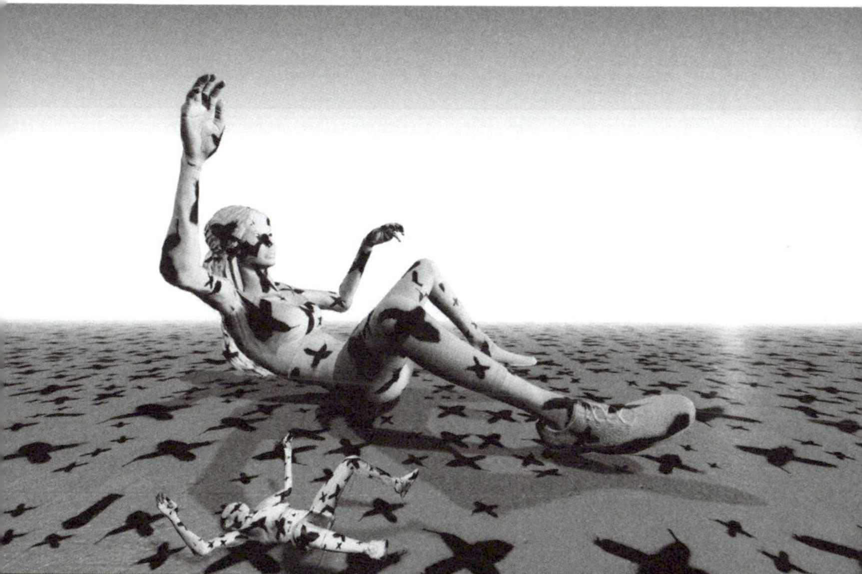

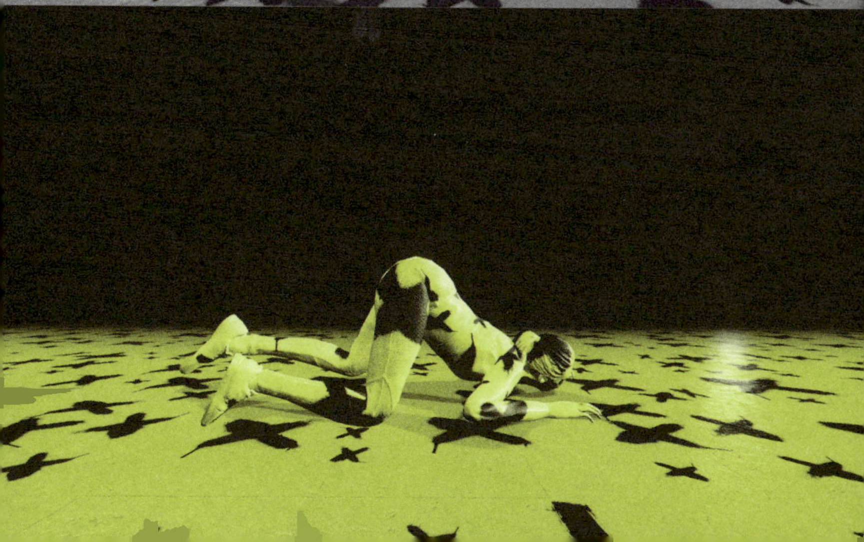

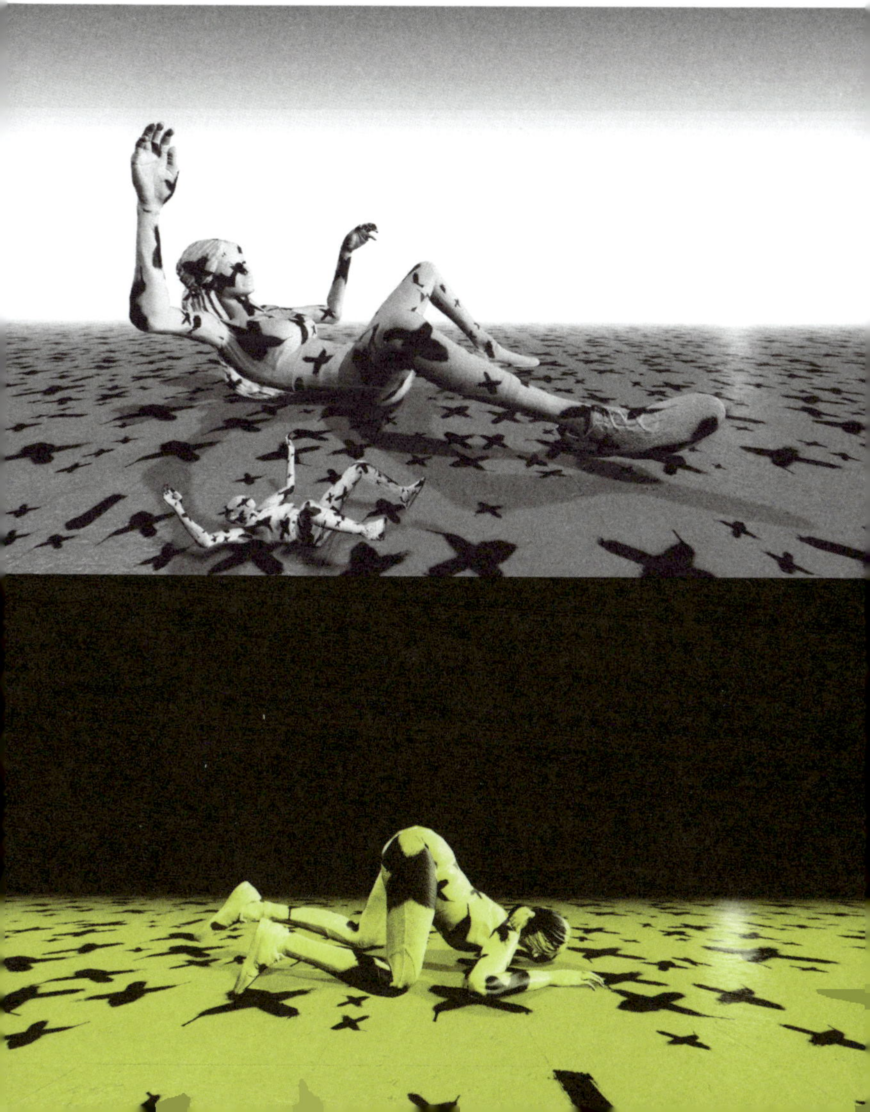

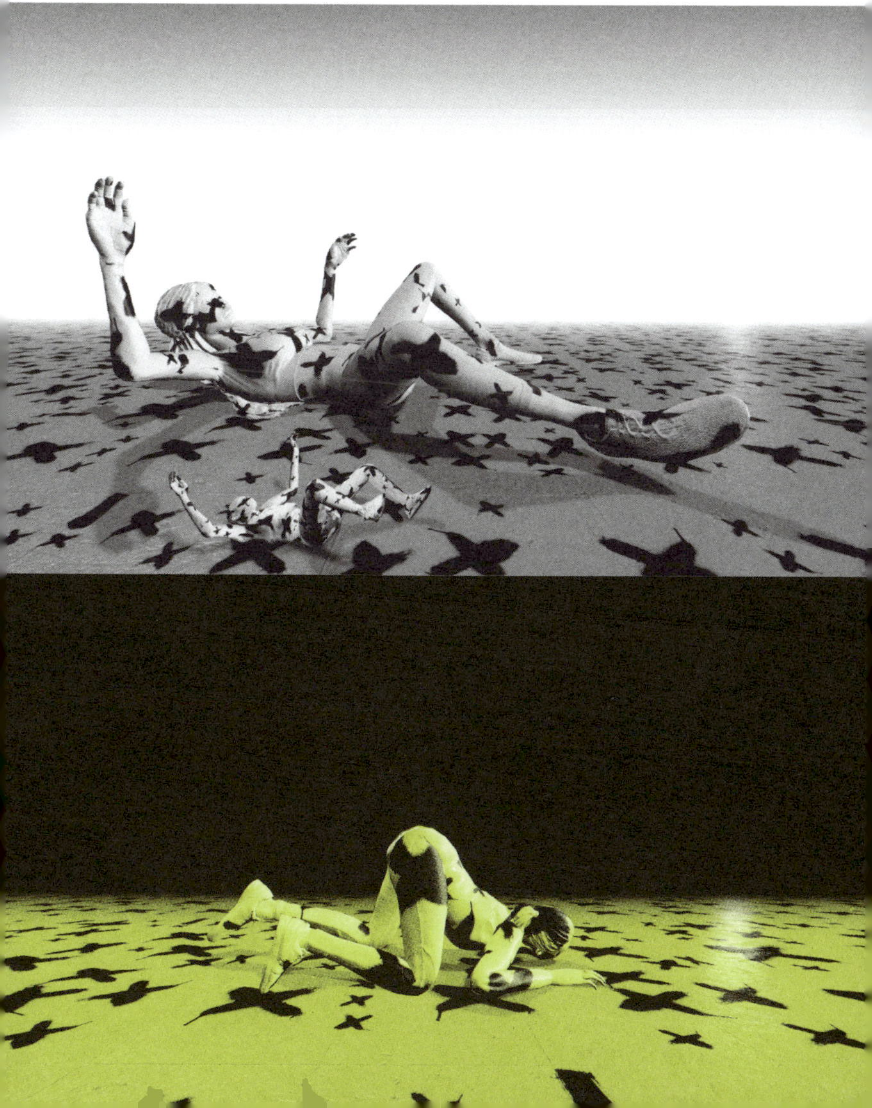

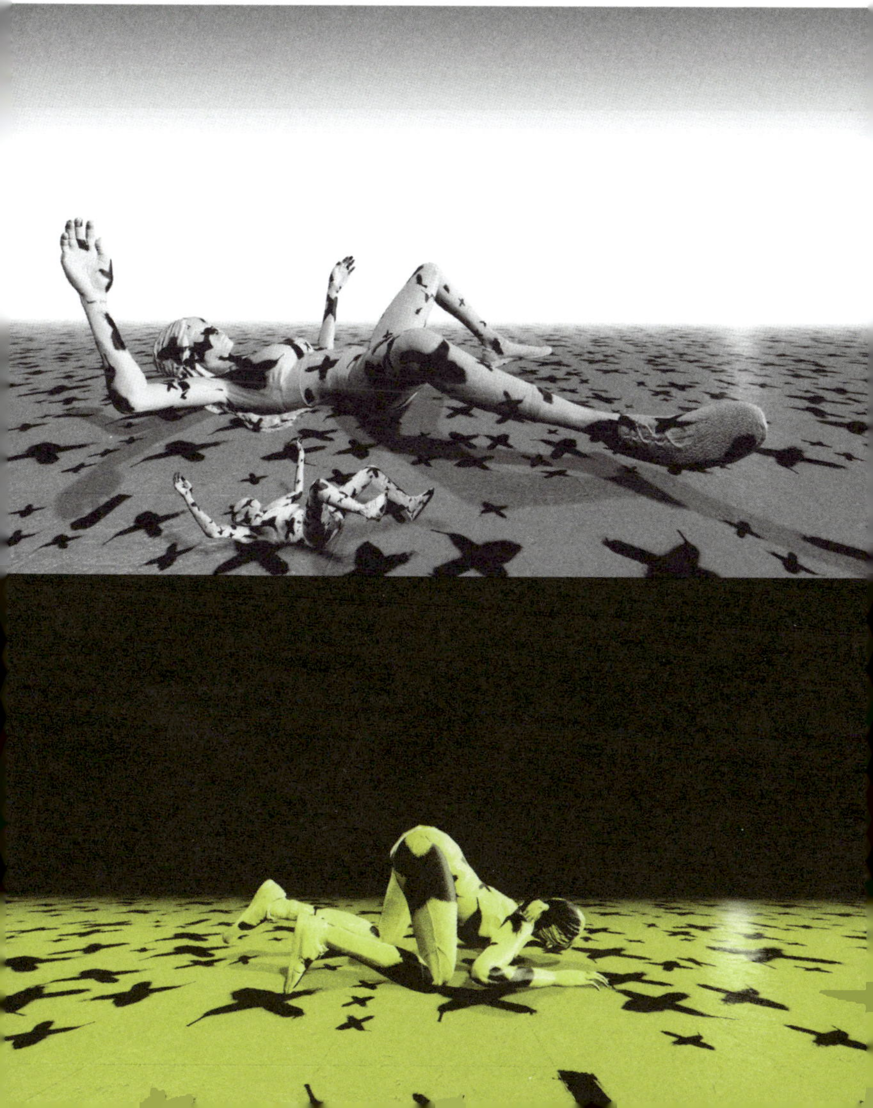

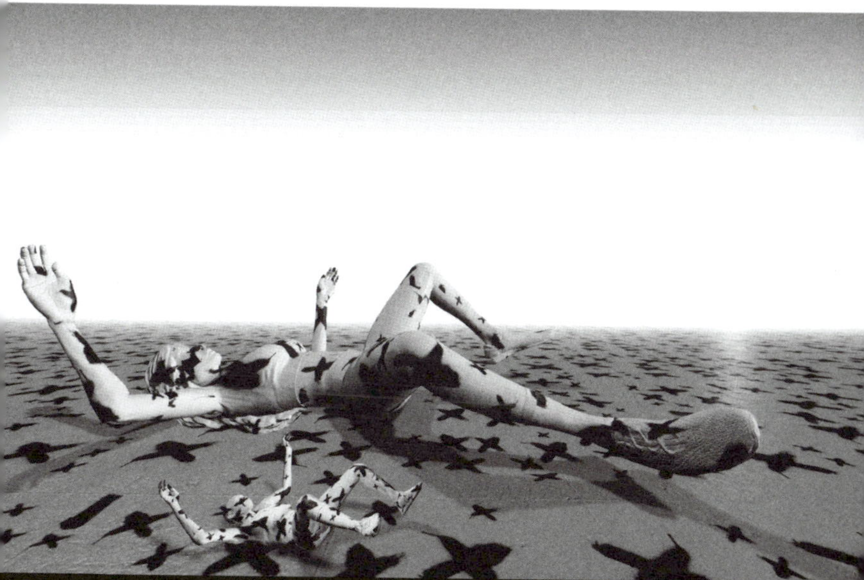

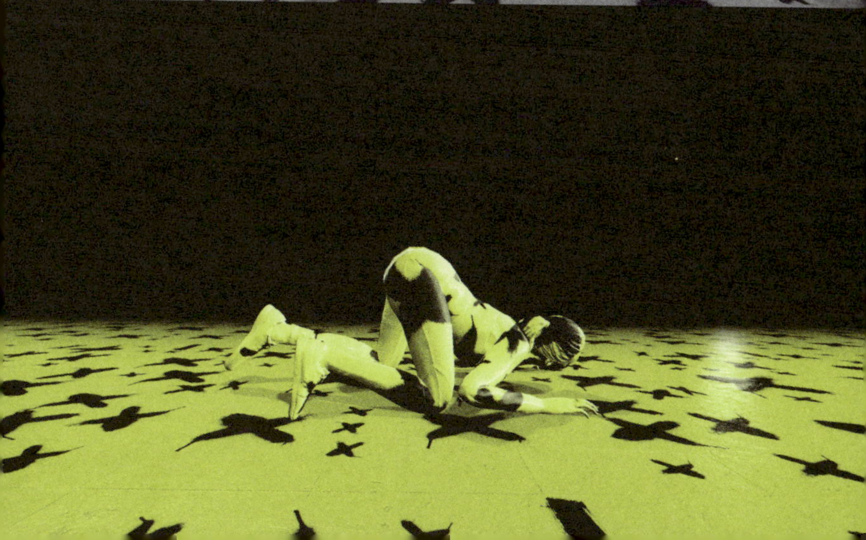

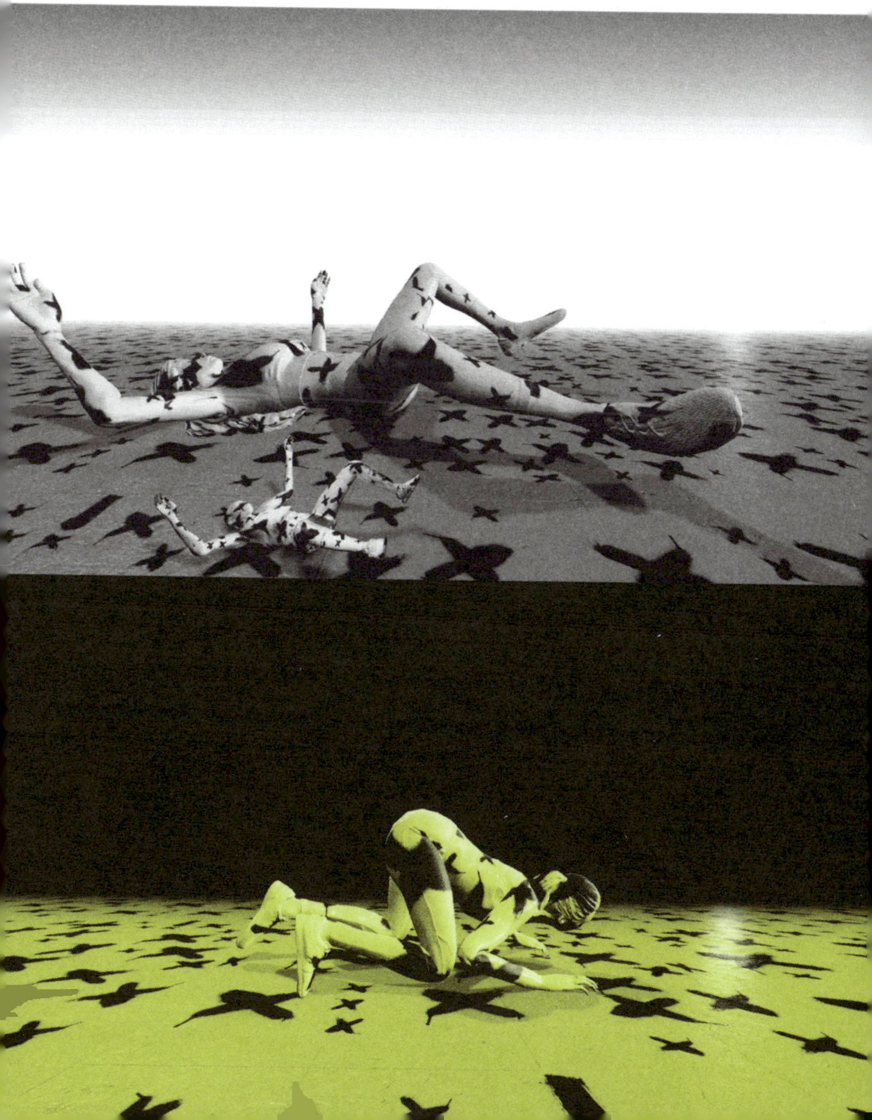

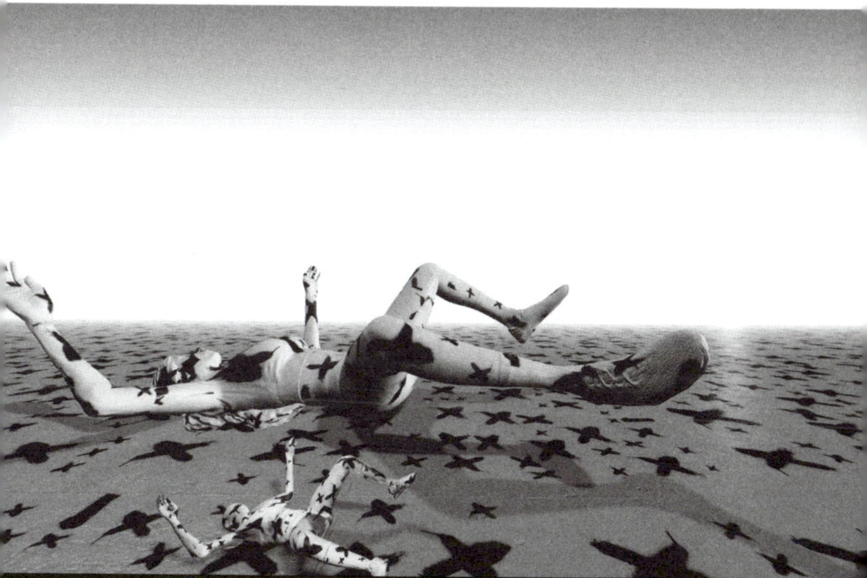

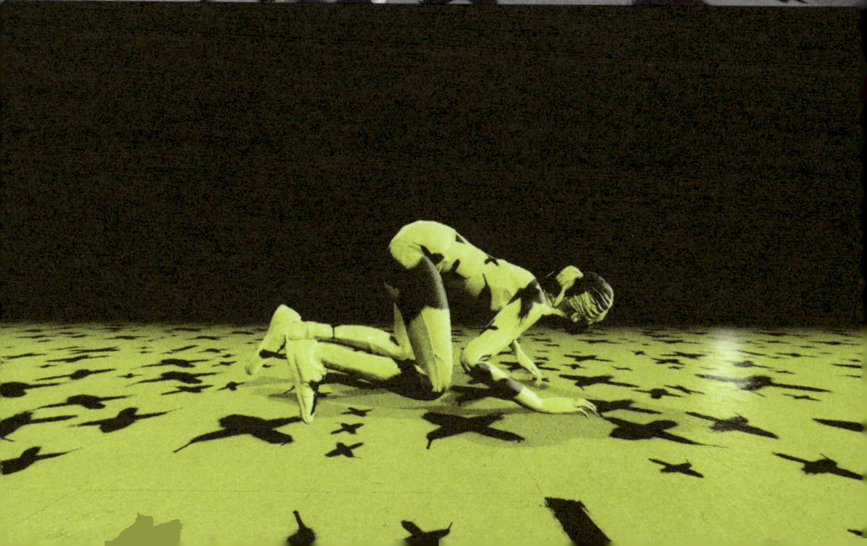

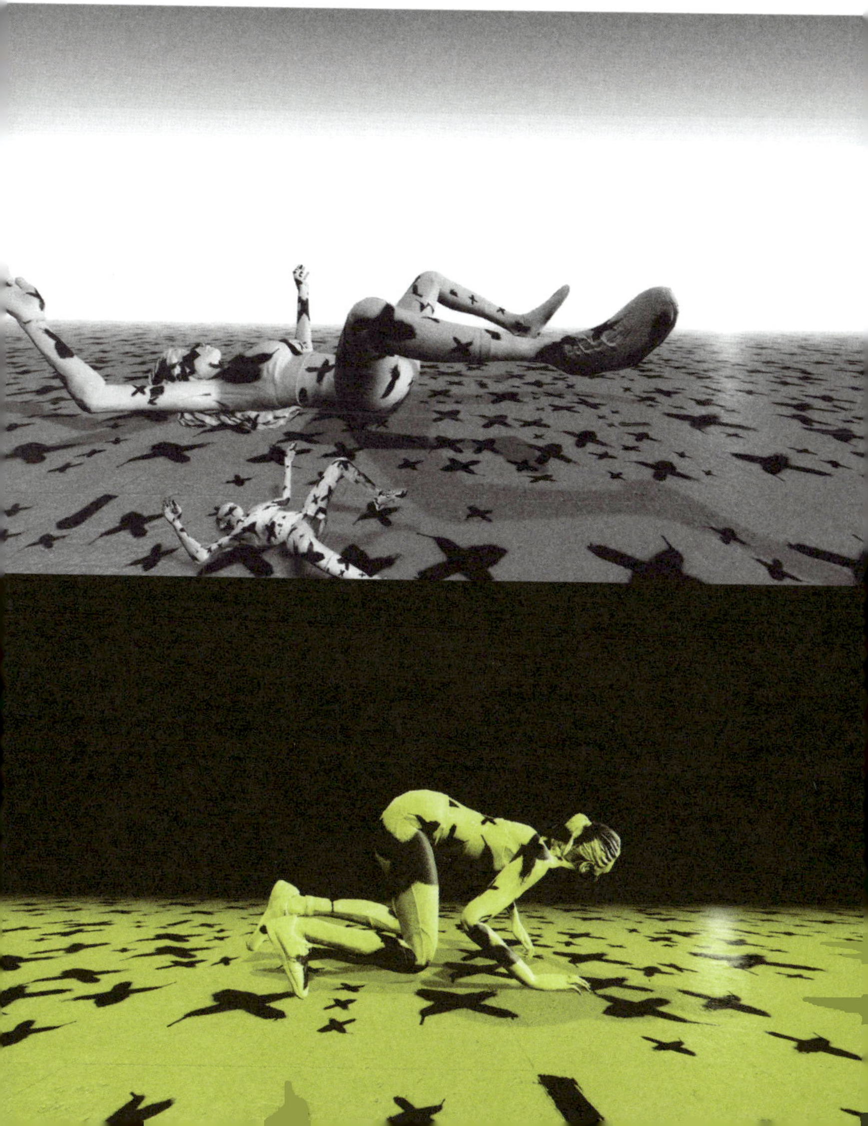

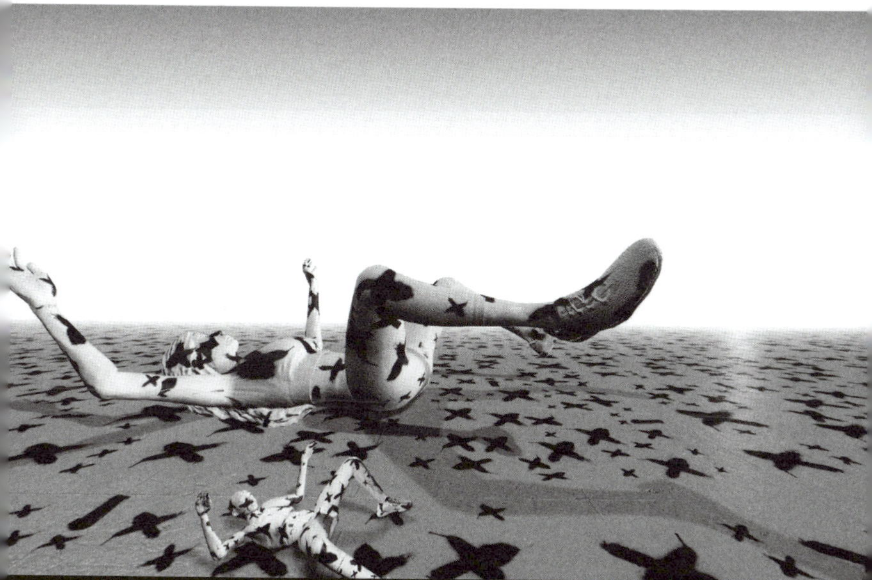
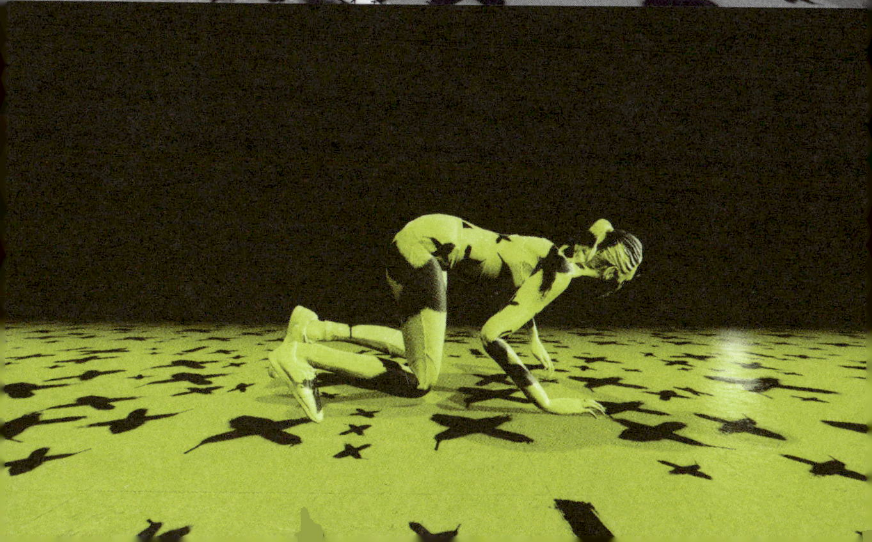

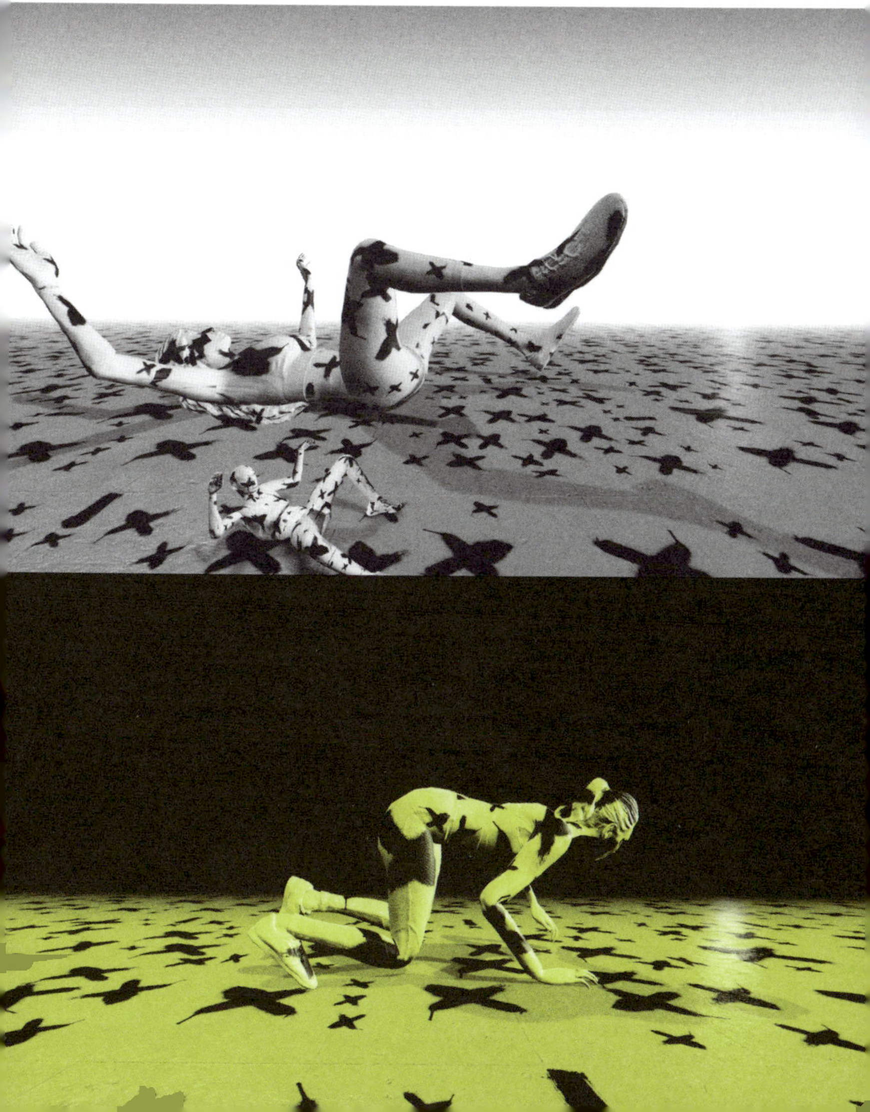

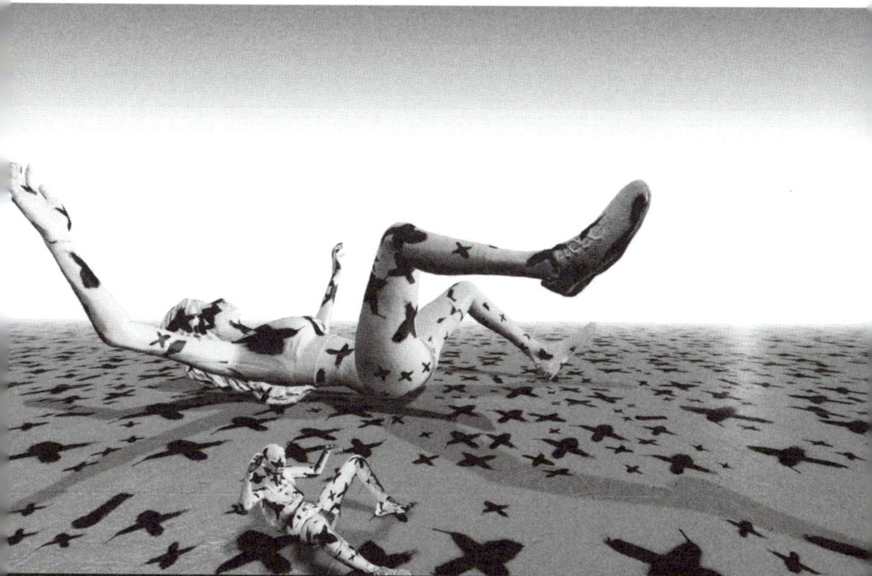

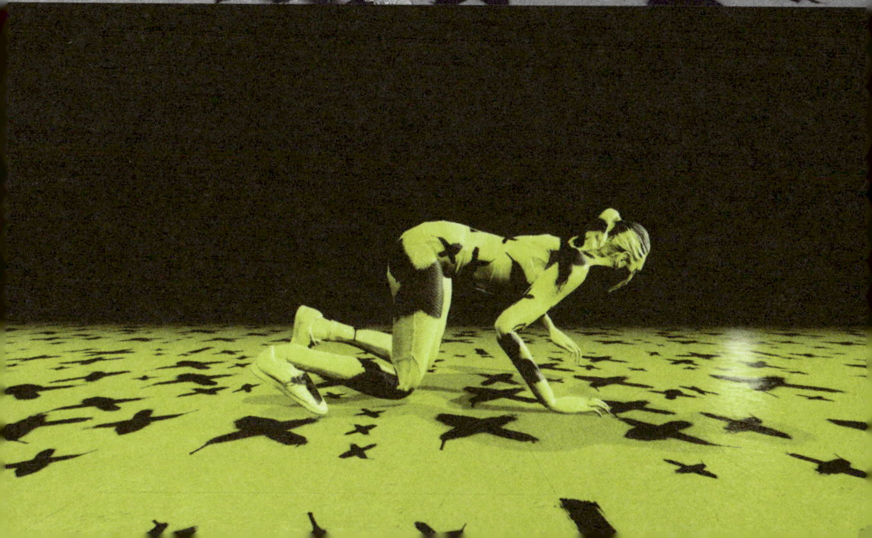

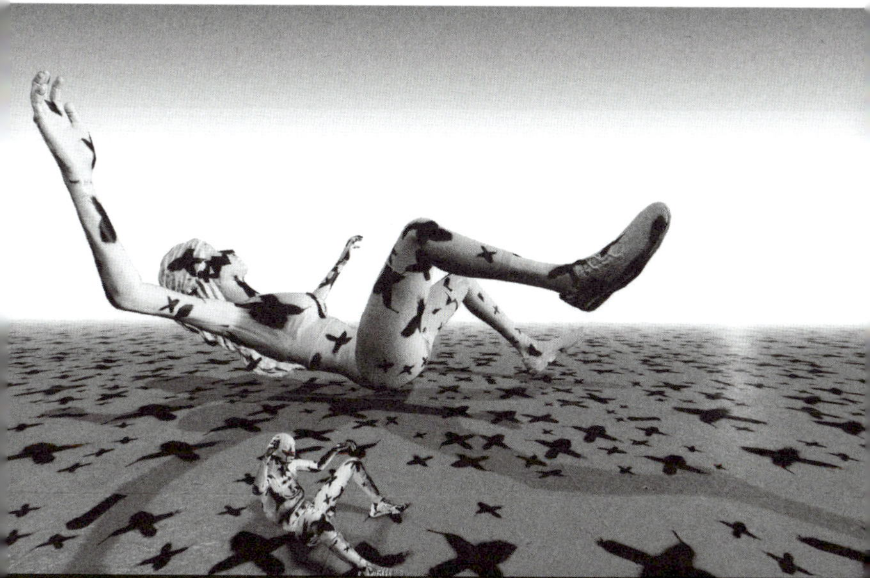
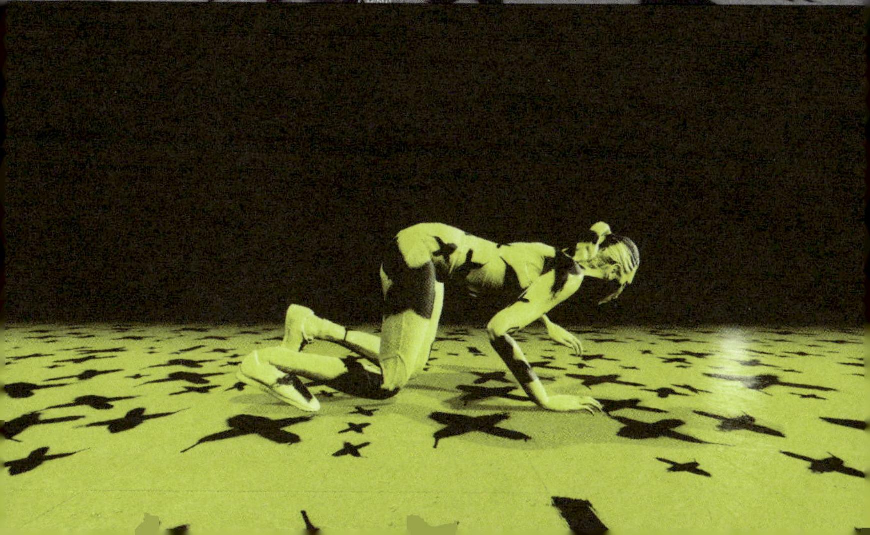

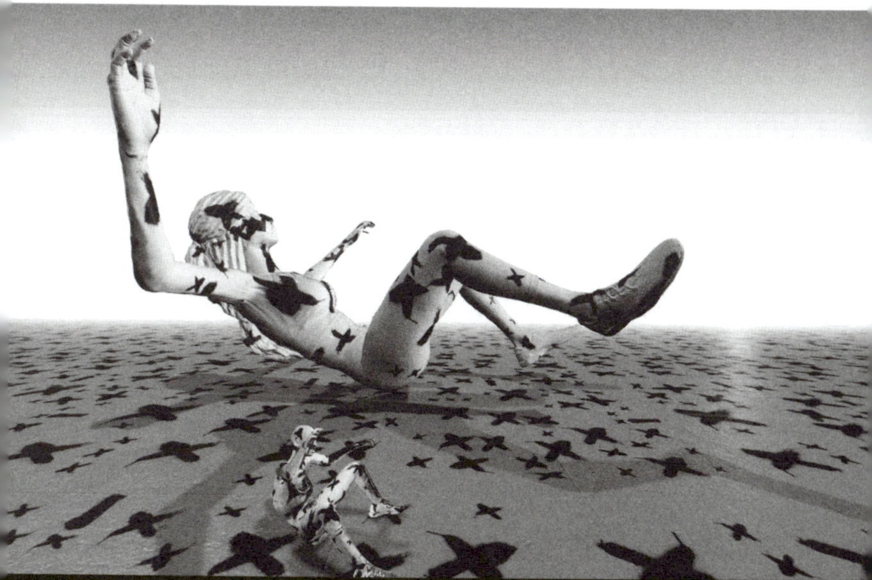

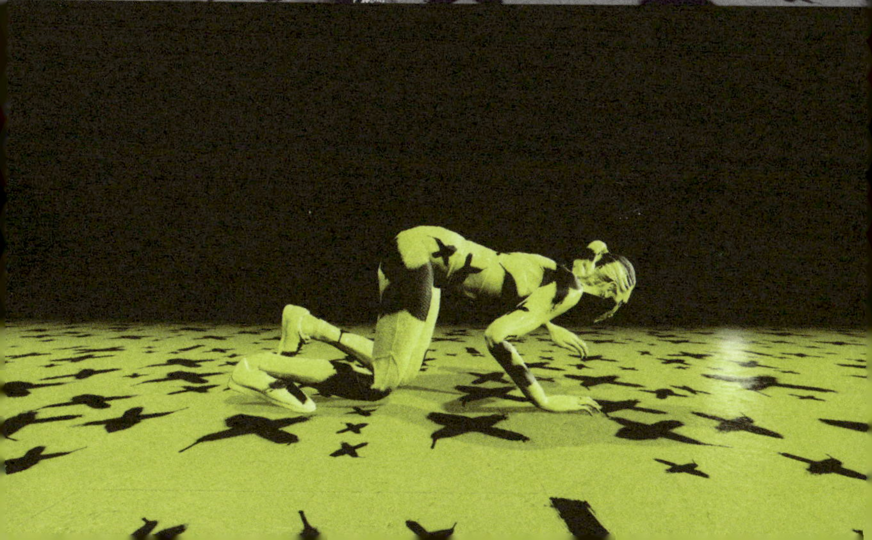

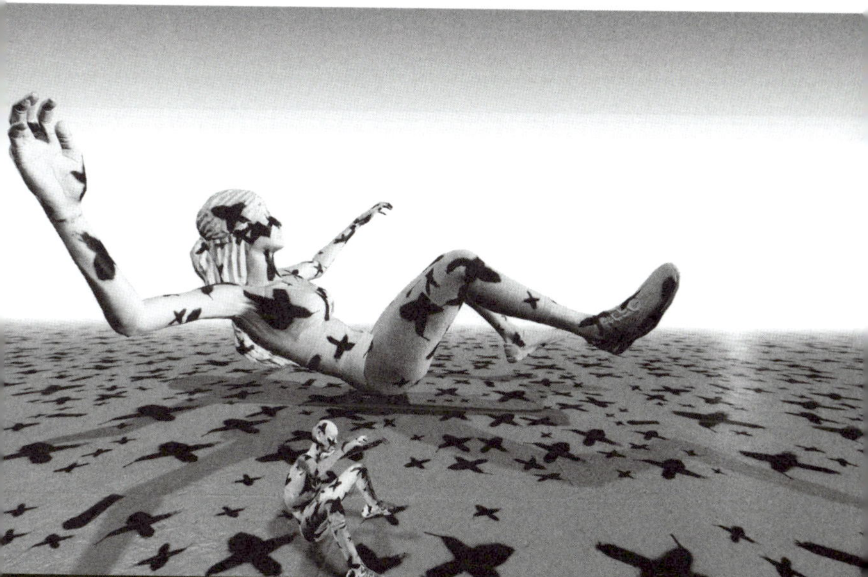
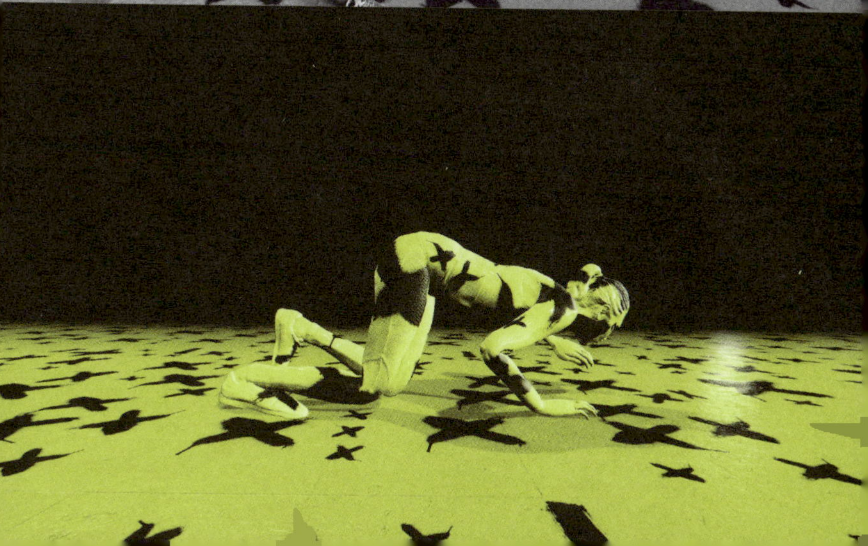

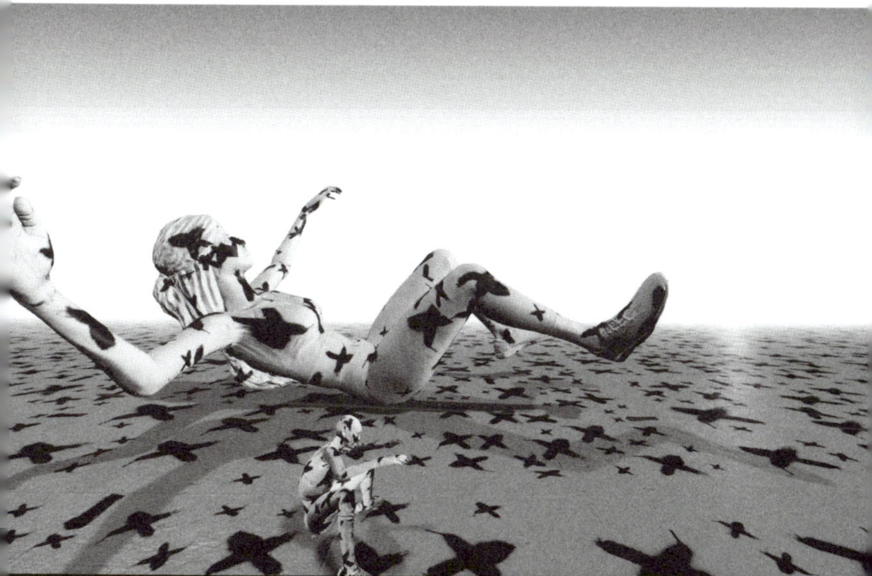
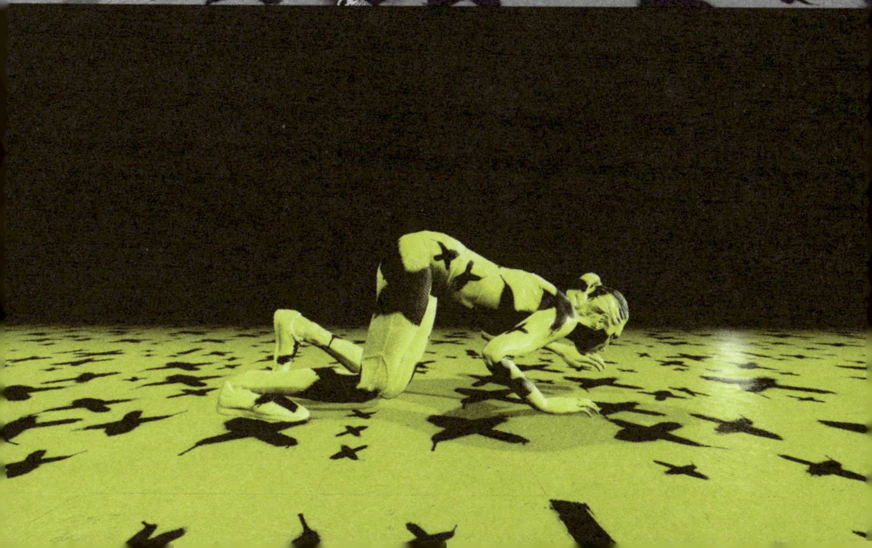

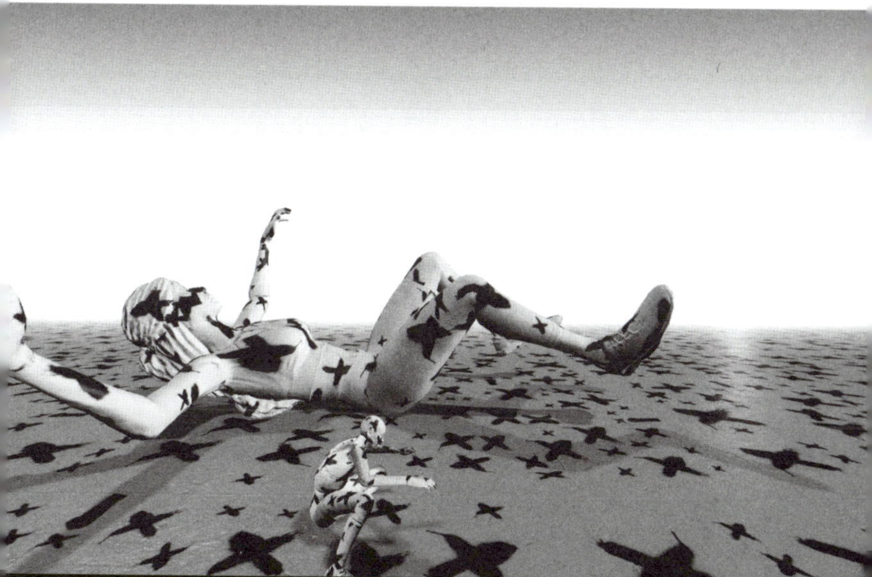

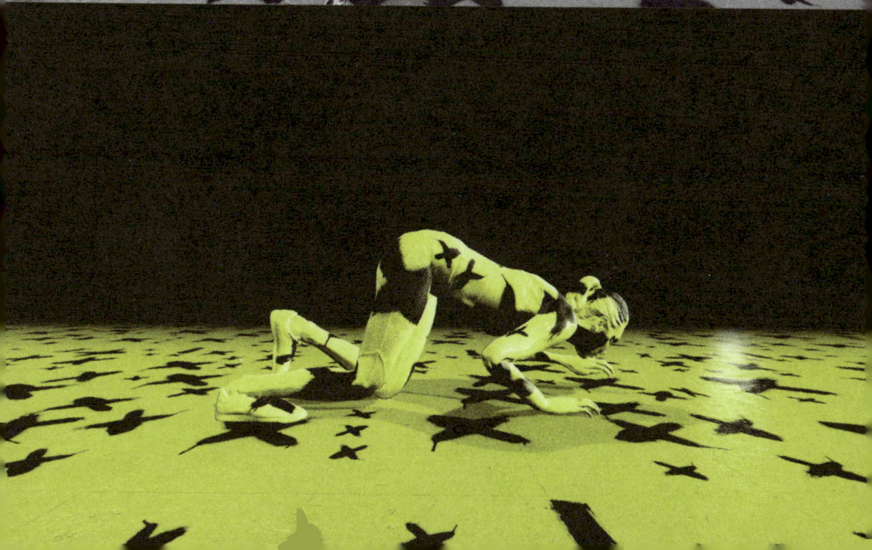

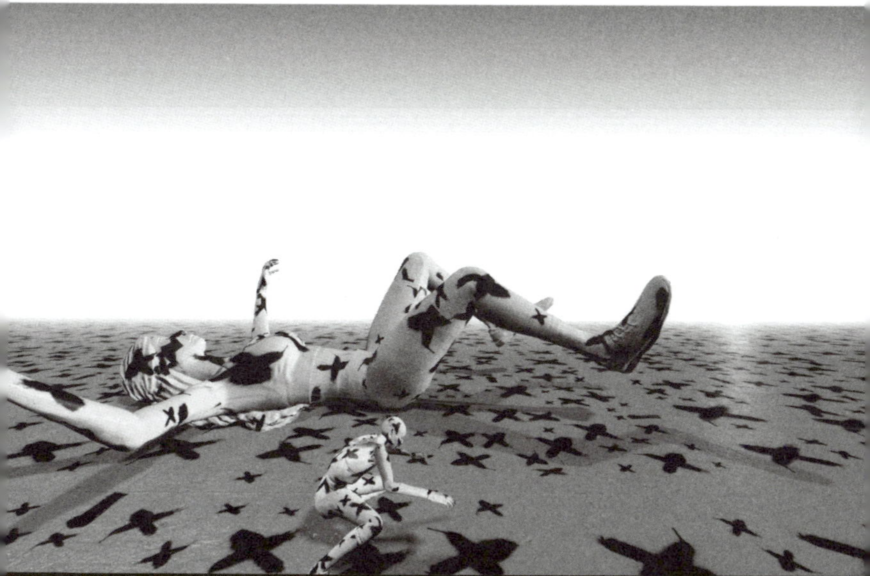

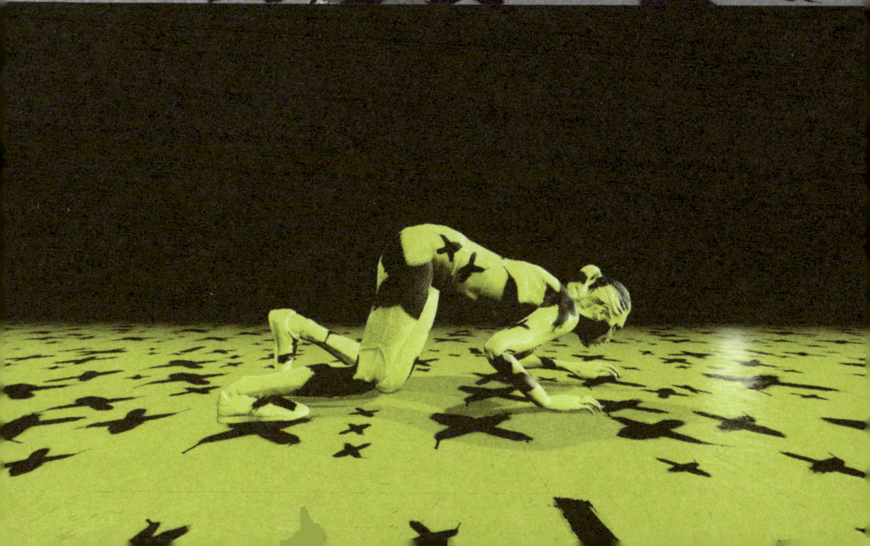

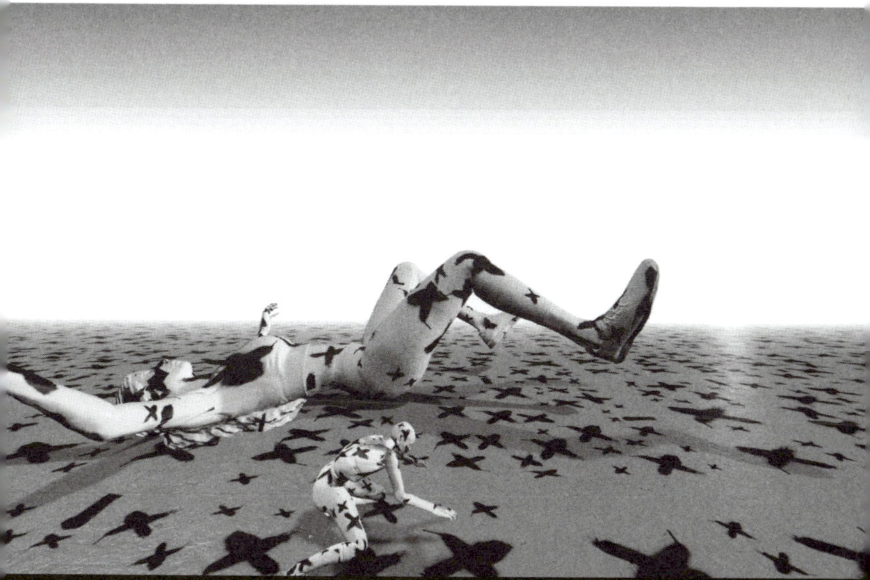

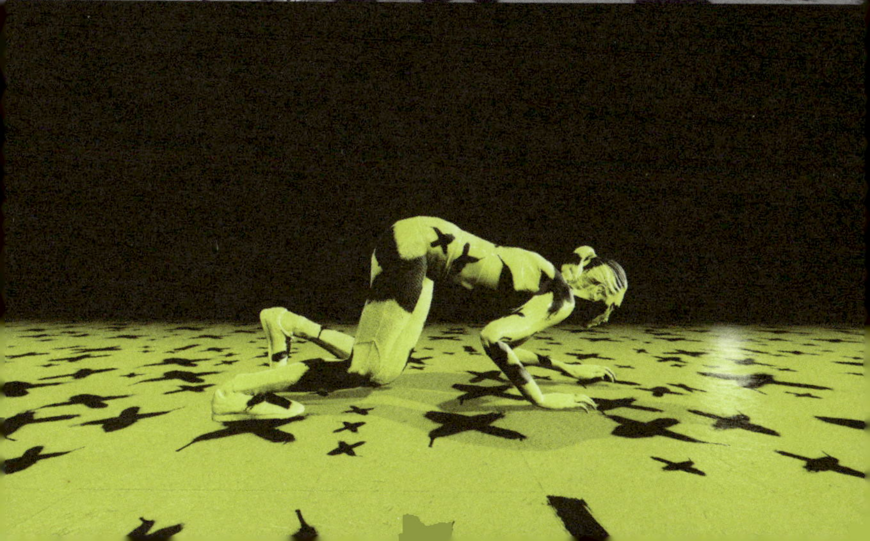

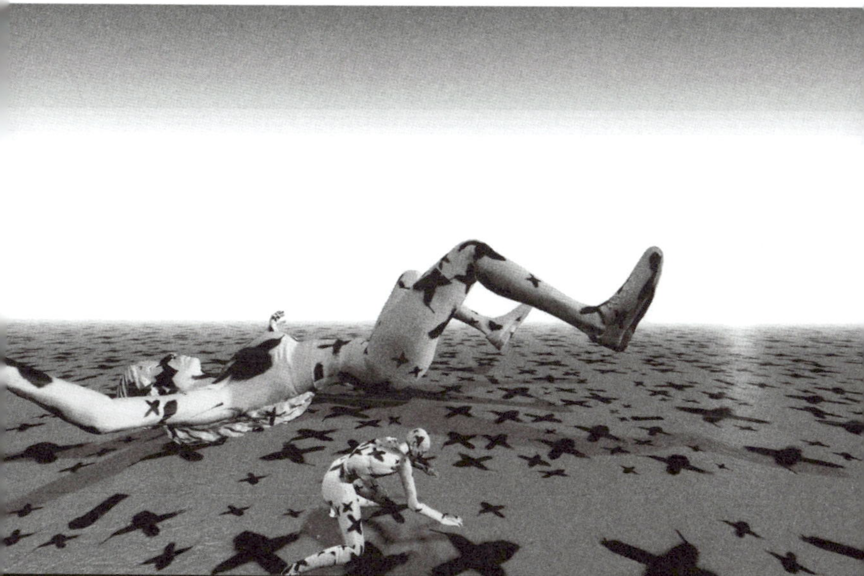

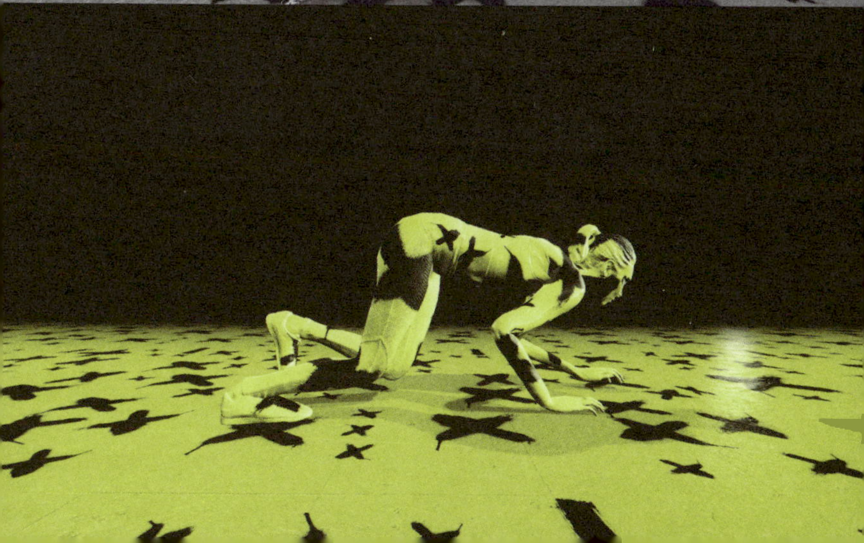

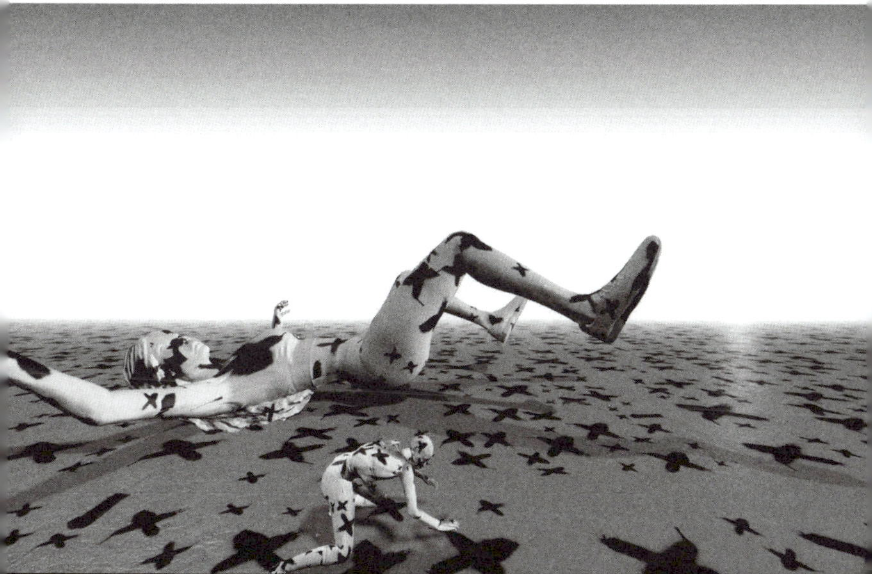

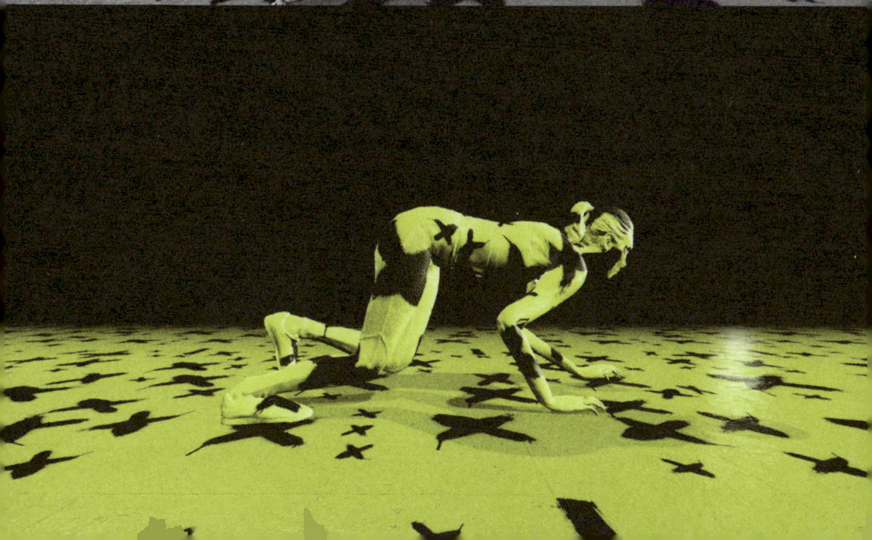

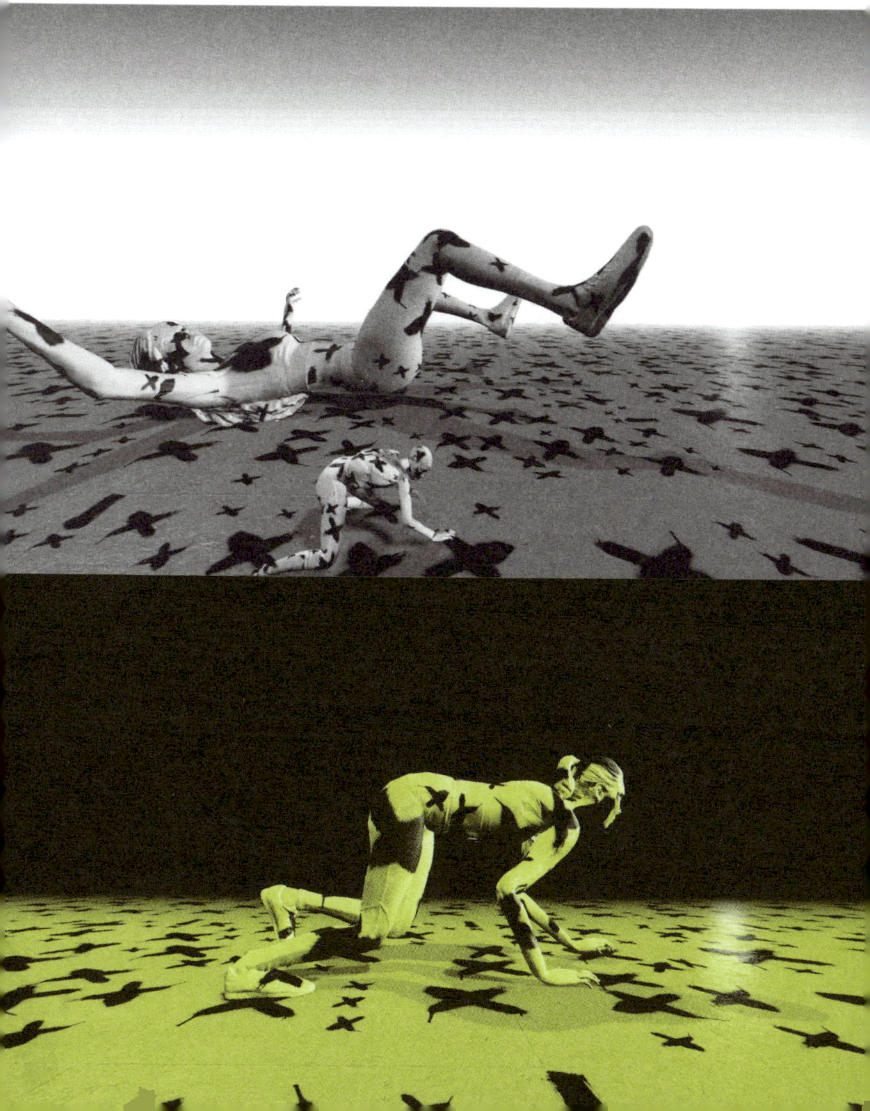

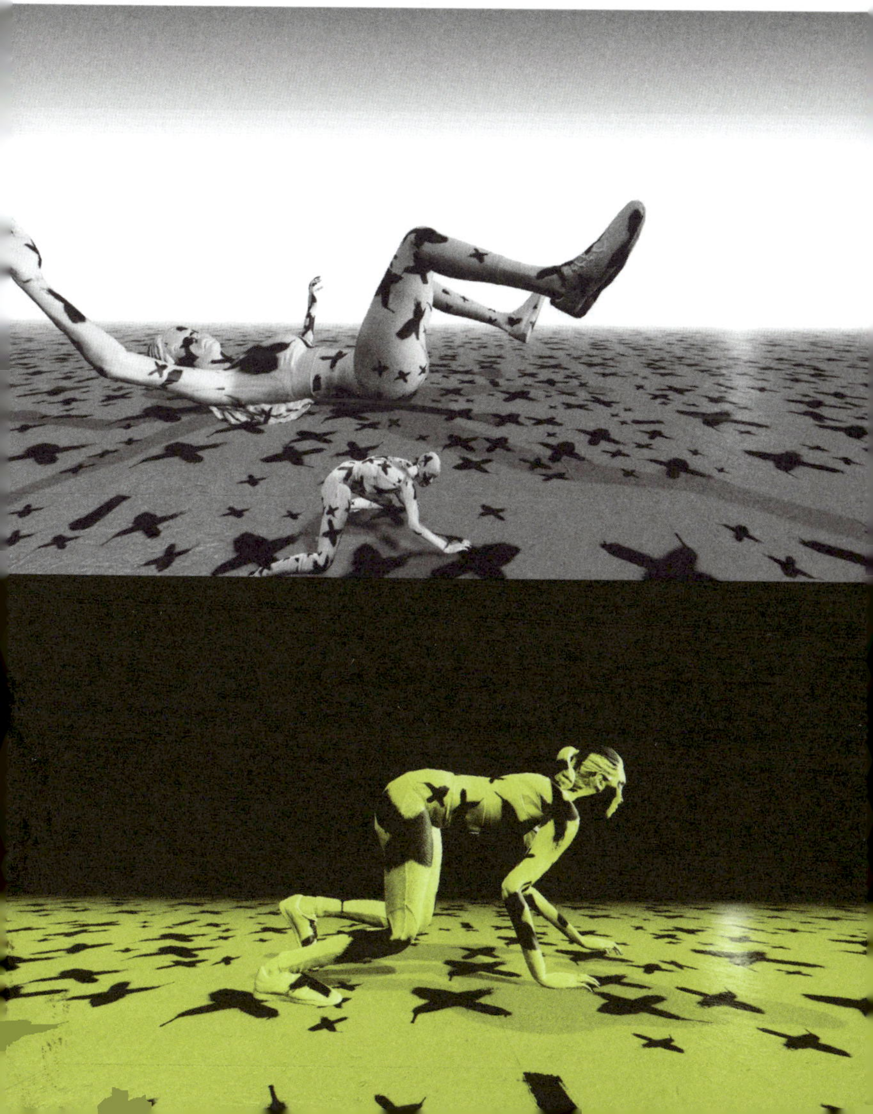

halfcheetah.xyz

Published and distributed by
Mousse Publishing
Contrappunto s.r.l.
Via Pier Candido Decembrio 28,
20137, Milan–Italy

Available through
Mousse Publishing, Milan
moussemagazine.it

Publishing Editor
Ilaria Bombelli

Design
Massimiliano Pace
Mattia Lombardo

First edition
2025

ISBN 978-88-6749-726-3
€ 25 / $ 30

James Bloom would like to thank Georgi Georgiev for his coding expertise, also Iván Rodríguez López for sound design and Sam Liddle for 3D animation.